Homo Sapiens Rediscovered

Paul Pettitt

Homo Sapiens Rediscovered

THE SCIENTIFIC REVOLUTION REWRITING OUR ORIGINS

On the cover: Types of teeth used as personal ornaments in the Aurignacian (M. Vanhaeren & F. d'Errico, 2006); Clovis points from the Drake Cache, Colorado, USA (accession numbers 1052917, 2043488 and 2049354, Department of Anthropology, Smithsonian Institution); Clovis projectile points from various North American sites (Center for the Study of the First Americans, Texas A&M University; courtesy Michael Waters).

First published in the United Kingdom in 2022 by
Thames & Hudson Ltd, 181A High Holborn, London WC1V 7QX

First published in the United States of America in 2022 by
Thames & Hudson Inc., 500 Fifth Avenue, New York, New York 10110

Homo Sapiens Rediscovered © 2022 Thames & Hudson Ltd, London
Text © 2022 Paul Pettitt

Layout design by Samuel Clark
www.bytheskydesign.com

British Library Cataloguing-in-Publication Data
A catalogue record for this book is available from the British Library

Library of Congress Control Number 2022931261

ISBN 978-0-500-25263-5

Printed in China by RR Donnelley

FSC
www.fsc.org
MIX
Paper from responsible sources
FSC® C144853

Be the first to know about our new releases,
exclusive content and author events by visiting
thamesandhudson.com
thamesandhudsonusa.com
thamesandhudson.com.au

Contents

Prologue

We had already been underground for five or six hours. Perhaps more. My sense of time always failed me in these places that were so far away from natural light. Those points of orientation we take for granted – sunlight, distant noise – held no sway here. My arms and legs ached, and a rumbling stomach reminded me that we'd not eaten since a light breakfast. We had been standing still for much of the time, staring at the cave's gritty wall, arms extended above our heads. There were six of us. We took it in turns to scrape the scalpel carefully over the glittering white surface, or to hold the test tube beneath it. Scrape, scrape, scrape. One of us would shine a torch at the spot on the wall on which all eyes were focused. One would take notes, another photograph or film. The shelly stalactite came off painfully slowly, a small accumulation of bright white powder no bigger than a pinch of salt built up at the bottom of the test tube. It was rock, after all. Scrape, scrape, scrape.

It was April 2016, and when we finally emerged into the light of day, and sat with the cold beers we'd been looking forward to, we had no idea how our results were to radically change what we thought we knew about the origins of art and Ice Age culture.

The process that led us here had begun some thirteen years earlier. One evening at a college dinner in Oxford, a friend of mine, archaeology writer and Ice Age art specialist Paul Bahn, expressed how he would love to look for cave art in the UK, but wouldn't know where to look. I would, I replied. A few weeks later I'd organized a four-day survey of the English and Welsh caves I thought were most likely to have any art if it was there. At Paul's request we were joined by Sergio Rippoll, an Ice Age art specialist from Madrid's distance learning university. I certainly didn't expect to find any art. It's lucky I'm not a gambler.

Our first stop was Creswell Crags, a narrow limestone gorge that straddles the counties of Nottinghamshire and Derbyshire in the English Midlands. Its several caves have long been known for their Ice Age archaeology; it seemed a sensible place to start our search.

Sergio is famous for his 'eyes', and he had before spotted Ice Age art in several Spanish caves. It was still an immense surprise when he called down excitedly from a ledge above our heads in a cave called Church Hole. He had found an engraving of a red deer, which could only be Ice Age in date. As news of the discovery spread, English Heritage paid for scaffolding in Church Hole, which allowed us to examine the higher parts of the cave's walls where any additional surviving art would most likely be found. We discovered several more examples – about a dozen in total, all engraved – including the outline of a bison and extinct aurochs and enigmatic human-like images.

That's when my colleague and old friend Alistair Pike came into the story. 'That art you've found in Church Hole,' Alistair asked, 'any of it covered in stalactite?' I answered enthusiastically: yes, I'd spotted several areas where the white stone had formed over the engraved lines of the cave's images. Our excitement was immediate. If that was the case, Alistair could use a special method called uranium-thorium dating to date stalactites that had formed over the art. If we ensured that we took our samples from the stalactite where it clearly overlaid the art, the results would provide a minimum age for the underlying engraving, or in other words a date that the art must have been created before. We were soon back in Church Hole, and busy with a drill. Back then – it's not that long ago but science moves quickly – we needed a relatively large sample, a circle of the stalactite roughly 3 cm (1 in.) across. When Alistair's results came through a month or so later, they showed that the stalactite had formed towards the end of the Ice Age, about 13,000 years ago. The art underneath must have been older.

Several years passed. Alistair and I began directing archaeological excavations at Creswell Crags in order to understand more of the behaviour of the Ice Age artists who had left their indelible marks on Church Hole's walls. There was a lot of cave art out there in France and Spain too. That's how we came to spend so much time underground in three Spanish caves, painstakingly scraping stalactite off dozens of examples of Ice Age art. Our main intention was to refine what we knew about how the art had evolved, and how it changed in theme and style over the course of the last 25,000 years of the Ice Age. But things would turn out differently. Much of the art we dated fell within the expected range, from a couple of thousand back to over 25,000 years ago. But some of the results inspired Alistair to telephone me at home one late evening. Several samples – from all three of the caves we'd examined – had come out surprisingly old. Much older than we'd expected.

The results showed that the stalactites overlying art in La Pasiega Cave in the north of the country, Maltravieso Cave in the centre, and Ardales in the south, had formed around 65,000 years ago. In all cases the art had to be *more than 65,000 years old*. The implications were profound: this doubled the age of Ice Age art overnight. But, far more importantly, it showed that the art could not have been made by *Homo sapiens*. We have a good understanding of when members of our own species first arrived in Europe during the Ice Age; in Spain as elsewhere, this occurred around 42,000 years ago. Even if the art we'd dated turned out to be 65,000 years old and not much older, it would have been created 23,000 years before *Homo sapiens* first arrived in Spain. It had to be the creation of another type of human, and in all probability it was made by the Neanderthals.

Thinking this through raised more questions. Were the Neanderthals the first to produce art? If so, we were wrong in thinking that it was unique to *Homo sapiens*. Was their art different? The examples we'd dated were all non-figurative: marks made by covering parts of the body with pigment and using them to colour the walls. Perhaps our *sapiens* ancestors can still lay claim to producing the first figurative art. But were they producing this art as they dispersed across the Europe and Asia for the first time, or did it come thousands of years later? What does this say about the cultural evolution of our own species?

Introduction

Who are we? How do scientists define *Homo sapiens*, and how does our species differ from the extinct humans that came before us and those with whom we were contemporary as recently as 40,000 years ago? In evolutionary terms we are a crazy experiment. We sacrificed some of the tough, muscular bodies inherited from our ancestors and came to rely more upon tools. We grew brains that are huge by primate standards, and so expensive metabolically that we needed highly nutritious packages of food in the form of meat to power them if we weren't to graze all day long. Obtaining this meat required the regular hunting of large, dangerous animals, which in the days before rifles was very difficult and often resulted in painful injuries. Why do this? As we will see, the changes that define our brains probably required only a few genetic mutations, but these had a profound effect, resulting in a possibly unique mental world. There must have been good reasons for such an expensive change.

We owe much to our Ice Age ancestors. Just to think of a few things common to modern life: sewing needles and tailored clothing, jewelry, burial of the dead, art, dogs, weapons, tents, lamps, and – as I shall show – villages and even a form of writing.

Archaeologists can't interrogate our distant ancestors directly. We're reliant entirely on the stones, bones and residues that have survived from the remote periods in which they lived. We have a battery of cutting-edge scientific techniques that we use to try to answer the questions we'd like to put to the people of the Ice Age. Many of these techniques are very new, and are only now opening up fresh lines of research which are radically changing what we think we know about our own origins. How difficult was it to survive the harsh and unstable climates of the series of ice ages scientists call the Pleistocene. How did you hunt those large, dangerous animals? How did you know how to find the mammoth herds in winter? How did you learn to make the hide-working and antler-carving tools, spears and javelins that were so essential to your survival? What was the purpose of your art? Was everyone allowed to produce it? Was your society one of equals, or were some more equal than others? Had you formed religious beliefs?

Researchers into human evolution often disagree about the answers to many of these questions as well as a host more that I will ask in the pages to come. Through the evolution of our peculiar brains and the imaginative spin they allow us to put on things, coupled with the story of how we learned to survive in remarkably small numbers in a truly hostile world, the story of our origins spins out of the Ice Age. This is the story I want to present here. It's a story that has benefitted from remarkable advances in biomolecular science, not least of which is the sequencing of ancient DNA, the revelations from which understandably hog the limelight. But I've always been interested in behaviour, and understanding one without the other is a bit like knowing that someone is a great author without reading any of their books. We are far more than our DNA; it's a great human blueprint, but in this book I want to bring out what our Ice Age ancestors created with it.

I should say very briefly who I am. I specialize in Palaeolithic archaeology, literally the Old Stone Age, the study of the archaeology of the oldest, most distant archaeological period. I went to university a little over thirty years ago, intending to specialize in Roman Britain, but ended up falling back and back in time until I landed with a bump in the Pleistocene. These days I leave the Roman stuff to my wife. I research the behaviour of our Stone Age/Ice Age ancestors, and in the following chapters I want to reveal the big picture of how modern science is used to study these people, and what I think we now know about them. I will pepper them here and there with stories of what I've researched and who I've worked with, in order to convey a sense of what research in field and cave, in museum and laboratory, is like. I'll be taking you back into a remote and alien past, to get under the skin (and furs) of the experience of Stone Age people. At times we'll be moving swiftly so as to set the scene, but I promise that in places we'll stop for a while and watch individuals at work. We'll do that particularly in Europe (as it's what I specialize in), where the period in question is called the Upper Palaeolithic. There are many untold stories to reveal. So, pull on your parka, leggings, mittens and boots (it's going to be very cold), pick up your javelins and pocket some smoked bison meat and putrefied fish heads for the journey. We've a long way to go.

Chapter 1

Skin and Bones

Cheddar Gorge is a magical place. It's a steep-sided limestone valley in the UK associated today with the eponymous cheese and with walkers attracted to the Somerset beauty spot. But its ancient inhabitants were interested in an entirely different local resource: wild horses. With a little planning the dangerous herds could be channelled through the gorge and ambushed where it narrows. In 1903 a human skeleton, an adult male, was excavated there just inside the mouth of Gough's Cave, nowadays a popular show cave. Radiocarbon dating of his bones has shown that he lived and died around 10,000 years ago, just after the end of the Pleistocene. His people were drawn from an ancient Ice Age stock, now adapting to the boreal forests spreading across Europe as the climate warmed into the Holocene (the current epoch). 'Cheddar Man' probably died violently – a large break is visible on his cranium – and whether he was buried or simply came to lie where he died, he was gently covered by naturally accumulating sediments, and there he stayed, until his accidental discovery ten millennia later.

I've often visited Cheddar, usually with university students, and I've always found this rugged landscape particularly evocative of the Ice Age world. In 2018 colleagues from London's Natural History Museum managed to extract surviving fragments of DNA from the densest bone in Cheddar Man's body: the petrous temporal bone, part of the base of the skull, which houses the machinery of the middle and inner ear. Their results painted the most intimate portrait anyone would have of the man since his death. Like all Ice Age humans he was lactose intolerant. That was to be expected; the ability to digest dairy products would arise only thousands of years later when early agriculturalists domesticated cattle, sheep and goats. But the real surprise was his appearance. In life he was dark skinned, blue- or green-eyed, and had dark brown curly or wavy hair. Much was made of the news in the little town of Cheddar, where today light skin and brown eyes are common, milk is drunk and cheese is made, as in the rest of northwest Europe. Several of the Cheddar locals shared some of his DNA, but important changes had clearly separated them from this man of our remote past.

Cheddar Man was not alone. Even as late as 7,000 years ago (the Late Mesolithic as archaeologists call it), pale skin was not the European norm.[1] Cheddar Man reminds us of a deep and distant ancestry we all carry today. He came back to us from the northwestern edge and youngest end of the Ice Age. But his skin and bones carried with him a far longer legacy, one that takes us back to the forests of Africa 7 million years ago, where the locomotion, diets and brains of quadrupedal apes were about to undergo profound changes.

African apes and human origins

We are all African apes. Although we have undergone important changes over the course of human evolution, we retain the major characteristics of our primate[2] roots. Our hands are dextrous at grasping and manipulation, and come equipped with the nails of tree-climbers rather than claws; and like other apes today we're a social creature, living in complex webs of relationships. We primarily rely on our sense of vision rather than smell, and as the primate nasal area reduced in size, our eyes became positioned in the front of the head, enabling binocular (three-dimensional) vision. For a mammal, however, we have a brain that's very big relative to the size of our body – with a correspondingly high energy demand. One of the major questions of human evolution is why we came to diverge from our ancestors and pay such a large metabolic cost for it.

Victorian scientists such as Charles Darwin and Thomas Henry Huxley noted the remarkable similarity between the skeletons of apes and humans and correctly inferred a close evolutionary relationship between them. It seemed that with a few modifications, a quadrupedally walking ape could be turned into an erect-walking human, and over the course of deep time, so they reasoned, this had happened by means of evolution through natural selection. From the mid-twentieth century, fieldworkers like Louis and Mary Leakey in Tanzania's Olduvai Gorge began to recover fossils of creatures apparently intermediate between living apes and humans, and to document the evolutionary experiments that lead to human distinctiveness. Today, we're able to draw on cutting-edge genetics to refine our evolutionary story. As one geneticist put it, new discoveries in human evolution are as likely now to emerge from a genetics laboratory as the East African Rift Valley.

Rather like researching a family tree, comparing the genomes of all four families of great apes traces them back to a common ape ancestor that lived in Africa between 10 and 16 million years ago. A branch leading to orangutans split off around 10 million years ago; another leading to gorillas split between 6 and 10 million years ago; and we still shared a common ancestor with our sister group, the chimpanzees, as late as 5 million years ago. We know very little about this common ancestor, but we can use comparative anatomy of existing and extinct apes to conclude that it must have been a knuckle-walking, branch-hanging and vertically climbing ape. The divergence between the chimpanzee branch and that leading ultimately to *Homo sapiens* occurred between 5 and 7 million years ago. Interbreeding between the two diverging groups probably continued for a million or more years, but it was infrequent enough for the genes to diversify, and in the case of early humans to spread the mutation that had caused the two chromosomes of one individual to fuse.[3] The non-human apes pursued successful adaptations of their own, but as an archaeologist my interest is in humans, and we will soon have to part ways with chimpanzees and gorillas.

We still share many traits with our living ape relatives, which is no surprise given that we also share over 98 per cent of our genome with them. The initial divergence was probably limited, but some gene regions came to diverge considerably more than others and we shouldn't underestimate the complexity of the differences that increasingly separated the two branches between 5 and 0.5 million years ago. A number of differences grew, including those that affect our susceptibility to diseases such as cancers, and those genes relating to brain development and function were particularly important. But long before they kicked in, other changes were quite literally afoot.

Walking on two feet

The bodies of all living apes are anatomically adapted for below-branch swinging, climbing and clambering, and when they're on the ground they knuckle-walk on their relatively long arms. African fossils dating to between 23 and 5 million years ago (the Miocene)

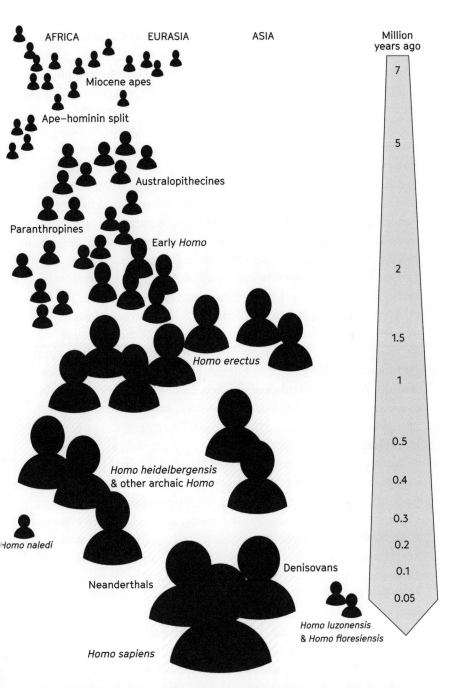

The diverse evolution of humans from >7 million years ago to *Homo sapiens*. Australopithecines and paranthropines shared more characteristics with apes than humans. By 4 million years ago hominins shared more characteristics with later humans: although they retained small, ape-like bodies they were habitual bipeds with considerable dietary diversity. More human-like body size and shape appeared with *Homo erectus*.

show that apes were already experimenting with variants of these types of locomotion. Some spent more time knuckle-walking on the ground, others experimented with minor tweaks to swinging and climbing. So why did some come to rely solely on two limbs for locomotion? The answer lies in a changing environment.

During the Miocene, Africa was covered in thick forests, broken only by rivers and lakes. Most primates lived up in the tree canopy. But around 8 million years ago temperatures began to fall as ice built up at the planetary poles, and as a result Africa went through a prolonged period of drying. The forests began breaking up and thinning out, increasingly separated by swathes of open grassland. The distribution of fruits and other foods became more patchy, and apes needed to cover more ground in order to obtain the necessary amounts of food. Some groups became extinct, others managed to survive by doing the same thing. But other groups developed a simple form of habitual bipedal walking on the ground: a compromise between arboreal climbing and swinging and terrestrial walking. It wasn't just these African apes that took to their legs, nor did bipedalism guarantee evolutionary success. Around 12 million years ago, *Danuvius guggenmosi*, a small ape known from Bavarian fossil deposits, was clambering along branches on two legs, an experiment which clearly did not lead to more human-like descendants.

For a relatively short-limbed primate, bipedalism is a more energy-efficient way of travelling on the ground than knuckle-walking. Chimpanzees and gorillas stand upright for short periods of time, particularly when they're feeding, and it's easy to imagine how some individuals simply took a couple more steps to reach another fruit tree. Early bipedalism may not have been *much* more efficient than quadrupedalism (or have looked particularly graceful), but a few extra steps here and there could amount to reaching the necessary quantity of fruit to survive. These initial steps started a process that would improve ape diet, balance the head on top of the body, and begin the walk towards humanity.

The African fossil record shows that a number of apes between 5 and 7 million years ago were tweaking these early forms of habitual bipedalism. Some of the earliest walkers, such as the 4.4 million-year-old *Ardipithecus ramidus* of East Africa, retained an ape-like body, with a few anatomical changes – such as shortened pelvises and feet that now resembled platforms for locomotion rather than a second pair of hands – that allowed something like a slow, bent-kneed, hip-rotating swagger. The new walking was occurring across much of Africa, although many groups would become extinct. Others, however, would continue to refine their bipedal anatomy, alongside – among other things – increased brain size.

Diet

The biological success of a species comes down to being able to maintain the body's functions and passing them on through reproduction. Understanding the food we eat and where we get it from is critical to understanding human evolution. Geological and ecological clues preserved in the sediments in which human fossils came to rest tell us what environments they lived in. But why did human diets become so diverse?

When Miocene apes began to establish themselves in Eurasia from 17 million years ago, their diets began to diversify as they adapted to the different environments they encountered, specializing in hard or soft fruit or a mixture of both. Diet diversification increased in the late Miocene as the forests continued to fragment, as the seasons became more pronounced, and as deciduous trees gave way to evergreens in Eurasia.[4] Preferred foods are all well and good when they're available, but fall-back foods – critical for surviving the seasons of scarcity – have been a major driver of human evolution. When the dietary going gets tough, the tough get chewing. As with modern chimpanzees and gorillas, it seems that while Miocene apes preferred fruits, they ate hard nuts and seeds when nothing else was available. Let's call these 'tough-times strategies'. We'll return to them later, as they were truly the making of *Homo sapiens*.

From 5 million years ago we can see growing dietary diversification among the early ape bipeds, the australopithecines (an early name for this group of 'southern ape-men'). Some bipeds, such as southern African *Australopithecus africanus*, have quite mixed microwear on their teeth, reflecting diets of various different plants; others, such as eastern African *Australopithecus afarensis* and *Paranthropus boisei*, have very homogeneous wear patterns, suggesting more specialized diets. One East African evolutionary path seems to have been from *Australopithecus anamensis* through

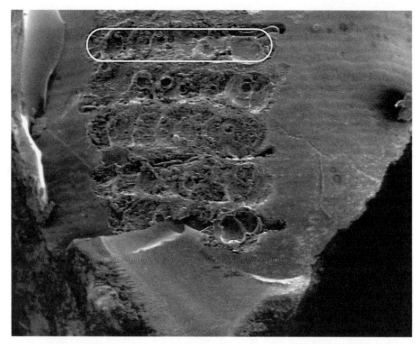

Micro-section through the growth enamel of a permanent molar of 1.8 million-year-old *Paranthropus robustus* from Swartkrans, South Africa. The thin lines to the right are enamel growth lines representing about one week each. The rows of superimposed circles are laser-ablated samples (the highlighted area is 1.6 mm or 0.06 in. across) from which stable isotope readings reveal dietary variation over some two months' of life.

Australopithecus afarensis to *Paranthropus boisei*, reflecting increasing efficiency at grinding tough food in large quantities. The southern African *Paranthropus robustus*, by contrast, adopted a lowland gorilla-like diet, preferring soft fruits but roughing it on tough foods during times of dearth.

Isotopic analysis can be used to look even more specifically at diet.[5] This is a versatile technique for examining the elemental or isotopic composition of solid materials. Colleagues and I used it to identify the sources of flint from which Ice Age tools were made in the UK, but it has also been used to reconstruct the diet of 1.8-million-year-old hominins from Swartkrans, near to Johannesburg in South Africa. Since its discovery in the 1940s, this site has been famous for its many remains of *Paranthropus robustus*. Tiny samples from the teeth of several specimens were subjected to laser pulses to ablate (remove by vaporizing) the isotopes of carbon in them.[6] Since different foods have different isotopic signatures,

Chapter 1

the researchers deduced that these hominins had a diet that changed with the seasons, from sedges, grass seeds and roots to a modicum of meat. It's easy to see how the energetic improvements brought about by bipedalism were of great use.

By at least 3.4 million years ago some early human groups were obtaining meat from animals. Animal bones from archaeological sites dating to this period bear the hallmarks of being smashed open so that their fatty marrow could be eaten. By 2.5 million years ago these smash marks are accompanied by straight cutmarks, showing that meat was being carefully removed from bones too. The consumption of meat, marrow and organs from small animals at least had become a regular part of the diet – there is plentiful evidence from this time of systematic carnivory. From a human point of view the salad days were over. The consumption of larger animals is also known, although their remains are more partial, and the over-abundance of their head parts relative to others on archaeological sites suggests that brain tissues were scavenged from the remains of carnivore kills of larger animals. Yum!

It may be no coincidence that the first signs of deliberate use of fire occur at around the same time as those of meat-eating. With the exception of fruits – a source of easily digested sugars – eating raw food is not energetically efficient, despite modern fads. Only a small amount of nutrients from raw carbohydrates and proteins are digested by our gut, and some of these are fermented by microbes which consume a proportion of the available energy themselves. During digestion we lose up to 50 per cent of carbohydrate nutrients and as much as 100 per cent of those from protein. Cooking, however, gets some of the digestion done artificially, and can improve calorific intake by up to 50 per cent. By breaking down carbohydrates in tubers and proteins in meat, cooking opens up a far wider range of foodstuffs for consumption which would otherwise be inedible or of limited nutritional benefit, and by destroying an army of potentially lethal food-borne bacteria such as *E. coli* it also makes meat-eating much safer. According to the anthropologist Richard Wrangham, cooking may have been the only way of guaranteeing survival through the dry seasons, and we can see it as another tough-times strategy. Fire also deters dangerous predators, making it possible for an early human to sleep safely on the ground for the first time, and provides light that can be used to extend the hours available for socializing. Ultimately, the net effect was to lengthen the amount of time spent on communicating and reinforcing relationships, leading to the growth of the brain beyond that of other primates.

Things begin to get really interesting by 2 million years ago. Back in 1962, the pioneering palaeoanthropologists Louis and Mary Leakey found the remains of an early hominin that seemed at the time to be the first tool user, hence they named it 'Handy Man', *Homo habilis*. Up to that point one of the few known hominin species had been the later 'Upright Man' or *Homo erectus*, discovered as far back as the 1890s in Sumatra (modern Indonesia). Since the Leakeys made their breakthrough, there has been a spate of new discoveries and a proliferation of differently named hominin species – particularly for our purposes those later than *Homo habilis: Homo rudolfensis, Homo ergaster, Homo georgicus, Homo erectus, Homo naledi* and *Homo antecessor*. The famous Neanderthals, *Homo neanderthalensis*, first identified in 1857 in the Neander Valley of Germany, appeared in Europe at much the same time as modern humans were evolving in Africa. We will encounter many of these names again as our story unfolds. But it's worth bearing in mind that researchers who spend many years hunting down these incredibly rare specimens often understandably have a tendency to want to give 'their' hominin a brand-new name to make it stand out. It is possible that some of these names will fall by the wayside in due course.

By 1.9 million years ago an ancestor to the earliest truly human-like humans had emerged in Africa, in the form of *Homo ergaster*. This species had smaller teeth, chewing muscles and bite forces. While the face was still large, the brain had enlarged to approaching half the size of our own – still a way to go but already above the ape range and growing. Its body was larger, its legs longer. It was now fully committed to life on the ground, and its finely tuned and efficient bipedalism allowed *Homo ergaster* to range over longer distances in order to obtain food, which now included significant quantities of meat. An adaptive watershed had been reached.

There are signs that these early forms of *Homo* had begun the dispersals out of Africa to which we shall return later. *Homo georgicus* was using an Oldowan toolkit (so named because the earliest discoveries of these simple stone tools were made in Olduvai Gorge) in the Caucasus by 1.5 million years ago, and *Homo erectus* had dispersed as far as China and Indonesia by 1.8 million years ago. These dispersals were short-lived and shut down when climates cooled once more, but the combination of an efficient bipedalism, weapon- and tool-assisted hunting and butchery, and controlled use of fire had created a successful and competitive colonizer.

The brain

We are metabolic prisoners of our large and expensive brains. They are 3.5 times larger than those of our closest primate relatives, the chimpanzees. They represent only 2 per cent of our body mass but they consume 15–20 per cent of our total resting metabolism, compared to all other primates' 2–10 per cent. Such an expensive tissue needs more energy than the life of a simple omnivorous primate can provide. There are several solutions: increase consumption of energy-rich foods (meat, particularly fat), render otherwise inedible foods edible and more foods easier to digest (efficient butchery and cooking), and trade off energy from other expensive tissues such as muscles or the stomach. These were all achievements of *Homo ergaster*.

As mammals mature into adulthood the complexity of the connections between their neurons changes as some are lost and others emerge. Chimpanzee and human brains develop in similar ways, both relatively slowly. Some neuron regions mature by the age of 3–4, while others don't until as late as 12, and fine-tuning occurs as late as 14. At the other end of the primate spectrum, macaques' brains mature quickly, shortly after birth. There is an important reason for our slow and ponderous neural maturation, which relates to what neuroscientists call 'neural plasticity', a rather grand term describing how numerous routes are created through the neurons while others are pruned back, which results in a very flexible way of thinking: we might call it effective problem-solving. A similar process may have occurred in other mammals who have evolved relatively large brains, such as elephants and some whales, but it's not just size that counts. As body size gets bigger so do brains, but not all regions of the brain scale up to the same degree. Our brains have grown particularly in the cerebral cortex (the outer layer), where much of our thinking and memory-related activities occur.

The need for flexible brain power must have been intense, but why? From an evolutionary perspective we must assume that the metabolic costs of enlarged brains were outweighed by the benefits.

Brains certainly come in useful for acquiring food, and for avoiding predators and infections, a sure sign of the dangerous world our ancestors inhabited. Cutting-edge genetic comparisons between human, chimpanzee and rhesus monkey gene expression in the brain and other tissues (the process by which DNA instructions are converted into a functional product like a protein) have established the differences that distinguish the human genome. Short DNA sequences called HARs (human accelerated regions) related to particular areas of the brain underwent rapid change (i.e. acquired more DNA substitutions), more than would be expected in comparison with other primates. Research is at an early stage, but it's looking like a number of HARs relate to the production of general-purpose cells that can turn themselves to many uses depending on what's going on in the environment, and a lot of these purposes involve cognition. A more specific example of a HAR is dopamine, a neurotransmitter related to improved working memory and the ability to plan and reason. Other cells relate to improvements in finger dexterity, social learning and tool use. Put simply, a neuronal rewiring, and the resulting ability to solve problems flexibly, seems to be what really separates us from our closest primate relatives. Archaic *Homo* was well on this road, but it was a road strewn with some danger. For example, modern conditions such as ADHD, epilepsy and dyslexia occur when a single gene, AUTS2, malfunctions. There is sometimes a cost to pay when playing with neurological fire.

It's not quite that simple, though. If this were the case, wouldn't all mammals find increasingly large brains desirable? This is where we read the evolutionary small print: all benefits come with an associated cost, in this case a metabolic one, and it doesn't come cheap. In evolutionary terms it's no use to have one brainy individual who is a little better than others at predicting where an edible animal might be; the benefit of intelligence will only outweigh its costs if the whole group benefits. The key has been provided by the evolutionary psychologist Robin Dunbar. In his 'social brain hypothesis' he has proposed that increased brain size allows the maintenance of larger numbers of social relationships, and hence the development of larger social groups. The more complex relationships with individuals become, and the larger the number of relationships that need to be maintained, the greater the mental cost. Thus the larger the brains, the greater the number of individuals who can live together cooperatively.

It's easy to imagine the benefits of living in larger groups: protection from predators and competitors is simpler, and the greater availability of mates could reduce the chances of inbreeding. But large groups come at a cost, and this would be prohibitively expensive if individuals were still deriving their metabolic energy solely from plant foods; vegetarianism works in modern varied diets, but not on a seasonally changing savannah. One solution to the problem of how to power larger brains would be to focus on smaller packages of nutritious food that were relatively easy to digest in smaller guts, and that's where meat enters the picture.

An important question is whether the differences that distinguish us from other apes arose gradually or abruptly. Recent research reveals that other great apes possess at least a rudimentary form of several aspects of the 'complex cognition' thought to be unique to humans. This implies that our mental abilities evolved gradually, at least in the early stages. The two-man team of palaeoanthropologist Tom Wynn and evolutionary psychologist Fred Coolidge have pioneered the study of our mental evolution, arguing that it all began in neural wiring that evolved to support the dextrous manipulation of objects: once you can do that, you can make and use tools, and the earliest archaeological evidence shows that stool tools were being made by 3.3 million years ago.[7] Stone tool manufacture is not easy, and requires much practice (I've never been any good at it).

Evolutionary researchers attach a lot of importance to technology. Unlike bones and other organic materials, stone tools are virtually indestructible. As a result they are fairly common archaeologically, and they can be used to establish how early humans were thinking as they solved technical problems. As we'll see later, language is another thing that distinguishes us from apes, but it doesn't fossilize and we can't study its origins directly. Thankfully, toolmaking and language share overlapping neural circuits in the brain, probably because they both involve complex, goal-focused action, and the increasing importance of teaching the skills of stone toolmaking probably played an important role in the cognitive development of language.

Today, sophisticated neuroimaging techniques such as MRI scans can be used to map the neurological demands of even the simplest stone technology. MRI scanners are big, however, and it's not possible to get students to knap stone tools while lying inside their claustrophobic magnets. Instead, they are trained to make

How human technology began. This series of images shows the gradual excavation of a core from which several flakes have been struck at the 3.3 million-year-old site of Lomekwi 3 in Kenya. (Top left) The core has been located and its extent carefully delineated; (top right and bottom left) the core is exposed gradually by excavation of the surrounding sediment; (bottom right) freed from sediment and flipped around, scars where sharp flakes had been removed 3.3 million years ago are visible once more.

stone tools of different technological sophistication, and while in the scanner they are presented with a series of technical questions that stimulate what they understand of particular techniques. In this way, the MRI and other scans build up three-dimensional maps of the areas of their brains that are active when thinking of each specific question. By scanning the students' brains at three points – at the start of their training, during it, and at the end – the palaeoanthropologist Dietrich Stout and his team were able to show that as knapping skills improved from the manufacture of random sharp flakes to shaped handaxes, structural changes occurred in the brains of the subjects (see PL. I). Activity increased as they practised intensively during the first two stages, then decreased in the third. The simplest technology requires little beyond an ape brain other than an ability to pay close visual attention to blocks of stone and a degree of dexterity in manipulating them as they are struck. But the manufacture of handaxes requires considerably more cognitive control in the brain's prefrontal cortex. It needs an ability to envisage a specific shape and to control the hands in three dimensions carefully enough to impose that shape on the material. To make a handaxe required the ability to plan sequences of actions. The technological brain had been born.

So far, the earliest known tools come from Lomekwi 3 in Kenya, and were probably made by one of those bipedally walking apes, *Kenyanthropus platyops*. In a mixed woodland and bush thicket, large cobbles of stone were struck against each other, rather like how chimpanzees use them to crack nuts. But in this case the sharp flakes that had broken off were used to cut foods. This is very simple technology and may not even have been that common, but it already required good motor control of the hands.

A huge mental leap occurred with *Homo ergaster*, with the inferior prefrontal cortex of the brain, which is concerned with attention and predicting the effects of actions, coming into its own. Now, the brain's increasing ability to perceive three-dimensional blocks of stone and to impose an imagined shape on them was brought to bear on the creation of the handaxe, a calling card of *Homo ergaster*. Handaxes are one of the perennial celebrities of early Ice Age archaeology, dispersed in the hands of this species and later archaic hominins such as *Homo erectus* and *Homo heidelbergensis*, which would ultimately see them distributed from their 1.8-million-year-old roots in southern and eastern Africa as far as Britain to the north and China to the east. Although of varied size and shape they were the dominant stone technology for 1.5 million years, an all-round general purpose tool. Why they varied in space and time is often debated, but their importance is that they mark a point when humans began a continuous process of reflection and evaluation about the technology they created. No longer were their stone tools quickly made, used and forgotten with little reflection; they were the creation of a mindset that had begun to think about functional efficiency in ways that are central to our modern experience.

We've come a long way in a brief chapter, and we'll have to wave goodbye to the apes, who of course swung and knuckle-walked along their own evolutionary paths. There is much, of course, that I've left out, but I've emphasized the evolutionary developments I think important to the story of *Homo sapiens*; these took a branch-swinging, fruit-eating ape and turned it over the course of 5 million years or so into a large-brained, human-bodied, omnivorous problem-solver living in increasingly larger and more social groups. Those tough-times strategies required by the fragmentation of forested ape habitats brought about simple and later effective bipedalism, and freed up the brain to begin growing. That growth was paid for with nutritionally rich foods, facilitated by technological solutions including stone-tool production and the control of fire. By half a million years ago something very new was about to appear.

Chapter 2

The Molecular Frontier

It is said that in the famous Oxford evolution debate of 1860 in which Thomas Henry Huxley debated Charles Darwin's notion of evolution through natural selection with Bishop Samuel Wilberforce, Wilberforce asked Huxley if it was through his mother's or his father's line that he claimed to be descended from a monkey. He should have referred to apes, of course, rather than monkeys, but the point was made. Monkey and ape ancestry, what a preposterous idea! Little did the bishop know that the idea of human evolution would gain traction, and in little more than a century the controversy would be settled, with our African ape origins clarified beyond doubt by molecular science. My own, albeit somewhat more modest, molecular revelation occurred another half-century after that.

In 2007 I had my mitochondrial DNA sequenced. I was co-leading a team investigating the biology of the earliest agriculturalists to spread into Europe and replace the old hunting and gathering way of life. We were undertaking various molecular and isotopic analyses of human remains from a small cemetery associated with the 7,000-year-old village of Vedrovice in the Czech Republic. We had the skeletons of some eighty humans to work with, establishing their biological origins by sequencing their ancient DNA. The DNA analyses were being conducted by Barbara Bramanti, now of Ferrara University, and the first thing Barbara needed to do was to rule out the possibility that any of our team had contaminated the ancient samples with our own DNA while we were working with them. So it was not for vanity's sake that Barbara sequenced my mitochondrial DNA, but to allow her to minimize the risk of contamination.

Barbara emailed me the results, congratulating me for the hunter-gatherer ancestry they revealed. The specifics of my DNA could not have been more pleasing. In technical terms, Barbara had discovered that I belong to Haplogroup U5a1, which is nowadays a relatively rare set of genes and found in largest amounts in Central and Eastern Europe. We can think of U5 as a family of genes that had appeared by 30,000 years ago among the earliest *Homo sapiens* populations to have arrived in Europe. Around 27,000 years ago this genetic family split into two groups, of which U5a is one, which then spread further across Europe from around 20,000 years ago from a source somewhere between the Pyrenees, Balkans and Ukraine, and fragmented into several smaller groups in the last few thousand years of the Ice Age. It is no exaggeration to say that the U5 haplogroup is the true genetic representative of hunter-gatherers in Europe, having survived dilution by subsequent waves of those new-fangled agriculturalists after the Ice Age. These findings revolutionized how I saw myself, just as the revolutions of science have in turn revealed new amazing insights into the African origins of *Homo sapiens*.

Frontiers of archaeological science

To study human evolution is to study human variation. What makes us all different has very deep roots, and these can be traced back to Africa, where in the case of *Homo sapiens* they began unfolding around 300,000 years ago. Some Ice Age specialists research biological variation: diet, ecology, anatomy, cognition. Others, like me, research behavioural variation: technology, settlements, survival strategies, art, treatment of the dead. Ice Age specialists have long been used to working with bones, stones and sediments, but when I started my career in the 1990s it hadn't dawned on me that I would need to become literate in cutting-edge science. The study of the Ice Age was changing rapidly. Although 'revolution' is an over-used word in science, it's justified to say that archaeology has gone through one over the last two decades, and because there is so little evidence preserved the further one goes back, Ice Age archaeology has always been at the forefront of scientific innovation. Science has transformed the field. Now, geneticists, isotope geochemists, climatologists, physicists, statisticians and a host of other hard scientists contribute to our understanding of humanity's long-term evolution. Not that it's an easy process: scientists form cliques like any other group, and the sudden explosion of radical new techniques, such as the sequencing of ancient DNA, and the totally new insights these often provide into our origins can ruffle more feathers than *Archaeopteryx* in flight. We're still developing a rapport between the extremely wide range of different sciences that contribute to the very foundations of archaeology.

The transformation began in the 1980s, towards the end of which I began to study archaeology at university. Archaeological scientists were beginning to talk of molecules – groups of atoms that form the smallest units into which substances can be divided. A battery of scientific techniques that can be deployed to analyse archaeological remains at the molecular level were starting to make their mark on the past. Among the topics of interest were isotopes – atoms of the same element that differ in their mass and physical properties – and by the time that I came to work as the resident archaeologist in Oxford's radiocarbon dating laboratory, stable isotope analysis was being rolled out to better understand the evolution of human diet. Ancient DNA analysis began at the same time, and by the late 1990s the first genetic sequences of extinct humans were being produced. It is hard to keep up with the stunning advances of palaeogenetics, accounts of which read like a sci-fi novel. By the 2000s, proteomics – the study of the complete set of proteins made by an organism – was also being used to establish to what species even the smallest fragments of ancient bone belonged.

Unstable things: what molecular decay reveals about human origins

Archaeologists researching periods when people wrote things down and put dates on coins and inscriptions can usually date things quite precisely, sometimes to a specific year. Even where sources differ, they can be compared, and accurate chronologies generated. We know that the boy king Tutankhamun died in about 1323 BC, the emperor Augustus in AD 14, and that England was conquered by the Normans in AD 1066. But Ice Age people didn't record dates that can be traced forward to the present. Specialists in this epoch deal with vast stretches of time: for the origins of *Homo sapiens* we have to look back at least 300,000 years; for the earliest dispersals of our species out of Africa at least 100,000 years; for the earliest dispersal into Europe at least 40,000 years; and even 12,000 years for the end of the Ice Age. Certainly, it's a fraction of time compared to the history of life on Earth, but it's still vast and hazy. In order to date sites, fossils and archaeological objects that pre-date written history, we're dependent on a variety of laboratory dating techniques that rely on radioactive decay in the materials we're interested in. They are expensive, but essential if we're to locate our sites and materials in time and make sense of it all. The beauty of these techniques is that we can analyse vast periods of time using minuscule amounts of material – millennia from molecules. Yet we can barely comprehend these extremes. Just think about it: can you really grasp how long 50,000 years is, or envisage one among 10^{15} atoms (one in a quadrillion or, if you prefer, one atom per fifteen thousand million millions)? To radiocarbon scientists these are everyday concepts.

The principle of radiocarbon dating, the most commonly used technique, is simple. Most dating techniques are based on radioactive decay. Some isotopes of particular elements are unstable and decay from one type of atom into another. Unstable isotopes decay at a predictable rate, so if we measure how much of the isotope has decayed, we can establish a sample's age. Radiocarbon (or ^{14}C) is produced in the upper atmosphere through the complex interaction of cosmic rays with nitrogen. It then rapidly disperses through the air and into water bodies and terrestrial ecosystems. It enters plants through photosynthesis, passes into herbivores eating those plants, and in turn into omnivores and carnivores. It gets into everything living, but it is death that's important to archaeologists, because that is when the constant replacement of decaying radiocarbon in living things ceases.[1] In theory radiocarbon dating can be used to date anything that once lived, such as human and animal bones and teeth and plant charcoal from Ice Age sites. But there are a number of potential pitfalls. Carbon from contaminants which might provide a misleading date needs to be eliminated, and the rate of radiocarbon production in the atmosphere can vary from time to time, so raw measurements need to be calibrated in order to turn them into real dates.

In the 1980s our understanding of how old human fossils were was very imprecise. The prospect of directly dating human fossils was extremely exciting, and soon in the 1990s I was travelling between museums in Austria and Italy with my colleague, Erik Trinkaus, drilling minute samples of bone from the skeletons of Ice Age humans for just that purpose. Erik, a genial American with an infectious laugh, had already established a reputation as the world's leading authority on the health and pathology of Ice Age humans, and as we worked together I admired the meticulous way he studied each precious fragment of bone. In the stores of Vienna's Natural History Museum we worked hard, he with callipers and me with drill, surrounded by dozens of boxes, each marked 'Mozart'. The great composer was buried in an unmarked grave, and the museum is required to keep all skulls brought to it as possibly belonging to him. There are a lot of contenders. But we were interested in the museum's much older bones: some turned out to be younger than expected (Bronze Age gravediggers have a lot to answer for), while others turned out to be some of the oldest remains of *Homo sapiens* in Europe. Soon, I was able to expand the project to some of the earliest known burials, including the 34,000-year-old 'Red Lady of Paviland' in Wales (who we will meet in Chapters 9 and 16) and the 29,000-year-old Lapedo Child from Portugal (see PL. XXV).

Radiocarbon dating takes us back to 50,000 years ago, but no further because in samples older than that almost all the radiocarbon has decayed and measurement of what is left is not possible. For earlier periods, or for non-organic materials, we need other dating methods. This is where my old friend and colleague, Alistair Pike, comes in, through one of those pleasant chains of connections that often arise in academia. We were researching two caves in the limestone gorge of Creswell Crags in the English Midlands where we had found engravings of animals and other themes that looked like Ice Age art. We'll return to these much later, but the point here is that we really needed independent verification that these were Ice Age and not much later in date. But how? Unlike charcoal drawings, which can be dated by radiocarbon, these were engravings.

Alistair noted that, in places, small stalactites had grown over our engravings. He suggested that he should have a go at dating them with the uranium-thorium method, as it could be applied to stalactites as well as bone. The uranium-thorium technique has been used for half a century in palaeoclimate research: it can date the long periods of time over which stalactites and stalagmites formed in caves and corals in oceans. Its great advantage is that isotopes of uranium decay much more slowly than radiocarbon, meaning that its range extends back around half a million years into the Ice Age. What's more, it requires samples as little as half a billionth of a gram of uranium in size, small enough for us to convince the powers that be to allow us to take our drills to the cave walls of legally protected archaeological monuments. A few months later, Alistair's results showed that the stalactites had formed in some places around 7,000 years ago and in others as early as 13,000 years ago. As the engravings were underneath the dated stalactites, the art must be older, and at the very least must be early prehistoric and in other cases demonstrably Palaeolithic. That was the independent verification we needed.

Let's not stop there, Alistair reasoned. We could extend our dating to the impressive cave art of Spain and France. So it was that we teamed up with European colleagues and began the project I introduced in the Prologue, which went on to demonstrate that the Neanderthals were also producing some of the earliest art. All thanks to radioactive decay.

There is one more technique I need to introduce that is critical to dating Ice Age sites. Luminescence dating can be used to establish the time at which mineral-rich materials like sediments and flints were last exposed to heat. As radioactive isotopes decay in them, they release radioactive charges which accumulate in the mineral grains; the longer the process of decay, the greater the accumulation of charges. Stimulating these with either light (optically stimulated luminescence – OSL) or heat (thermoluminescence – TL) releases these charges, resetting the clock to zero. The relevance to dating is that sediments can be reset by daylight as they are being laid down by rivers or streams, and flints can be reset as they are thrown into hearths. After some complicated chemistry, stimulating a sample once more with either light (OSL) or heat (TL) in a dark laboratory releases the charge that has accumulated since their last heating. As the rate of accumulation is known, the age since the sample's last reset can be established, and hence, the date that a hearth on an Ice Age campsite burned or the sediments in which the archaeology accumulated were laid down.

Luminescence dating has proven to be critically important for dating the African archaeological sites that demonstrate the biological and behavioural evolution of our own species. Most importantly, it has shown that the earliest known fossils of *Homo sapiens*, found in the cave of Jebel Irhoud in Morocco, are more than 300,000 years old. This is a remarkably early date for the first dispersal of our own species, and as we have similar dates from eastern and southern Africa it reveals that from this time we had spread across the entire continent. But it's not just about dispersal; the illustration opposite shows what luminescence dating reveals about how our very behaviour was evolving towards something distinctly human too.

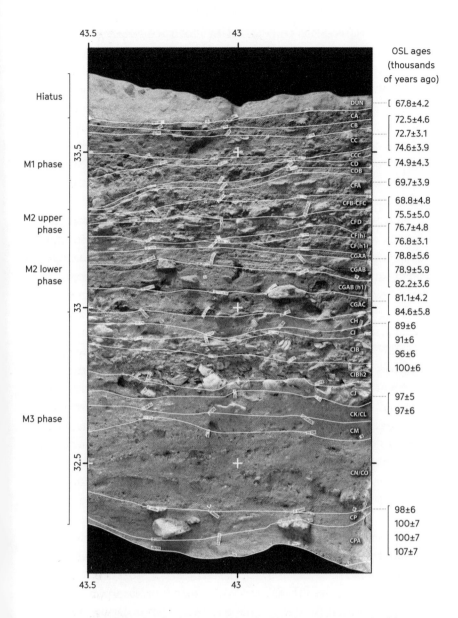

OSL and TL dates for the long sequence in Blombos Cave, South Africa. The white lines denote changes between distinct sedimentary levels in the cave. The dates for these are shown to the right (getting older with depth), in thousands of years with an error (imprecision of a few thousand years), hence level CP towards the bottom of the sequence dates to somewhere around 98,000–100,000 years ago. These dates are particularly important as level CP contained two mortars of natural sea shell, found with stone pestles, all stained with ochre, showing that the production of red pigment by grinding was being practised by our own species at least 100,000 years ago (see PLS II & VI).

Unstable things: what isotopes reveal about prehistoric diet

It was the late 1990s and Mike Richards and I had begun to roll out his skills to look at the stable isotopes in human teeth and bones and what they revealed about Ice Age diet. Mike and I had become friends in Oxford, where he was undertaking his doctoral research on the analysis of isotopes in human bone. Soon after, he had established himself as the world's leading authority on Ice Age human isotopes and what they reveal about past diet.

Biology constructs our bones in a clever way. Our bodies digest proteins, absorbing amino acids, and then build the proteins that give our bones a tensile strength (the ability to withstand forces that pull them apart), interwoven with various minerals that give our bones their ability to withstand forces that compress. The main structural protein, collagen, is of importance here, as isotopic analysis of small amounts of collagen sampled from a human or animal bone can reveal where the protein was derived from. The ratio of the stable isotopes of carbon ^{12}C to ^{13}C reflects the relative proportions of terrestrial and aquatic protein in the diet, and nitrogen ^{15}N levels the amount of protein obtained from an animal diet. Together, the isotopes will tell us where an organism that once lived got its dietary protein from. The bones on archaeological sites can thus tell us a lot about what animals were being eaten while the sites were occupied, and if we're lucky the odd fragment of plant remains will tell us about the contribution of seeds, nuts and fruits. This is all good, but as Ice Age hunter-gatherers were highly mobile, the isotopes don't reveal what people were eating during the course of a whole year, over which diets likely varied considerably. Isotopes will average out the protein sources of the diet, either early in life (teeth) or in the last ten years or so (bones).

Mike had analysed the isotopes of a number of European Ice Age human bones that I'd been sampling for radiocarbon dating. We'll return to some of them in Chapter 8. His results showed us the first nuanced picture of Ice Age diet, in this case between 20,000 and 30,000 years ago. Meat was by far the most important source of protein, which was not surprising as there are few plant sources of protein on the Ice Age tundra. But what was surprising was that river fish formed a far more important source of protein than we had realized. It doesn't pay to stand in a freezing river trying to spear the odd fish: that's fine for the occasional treat, but it is too hard a price to pay for limited returns. Our evidence that fish did nevertheless form an important source of protein must indicate that some kind of trapping technology was in use that increased the nutritional returns while staving off the chilblains. Most importantly, it showed that food was obtained from a variety of sources (known as a broad spectrum diet), which had probably given *Homo sapiens* an evolutionary advantage over the preceding Eurasian Neanderthals by way of its in-built 'insurance policy'. In the modern world, if a whole aisle in the supermarket is closed, we can simply buy from another aisle. But hunter-gatherers are entirely at the mercy of the wild resources they hunt, gather and fish: if their selection is relatively limited – say the animals that Neanderthals relied upon – even modest fluctuations in availability could prove fatal. A broader set of resources adds a degree of resilience: if one source fails, others can be turned to. These are simply more flexible tough-times strategies. The suggestion is that a critically important evolutionary transition had come about. Even though fish bones had been recovered from the archaeological sites from which the bones we'd analysed came, they were not abundant, and we'd have totally missed this important development if it weren't for the isotopes.

Genetics and human evolution

What can you do with a scrappy little bit of bone? One that otherwise might languish forever in a museum store? When I was a student the answer would have been 'nothing much at all', but today, thanks to remarkable biomolecular advances, the answer is more likely to be 'a great deal, including discovering extinct human species'.

As Ice Age sites accumulate in natural sediments they are subject to various processes of erosion, which means that bones are often broken, softened, scoured and otherwise reduced to worn little fragments. But while their shape may offer us little, they still contain their proteins, and these have much to reveal, especially when it comes to genetics.

DNA from both living and ancient populations can tell us a lot about evolution. The patterns in our genes reflect ancestral relationships, which can be traced back like family trees. Ancient DNA provides comparable points in deep time. In theory, DNA can be extracted from anything that once lived, from human bones and mammoth hair, ostrich eggshells and reindeer antler, and even traces adhering to grains of sediment and soil. It is truly the ghost of Ice Age individuals. If you think it is difficult wrapping your head around the lengths of time we deal with in the Ice Age, try genetics for size. Each of our bodies is comprised of *trillions* of cells. Every single cell contains identical copies of our DNA. Most of it is found in the cell's nucleus, its command centre (nuclear DNA); some of it is found in mitochondria, structures which generate chemical energy for cells. In every cell, genetic information is stored in pairs of two of four chemical bases, joined together like the rungs of a ladder, and each base pair, along with a sugar and a phosphate structure (the rails), comprises a nucleotide. Sequences of nucleotides group together as two long strands which spiral together into the famous double helix. Along the double helix, groups of base pairs of a few hundred to more than two million in length form genes, and a long strand of DNA containing multiple genes is known as a chromosome. Genes are the blueprint for producing proteins, and as such are the basic units of heredity: their specific instructions are coded as a specific sequence of base pairs (hence to reconstruct these is called sequencing). The sum total of genes in the human body – up to 25,000 – comprises the genome. Today, our individual genomes are 99.9 per cent identical to everyone else. In terms of variation it's the small differences that count.

The differences between single nucleotides are called single nucleotide polymorphisms or SNPs (pronounced *snips*), and occur in roughly every 1,000 base pairs. There are roughly 4–5 million of them in our genome, and they are important since they are the most common form of genetic differences between people. Along with deletions and repeats they are what make each of us individuals. A set of genes which tend to be inherited together is called a *haplotype* – and a set of these inherited by a number of individuals from a common parent is a *haplogroup*. As these reflect a single line of descent, they form a basic unit of analysis in population genetics. The most commonly studied haplogroups are Y-chromosomal (Y-DNA), passed from father to son, and mitochondrial (mtDNA), passed from mother to her offspring of both sexes. Most chromosomes swap stretches of DNA with each other when eggs and sperm are being made. But the Y-chromosome doesn't get involved with that swapping, and mtDNA is sealed away inside the mitochondria, which means that when geneticists spot changes in them, they can only have occurred through random mutation (copying error) over time. Genetic diversity comes about when individuals who possess one or more mutated genes pass them on. In this way, individuals not only inherit their haplogroup, but can themselves found new subgroups.

If you focus on your own mtDNA you will trace your inheritance back to a different ancestor than if you look at your Y-DNA. It's only by using sophisticated statistics to view these different trees together that geneticists can understand the complexity of evolution. We just need one final level of organization before we can begin to understand what genetics tells us of our Ice Age origins, and that is the so-called structured metapopulation, which only means the interactions between populations. Subpopulations (genetic family groups) connect together as one metapopulation through sharing of DNA brought about by individual movement, population movement and isolation, as well as local population expansions and extinctions. As we will see, such movements over vast periods of time are the stuff of Ice Age hunter-gatherer research, and, most importantly, metapopulations should correspond to the beautiful variations in our own species.

Genetics is a far from simple field, and there are many pitfalls that ingenious ancient DNA researchers have overcome. The first problem is that of age: the further we try to trace our genetic ancestors back, the weaker the information becomes, until it blends into the shadowy world of 300,000 years ago. The key to the frontiers of ancient DNA is to understand the changes that occur to its structure when it decays in bones over time. Ironically, most ancient DNA found in a bone does not originally derive from the owner of that bone: most of the DNA in a mammoth tusk, for example, will not be mammoth. The majority of it will have been introduced by microbes and fungi; the relatively little left that actually derives from the bone itself remains only in very low numbers of small, scrappy fragments – some sections less than 30 base pairs in length (to put this in perspective, Chromosome 1 has 249 million base pairs) – which themselves may have been damaged. As time passes, the double helix effectively breaks up into sharp-ended segments (think of sawing up that ladder), and the overhanging broken ends of the 'rails' undergo chemical changes which can change their identity and lead to misleading sequences. It took some time for geneticists to work out a way around this, but it can now be done. Some bones preserve uncontaminated DNA much better than others, such as the petrous temporal bone, as we've seen. Contamination is always a worry: handling or breathing on ancient bones can introduce our own DNA into the mix, but modern excavations use sterile excavation and laboratory techniques to minimize this risk. While we can never be sure that all contamination has been removed, methods of analysis take this uncertainty into account.

The first step on the road to this genetic revolution came in 1984, when 229 base pairs of ancient mitochondrial DNA were sequenced from the dried muscle of a quagga, an extinct form of zebra. The signs of a scientific revolution spread like wildfire, and sequences of human ancient DNA followed swiftly, commencing in 1985 with the 2,400-year-old mummy of an Egyptian child. In 2005 it became possible to reconstruct long sequences of DNA from several shorter fragments, with short sequences of DNA matched up where they overlap, and then cloned (copied many times). In 1997 the DNA of an extinct human – *Homo neanderthalensis* – was sequenced, and by 2010 its whole genome was published. The mitochondrial genome of the extinct woolly mammoth followed in 2006, and by 2014 – in terms of genetic science a lifetime ago – 19.4 *giga-* (19,400,000,000) basepairs were sequenced from the hairs of another quagga. And it is fair to say that the genetics of Ice Age humans and animals are today light years ahead of even these remarkable achievements.

We are indeed at the frontiers of palaeogenetics. This is the era of personal genomics, in which the 3 billion base pairs in a single human genome can be sequenced. As costs drop for high-throughput sequencing, it will become fully automated, better at dealing with damaged and minuscule fragments and hence able to reach back further in time or into bones which have so far failed to yield any surviving DNA. This will be particularly important for human fossils from Africa, where relatively warm and moist soil conditions can accelerate decay (just like food left out of the fridge). Increasing use of computer modelling and artificial intelligence will also allow far better control over damaged DNA and the elimination of contaminants. While a cloned mammoth or sabre tooth cat may still be the stuff of fantasy, we're getting a lot closer.

We are also able to extract proteins from bones, the success of which has been just as revolutionary as ancient DNA. There are several ways to extract and examine tiny amounts of ancient proteins. One of these was developed by Matthew Collins, a world-leading biomolecular archaeologist, and his then doctoral student at York University, Mike Buckley. This goes by the catchy acronym ZooMS (Zooarchaeology by Mass Spectrometry) and can 'mass fingerprint' collagen from scrappy fragments otherwise useless to archaeologists. A laser is used to release molecules from solids by vaporizing a small part of them, ionizing them, and measuring their mass in a particle accelerator.[2] Peptides – the constituent parts of proteins – vary a little from species to species, and hence can be used to identify the species to which fragmentary bones belong. This is of immense use to the study of our interaction with animals over time, as some animals, such as bison and the extinct wild cattle aurochs, or sheep and goat, are often difficult to tell apart. ZooMS has solved that issue.

Archaeologists such as Katerina Douka, a scientist at Germany's Max Planck Institute for the Science of Human History, and my successor at Oxford, Tom Higham, quickly realized the potential of ZooMS for Ice Age archaeology, and were soon trawling museum drawers for bones to characterize with the technique. Their labours repaid the effort dramatically: one fragment excavated from Denisova Cave in Siberia was shown to be human. Subsequent DNA sequencing revealed that Denny – as it came to be known – belonged to a previously unidentified human species, the Denisovans. If this weren't enough, Denny's DNA had other secrets to reveal, as we'll see in Chapter 5. ZooMS is a stunning scientific advance: it's relatively cheap, and hundreds of bone fragments can be checked quickly. It continues to surprise; recently it revealed that 8,000- to 9,000-year-old harpoon points dredged up from the North Sea were made of human bone, and there will no doubt be many more shocks in store. Soon, it will probably be used to identify what animals (or humans) have been butchered by Ice Age stone tools, through analysis of the proteins left on them.

Genetics and African origins

Since Darwin, Huxley and others pointed to the anatomical similarities between us and the African apes, we've known that human origins can be pinpointed to Africa. The degree to which the origin of *Homo sapiens* could be restricted to Africa was, however, debated until the late 1980s. The few human fossils from that vast continent suggested we'd been around there longer than everywhere else, but since fossils were lacking from many other areas of the world, how could we be so confident that the picture was that simple? It was genetics that finally answered that question, and we now know that *Homo sapiens* evolved in Africa, dispersed across the continent by 300,000 years ago, and then out of Africa during several periods of expansion from around 100,000 years ago. It's less clear where exactly in Africa we originated. A comparison of 580,000 SNPs (those snips!) from modern African hunter-gatherers shows that it is most likely that if there is any one region we can pinpoint our origins to, it is southern Africa. We have to remember that while lineages in a genetic tree relate to parent–offspring descent, they *don't* relate

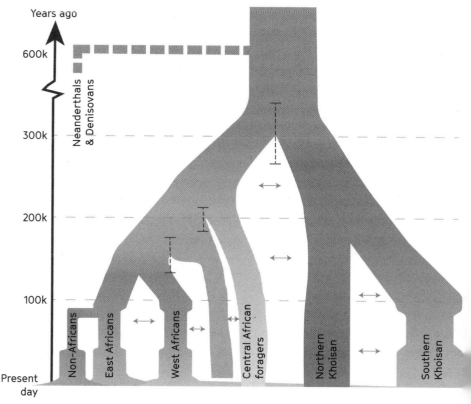

Ice Age population divergences in Africa according to haplogroup differences in the genomic sequences of living and archaeological Africans, from around 600,000 years ago (top) to the present day. The first major divergence into southern African Khoisan hunter-gatherers and more northerly Bantu farmers occurred around 300,000 years ago (with the vertical dashed line showing the error margin). Further divergence occurs within these two major haplogroups between 200,000 and 75,000 years ago. Arrows between these later haplogroups show major migrations.

to populations as a whole. Nor do the splits in the branches where lineages diverge correspond to actual population divergences. Add to this the fact that populations have never been static – far from it in the case of Ice Age ancestors – and we're probably underestimating how much genes have been shared over huge distances and between various human groups.

Most of this information has come not from ancient DNA but from that of living people. Given that genetic diversity accumulates through random mutations, insertions and deletions over time, it's easy to see that in most cases, the greater the observable genetic diversity in any given region of the world the longer its population has been around: they have simply had more time for diversity to accumulate. Whether it's mitochondrial, nuclear or genome-wide, the Khoisan[3] populations of southern Africa are genetically the most diverse on Earth. There is more variability today between Khoisan people than there is between Europeans and Asians. Their genes are an echo of our ancient, pre-agriculturalist origins, and the Khoisan use of clicks – like our *tut tut/ tsk tsk* and similar sounds – as consonants are probably some of the oldest known human communicative sounds.

Our origin in sub-Saharan Africa is thus clear. Following that, the earliest genetic divergence identified in African *Homo sapiens* groups is between the southern Khoisan and East African populations, when the Y-chromosome split into two haplogroups deriving from a very early split between Khoisan- and Bantu-speaking groups respectively. Each of these then became further divided into sub-branches that are characteristic of different groups and regions of southern, central and eastern Africa. The results indicate a very deep population structure in southern Africa stretching back at least 260,000 and possibly as much as 350,000 years ago.

It is worth mentioning here that 'race' is a social, not a biological phenomenon: it's a classificatory system that emerged out of – and helped to support – European colonialism, and it came to be used to structure social groups and betrayed entirely subjective prejudices over the course of several centuries. As the understanding of human origins and variability grew during the Enlightenment, 'race' became entwined with the colonial powers' notions of cultural (and therefore biological) supremacy. Race has no genetic foundation. Characteristics such as skin, hair and eye colour, and cheek, chin and nose shape, which have been used in the past to pigeonhole people, have minuscule genetic triggers which serve largely to adapt people to different environments where certain traits may be favourable (it's why the Dinka of Sudan are tall and the Inuit of the Arctic are shorter, reflecting the need to keep cool or keep warm respectively). There is more genetic variation within modern populations in the USA or China than there is between them. Genomic data clearly refute the notion that distinct groups can be genetically distinguished from each other. They can't, and 'race' is simply an unhelpful concept.

By the way, Huxley's reply to Wilberforce's question that I began this chapter with was that he would not be ashamed to have a monkey for an ancestor, but would be ashamed to have an ancestor who (like Wilberforce, he implied) used his intelligence to obscure the truth. The seeds of modern science had been sown, and attention focused on Africa as the source of monkey, ape and finally human evolution. We now know definitively that by 300,000 years ago groups of *Homo sapiens* were spread here and there across Africa. As Ice Age climate changed from cold and dry to warm and wet, regional environments followed suit, and along with them so did regional ecology. Subpopulations of humans and other animals expanded, contracted and moved around the continent: groups met and individuals mated, spreading the haplogroup around and contributing to the developing subgroup variability. Some groups thrived, expanding in numbers and increasing their gene flow: others failed, becoming locally extinct as their resources shut down.[4] A complex set of biological traits, inherited from more archaic ancestors at least half a million years ago, was shared and put to the evolutionary test. The more successful of these included our large, globe-like brains, long-legged and small-armed bodies, small faces and distinct chins. Behaviourally, they included a flexible way of thinking and problem-solving, a growing set of resources to draw upon, an ability to live in larger and increasingly more social groups, and, perhaps, an imaginative desire to see what was over the next hill, at least when the weather allowed.

Chapter 3

Climate Change and Environment

I was standing with a number of palaeoenvironmentalists and archaeologists in a walk-in freezer, as if Copenhagen wasn't cold enough already. We'd entered it willingly, and despite the shivering we were excited to be there. It was 2009 and I was attending a conference on the late Ice Age. During a break we were treated to a tour of the Niels Bohr Institute of Copenhagen University, or, to be specific, what must surely be the university's coldest room. My teeth chattered as I watched a glaciologist carefully uncover what looked like a gigantic ice-lolly. Holding the cloudy tube up to the ceiling light, the banded ice sparkled like jewelry. It was a section of an ice core, drilled through the Greenland ice down to bedrock over 3 km (2 miles) down. This section was particularly special for me: it was laid down some 20,000 years ago, first as snow and then slowly compacting into layers of ice, during the last severe cold snap of the Ice Age. At the same time this snow was falling on Greenland, hunter-gatherers elsewhere were being put through their toughest survival challenge. In Africa, arid climate favoured the growth of seasonally dry grasslands, and in Eurasia sub-arctic environments were mantled in snow for much of the year. In a long line of challenges it was the last severe test of the Ice Age that humanity faced.

Secrets of the ice

It all begins with water. We don't call Earth the blue planet for nothing. For billions of years it has stored water in three forms, vapour, liquid and solid, which makes our home unique in the Solar System. Most of it – nearly 97 per cent – is stored in the oceans; the rest in the cryosphere (glaciers and ice), terrestrial reservoirs (groundwater, lakes and rivers) and atmosphere (vapour in clouds and greenhouse gases). Life on Earth originated in water and living species still reflect that: on average the human body comprises 60 per cent water, and 73 per cent of the brain and heart are water. Its influence is everywhere. Water vapours determine planetary temperature, which in turn determines habitability; oceanic waters transport heat and nutrients around the planet; precipitation sustains life; and the great ice sheets at the planet's poles help regulate climate and weather, which in turn determine the water cycle. The heat released as water cycles between vapour, liquid and solid determines global climate and weather, and on land this determines the terrestrial environments in which species evolve and adapt.

Water, climate, weather and life are locked together in a close symbiosis. Changes in the way the Earth orbits the Sun – the shape and extent of its orbit, the angle at which it tilts, and the degree to which it wobbles like a top – cause substantial shifts in the distribution of water within and between its reservoirs and in the interplay between fresh and saline waters. These drive climate change. In terms of Earth history, climate change of this nature is not new: it is *human-made* effects that are. Earth has gone through ice ages every 200 million years or so, some of which were far more destructive than the most recent. Around 430 million years ago, during the Ordovician, a massive refrigeration of the Earth occurred as a glacier over what is now Africa spread across the entire planet. Life on Earth at the time was restricted to the oceans, which froze on the surface. Well over half the living species became extinct. It was the first great cull of Earth's life, although the surviving ecosystem evolved, with many losses along the way, into the species of the Ice Age and of the present day.

Humans have been on Earth for only one broad Ice Age: its most recent. This is the 2.5-million-year-long Pleistocene, which was actually a series of climatic shifts between severely cold glacials and warm interglacials (such as the one we've been in for the last 11,700 years). For much of the Pleistocene the climate was colder than today, but not severe; the extreme glacials and interglacials account for only 20 per cent of Pleistocene time. But there was incessant change on less extreme scales between these peaks, and it is this instability that formed the background to our evolution. Cores drilled through polar ice reveal snows that fell hundreds of thousands of years ago, the layers of which contain the chemical clues to unlocking Earth's palaeoclimate and, by extension, weather. This is supported by evidence from ocean and lake sediment cores and other sources.

Dr Dirk Hoffmann reconstructs Holocene and Pleistocene climate based on isotopes that have accumulated over time in cave flowstones (stalactites and stalagmites), which can be correlated with records from ocean, lake and ice cores. Here, he is about to sample an impressive stalagmite in the Almonda karst system in Portugal.

Climate Change and Environment

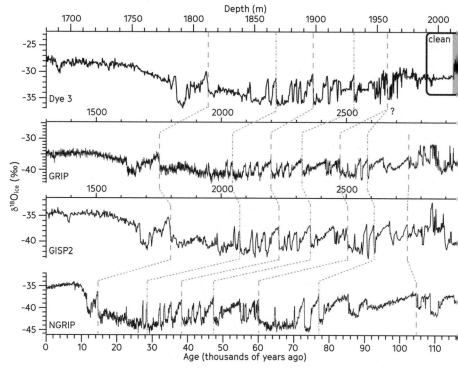

Climate change, Ice Age style. Oxygen isotope ratios of four Greenland ice cores plotted by depth in metres (top) and age in thousands of years before present (bottom), matched on the basis of oxygen ratios (dotted lines). All four cores sample the same period of time from the present back to over 100,000 years ago, but as these were drilled at separate locations where ice accumulations varied, they grew at different rates.

The Antarctic and Greenland ice sheets were, for most of the Pleistocene and succeeding Holocene, kept in a complex balance between the snow that accumulates (compacting to about 6.5 mm or 0.25 in. ice annually) and the amount that is lost to melting at their edges. But since 1990 the amount of loss has far outstripped gain. The vast ice reservoir is melting, and when it has completely melted, global sea level will have risen by 70 m (230 ft). That would put the highest point of my hometown, Portsmouth, 67 m (220 ft) under the sea. Climate-change deniers: don't say you haven't been warned.

Ice contains many elements and molecules deriving from when it was laid down, and among these are the stable isotopes of oxygen ^{16}O and ^{18}O, in a ratio that reflects the air temperature at the time it was snowing. Since ^{16}O is lighter it is more likely to turn into vapour than ^{18}O, which being heavier is more likely to turn into rain or snow. The difference between the two becomes far more marked in cold

Chapter 3

temperatures, which is where it becomes very relevant to the Ice Age, as a reflection of annual air temperature. Deep cores have been drilled through the ice on all continents, but in large numbers near to the planetary poles on Antarctica and in Greenland. Some of these stretch down nearly 4 km (2.5 miles) and back in time half a million years or more. Individual layers corresponding to annual snowfall can be seen very clearly: the densest layers reflect winter, the lightest summer. They can be counted back, year by year: this gets more difficult with increasing depth as the layers are compressed by the weight of ice above them, but grey layers of dust accumulated during times when the Earth's climate was cold, dry and windy can be used to separate annual layers further back down to bedrock. Points along the cores can be dated by using yet more dating techniques using radioactive isotopes.

The freezers of the Niels Bohr Institute contain some 15 km (9 miles) of ice from a number of drilling projects. The GRIP project drilled a core through the highest (and therefore deepest) point of the Greenland ice sheet, hitting bedrock 3,029 m (9,940 ft) down, where the lowest ice was formed from snow that fell 200,000 years ago. It matches other cores exceptionally well, and together these provide a remarkable record of climate change from the point at which *Homo sapiens* began to disperse out of Africa. Climate alternated dramatically over this period, from severely cold stadials to relatively mild interstadials, each lasting anything from one century to several thousand years. These fluctuations seem to be caused by changes in heat circulation between the oceans and the ice sheets, and show a repeated pattern of rapid warming of as much as 16°C (29°F) in a few decades, followed by much slower cooling over the course of centuries or millennia. They vary from region to region, but their effects spread rapidly and they are, therefore, global events.[1] We will see how these and the corresponding changes brought about in terrestrial environments played a major role in the repeated success and failure of human dispersals across Europe and Asia. For now though, it's time to return to Africa.

Climate and African tough-times strategies

We were standing nervously in the middle of thick bush, a few armed guards on the fringe of the small group, and our expedition leader, the human evolution specialist Lee Berger, rifle slung over his shoulder, was laying down some basic bush safety.

'Most things out here can kill you; if they don't, they'll make you very ill.'

Our South African, American and British team were near the border with Zimbabwe, surveying the banks of the Limpopo River for Ice Age remains. The guards were there to protect us from lions, hippos, and perhaps the most dangerous animal of all, poachers. Lee and my other co-team member, physical anthropologist Steve Churchill, were well used to conducting fieldwork in the bush. I, on the other hand, worried ceaselessly about the myriad animals that could, as he spoke, already have their sights on me. *If it's dangerous enough for me*, I thought, with our camp surrounded by a carnivore-proof ring of lit braziers and patrolled by rifle-wielding guards, *what would it have been like for our ancestors?*

Early humans in Africa had to deal with two extreme environmental consequences of the Ice Age. In tropical latitudes such as Africa the cool temperatures of glacial periods meant less rainfall and hence greater aridity. As a result, seasonal, arid savannah environments began to develop in the later Miocene (around 5 to 8 million years ago), initiating the process of diversification and isolation in ape populations which formed the backdrop to human evolution. By contrast, the increased temperatures during warm interglacials saw major precipitation in the tropics, leading to the greening of deserts, expansion of rainforests, and high lake-levels. During these periods the resources available for a human omnivore diversified and spread, as did the ecosystems of which small human groups were part. Humans first dispersed across the entire African continent, and later out of it. Then, as conditions declined once more and favourable environments disappeared, local extinctions followed. Imagine those human-friendly environments, mixed grasslands and woodlands with access to fresh water, expanding and contracting on centennial and millennial scales, constantly stirring Africa's ecosystems. At times, human groups were widely dispersed and probably highly mobile, while at others they were low in number, restricted in distribution and more isolated from each other. Such flux explains how the set of anatomical traits that define *Homo sapiens* came to spread across our home continent and by 300,000 years ago had coalesced to form a new human species.

Humans did not evolve in rainforests. Although they are the most productive ecosystems on Earth, their rainfall is highly seasonal and their productivity unpredictable. Most of their nutrients are available as only woody plants high up in the canopy, and animal fat and protein are rare. While they may be good for vegetarian and omnivorous monkeys and apes, they cannot sustain large human populations. Instead, it was those expanding grasslands and open woodlands that offered a diverse and easily accessed set of resources, and provided refuge for our early ancestors in eastern and southern Africa. We can reconstruct the environments they were living in through analysis of the microscopic remains of plants and bones of animals that have been recovered from archaeological sites or found in cores drilled through lake sediments. The sediments that archaeological sites formed in will tell us whether they were located in proximity to river or lake banks, or in upland plateaux. Putting all of this information together tells us

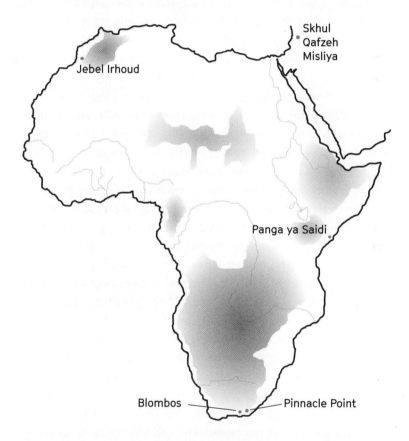

African cave sites with major archaeological remains documenting the period from 300,000 to 50,000 years ago. Upland areas, which separate the different regions in which our species evolved, are shaded. Enough contact between groups at a continental scale ensured that the emerging large-brained humans remained genetically similar.

a lot about the types of environment that were crucial for sustaining early *Homo sapiens* populations. Laura Basell of Leicester University has shown how surviving archaeological sites in East Africa cluster around the margins of lakes such as Turkana and Victoria, in scrubby treeless grasslands or those with a few trees (savannah), and in montane and open woodlands. A wide range of plant resources was available in the grasslands and woodlands, and grazing and browsing animals could predictably be found close to water, which also offered aquatic resources.

These environments were always temporary, lasting perhaps a few centuries or millennia before shrinking once more. On occasion they could be wiped out completely. Around 100,000 years ago many of the volcanoes lying along the axis of the volcanically active 2,000-km- (1,250-mile-) long Rift Valley of Kenya and Ethiopia collapsed into calderas. These were huge eruptions that deposited vast amounts of lava and ash over land and sea, traces of which can even be found in the polar ice cores. It blanketed Africa's lakes and grasslands, profoundly altering ecosystems. We all know from Pliny what the eruption of Vesuvius did for the inhabitants of Pompeii, and there are similar accounts of the destruction of 70 per cent of the island of Krakatoa, Indonesia, and its surrounding archipelago when that volcano collapsed violently into a caldera in 1883.

The rising sea levels of temperate periods acted as the southern African equivalent of the volcanoes, swamping large shrublands which had supported diverse animals from molerats and tortoises to zebras and hippos. Analysis of phytoliths – minuscule particles of silica that are often the only remains of ancient plants – reveals that in the caves of Pinnacle Point on the coast of the Western Cape, grasses, shrubs and tree wood were employed as early as 170,000 years ago as fuel for small, fast-burning hearths used to cook shellfish. In subsequent arid conditions, dry wood was gathered, probably to fuel small hearths for baking stone from which to make tools. Microscopic changes to the stone's structure caused by this early form of heat treatment improved the way the material behaved when it was hit with a stone hammer, giving the toolmaker or knapper finer control over its shaping: a small, but nevertheless significant early sign of human modification of the environment.

For at least 200,000 years, these temporary expansions and contractions within Africa were the norm for the new humans, and when one expansion first saw them venture beyond Africa this was merely a brief appearance in the adjacent areas of the Arabian Peninsula and Levant. It would be wrong, however, to view this as a failure or as some kind of false start. Dispersals in the natural world are not one-way; expansion and contraction, often with associated extinction, is the norm, and this applies equally to humans as it does to animals and plants. Two of the crew of Apollo 11 spent a mere one day on the Moon's surface, a temporary dispersal dictated by available resources (oxygen, food and fuel). But we would hardly describe it as a failure: we'll be back very soon, right?[2] Africa has a vast and remarkably complex range of environments on which a profusion of factors influenced Ice Age climate change, including sea surface temperatures, monsoon weather systems, landmass uplift, volcanism, and expanding and contracting glaciers and lakes. No wonder regional variations on the ape, australopithecine and human themes arose as a result.

Eventually, ecological expansion took humans and other animals out of Africa a number of times, several of which we can see archaeologically. There is nothing implicitly sophisticated about dispersing out of Africa; Miocene apes did it, as did early members of the genus *Homo*, and another success of the African Miocene, the biped *Struthio* – the humble ostrich – which, like *Homo erectus*, dispersed across the Eurasian grasslands as far as China.

Today, we're used to the idea that the sands of the vast Sahara Desert form a barrier between north and sub-Saharan Africa. But it hasn't always been that way. At various times during the last 8 million years, the region was green for several millennia. During those warm and wet periods this 'Green Sahara' and the adjacent 'Green Arabia' supported a mix of lush and semi-arid grasslands crossed by myriad rivers and lakes amounting to thousands of square kilometres of water. This would have offered repeated opportunities for our ancestors to disperse out of Africa, either during population expansions or when these environments closed down, 'pumping' their occupants not southwards but northwards and eastwards out of the continent.

We can get a good glimpse of early *Homo sapiens* during one of these Green Sahara episodes at Jebel Irhoud in Morocco, where a series of caves and hollows continues to produce a treasure trove of human bones, teeth and archaeological remains of their stays at the site (see PL. III). Most of these derive from a single layer rich in bone towards the bottom of the site's sediments (called Layer 7). The stone

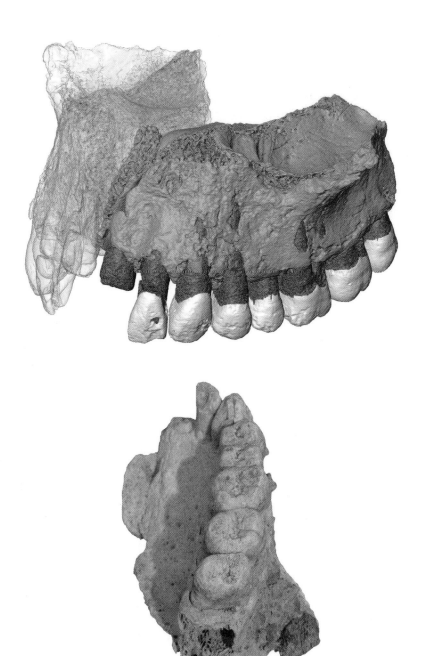

An approximately 200,000-year-old half upper jaw bone (bottom) from Misliya Cave in Mount Carmel (Israel), and its three-dimensional digital reconstruction (top). Note how the dark staining of the cave sediments adhering to it have been removed in the digital image. Morphologically this bone can be identified as *Homo sapiens*, reflecting an early dispersal into the Levant.

tools, also scattered around the site, are similar to those produced around the same time elsewhere in Africa, suggesting that *Homo sapiens* shared a continent-wide culture by this time. Thankfully, some of these tools had become heated by the hearths, allowing their dating by thermoluminescence (TL) to at least 315,000 years ago. The group probably lit small hearths, charcoal from which was scattered around the layer, and if the site's zooarchaeological remains are anything to go by they ate well. The bones and teeth of gazelle, zebras, wildebeest and hartebeest bear the telltale marks of butchery for meat and marrow. But the remains of other predators – leopards, lions and smaller cats – remind us of the challenges our early ancestors faced daily in these dangerous environments. The human remains recovered from the site show that many aspects of our anatomy had already emerged (see PL. IV). The Irhoud people, as with all *Homo sapiens*, differed from the Neanderthals (mainly found to the north in Western Eurasia) in having faces that were tucked under an expanded braincase, and while they retained fairly marked brows these had begun to separate from a single ridge into two distinct brows (PL. V).

The archaeology of the caves that riddle the coastal range in northern Israel has recently shown how *Homo sapiens* expanded its range outside of Africa much earlier than was previously thought. In Misliya Cave on Mount Carmel's western slopes, part of a human jaw dating to at least 180,000–200,000 years ago was found amid the stone tools and other remains left by the cave's inhabitants. Recent uranium-thorium dating of a fragment of *Homo sapiens* cranium from Apidima Cave in Greece to around 210,000 years ago suggests that the southeasternmost tip of Europe was also inhabited in this period.

We've seen how the dramatically unstable climate of the Ice Age drove constant environmental change, and how early groups of *Homo sapiens* dispersed and contracted across African environments as favourable conditions opened up and shut down on millennial scales. By 300,000 years ago, in warm and wet periods when even the Sahara was green, our species had already dispersed across the entire continent, and to similar environments in neighbouring parts of the Levant by 200,000 years ago. More dispersals followed, perhaps each one a little farther, like the Apollo lunar missions. But the grasslands favourable to human hunting and gathering did not end in Western Eurasia. At times of opportunity they could stretch as far east as China, which is where we will now track our intrepid ancestors.

Chapter 4

Dispersal:
from Africa to Asia

The little shells were tiny, and so fragile, cupped in the palm of my hand. It was still early, but already the South African sun was hot. We knelt in the shade of the mouth of Blombos Cave, and looking out across the ocean I thought, excitedly, that from a human perspective *this is the edge of the Ice Age world.*

We were a group of around fifteen, and had travelled some 250 km (160 miles) to the east of Cape Town, where we had been discussing the origins of human symbolism at a workshop organized by the cave's excavating team, Christopher Henshilwood and Francesco d'Errico. Now we were being treated to a personal tour of an archaeological site that has become iconic in the story of the origins of *Homo sapiens.* The little cave, its mouth now protected by a wall of sandbags, would have offered a spectacular view of the coastal plain during the Ice Age. As sea levels were lower than today's, the ocean would have been more distant and waking inhabitants could rise, clear the sleep from their eyes, and glance over a rich plain full of gatherable resources such as molluscs, some edible, some less so but with decorative shells.

The little shells that Francesco held in his hand, which had been excavated from the cave's Stone Age layers, were those of the whelk *Nassarius kraussianus.* They had been carefully heated to blacken them, and delicately pierced to be strung or sewn onto clothing. Someone had dropped or discarded them when the camp was abandoned, and there they lay until they were excavated 75,000 years later.

Very similar shells to the Blombos examples, of *Nassarius gibbosulus*,[1] also perforated, have been found in Skhul Cave on Mount Carmel in Israel, dating to over 100,000 years ago, and at the site of Oued Djebbana in Algeria, probably of a similar age. These sites are more than 6,500 km (4,000 miles) north of Blombos Cave. The same shells have also been found in Üçağızlı Cave on Turkey's Levantine coast, dating to 40,000 years ago, which all suggests that this tradition

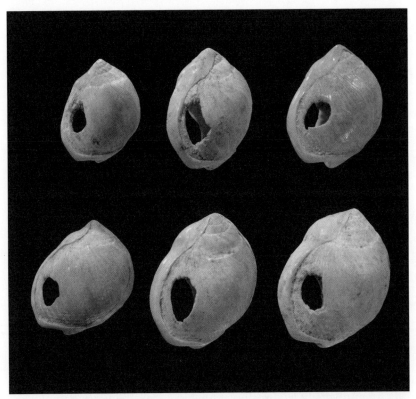

75,000-year-old shells of the common tick mollusc *Nassarius kraussianus*, perforated for suspension, from Blombos Cave, South Africa.

of jewelry based on very specific shells was widespread and persisted for tens of thousands of years.

My colleague Marian Vanhaeren has made a detailed study of Ice Age jewelry and has established that the shells were not randomly collected from beaches but were deliberately chosen because of their size. She has also replicated them experimentally in order to understand how they were made and how specific patterns of wear accumulated on their surfaces as they were worn. I once spent a day with Marian in a quarry south of Paris, sieving fossil shells out of sand. I came away with a number of beautiful belemnites which now decorate my bathroom, but I was not there for hobby purposes. By collecting all of the shells she found, Marian was able to establish the variation in size of shells in a natural population. She then compared her figures with those of the Ice Age pendant shells; if the sizes of the perforated shells were as varied as those from natural populations, it would mean that they were randomly collected. In fact they exhibit a much tighter size range, revealing that shells of relatively large size were preferred at Blombos and in the Levant, another indication that they had very specific meaning and were not simply chosen at random. It also seems they were worn for long periods, and were probably in daily use rather than being used for special occasions only.

These little objects, at the southern extreme of the Ice Age world, were not one-offs made by a local group concerned solely with their own style: they actually offer the first glimpse of an emerging human culture that was already prodigious in extent. If this was fashion, it was very popular. The wide spread of these shells leads us to look further into how *Homo sapiens* repeatedly dispersed out of Africa from at least 200,000 years ago, each pulse taking a growing population further away from the continent of our origins until ultimately a dramatically different set of environments had been encountered in the far east of Asia.

Dispersals

My first university lectureship at Sheffield University was initially temporary, replacing Robin Dennell, who was away on a three-year period of research leave writing a major book on the Palaeolithic of Asia. In my opinion he is one of the greatest critical thinkers in palaeoanthropology. My position was made permanent, and when Robin returned we became close friends. Together, we developed a course for postgraduate students on Pleistocene human dispersals and bounced a lot of ideas off each other. Robin has particularly concerned himself with the numerous human dispersals out of Africa eastwards through Asia, and has developed our ways of thinking about what dispersal actually requires, how climate can facilitate as well as constrain it, and what the evolutionary consequences of it were. I'll be drawing on his perspectives in this and the next two chapters.

We were African first, then Asian. Asia has some of the most dramatically diverse environments on the planet, and its three major climates determined the nature of the earliest dispersals of *Homo sapiens*, first into the Arabian Peninsula and Levant, and later through Central Asia and into the east. Biogeographically, the world's landmasses can be divided into eleven main zones. Although we inhabit them all today, we evolved only in the Afrotropical region, dispersed first into the adjacent Saharo-Arabian region, and subsequently extended our distribution into the Oriental region. Only later did we expand northwards into the Palaearctic region, south into the Australian, and even later to the three regions of the Americas.

There is nothing intrinsically special about long-distance dispersal. After all, birds do it, and bees do it. The important things are to be able to compete with existing fauna for resources and to adapt to new environments, in some cases as diverse as rainforests and arctic tundra. Still, human dispersal into Asia was important. We should not underestimate the vastness of this continent: Iran alone is six times the size of Britain, Arabia twelve times,[2] and at 9.6 million sq. km (3.7 million sq. miles) China is almost the size of Europe (10.18 million sq. km or 3.93 million sq. miles), something I have time to reflect on for nine hours when annually I fly its length to work with a colleague in Japan. Slowly, a panorama passes of the geographical features that would have guided or impeded our first steps eastwards. Mountain ranges such as the Hindu Kush and Himalayas and upland regions with harsh winters such as the

The first attempt to define areas of the world in terms of the distribution of species was made by Alfred Russel Wallace in 1876, who divided the world into six biogeographical regions. The above map results from a recent revision of his work based on over 21,000 vertebrate species, now with eleven major biogeographic regions based on species distribution and evolutionary history. The boundary between the Oriental and Australian regions is called Wallacea in his honour. Note how the African region extends towards Central Asia.

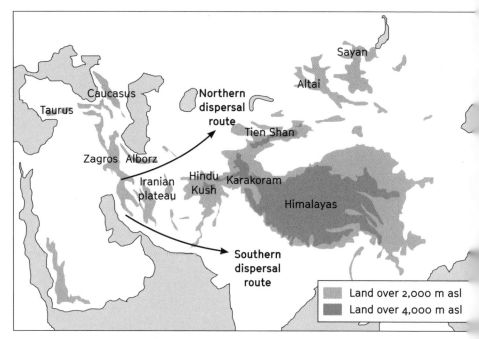

The dispersal of *Homo sapiens* across the vast continent of Asia in its geographical context. Upland areas provided considerable obstacles to Pleistocene hunter-gatherers; dispersal routes eastwards skirted to the north or south of these.

Anatolian, Iranian and Tibetan plateaux would have formed obvious and often permanent barriers. Humans and other animals would have needed to move around these, through corridors offered by low mountain passes such as in the western Zagros, and water courses such as the Ganges, Narmada, Yangtze and Yellow Rivers and their tributaries as well as those originally running through 'Green Sahara' and 'Green Arabia' that have long since run dry. These corridors connect major geographical regions, and where two corridors converge they could act as contact zones between different populations. We will see in Chapter 5 how distinct human groups met and interbred at these intersections. All the while, climate acted upon this dramatic topography. In severe conditions even low mountain passes would become barriers, whereas in warmer, wetter periods some deserts, such as the Thar (Great Indian Desert), would become green and habitable.

Let's remind ourselves that in the Ice Age, climate was colder and drier than today, in addition to being unstable, so the effects of weather systems would have been more pronounced. The key issue

Chapter 4

was rainfall, or, more importantly, its unreliability. As a result, from our perspective of hindsight, dispersal was high-risk: relatively familiar grasslands could shut down as heavy winters set in at the onset of cold periods. But other than an inherent curiosity to see what is beyond that distant hill, dispersals were not planned in the way that early modern voyages of discovery were, nor was anyone weighing up climate change. Our evidence for our eastwards dispersal from Africa is still relatively scarce, but a number of ambitious field projects are slowly remedying this, and we can glimpse activity in the Levant before 100,000 years ago, in Arabia shortly afterwards, and as far east as southern China by 80,000 years ago. In the Near East, populations seem to have split into two possible dispersal routes: a northern route into Palaearctic southern Siberia and Mongolia, and a southern route across the Saharo-Arabian region, the Oriental region from India to Indonesia, and ultimately to Australia. We will accompany them as far as China in this chapter.

Westerlies: the Levant, Arabia and Central Asia

The Levant spans the eastern Mediterranean from the Taurus-Zagros Mountains of Turkey, northern Iraq and Iran in the north to Egypt's Sinai Peninsula in the south, and from the Mediterranean coast eastwards into the deserts of northern Saudi Arabia. Westerly winds bring abundant rains to the region in winter and spring, the amount of rainfall decreasing dramatically the further one gets away from the Levantine coast, from which point one is dealing with semi-desert throughout Central Asia.

The Levant also has a spectacular assemblage of *Homo sapiens* fossils, including a number of complete skeletons. Thanks to a long tradition of research, particularly in Israel, we understand a good deal about the Ice Age humans of the area. We'll have to wait for Chapter 5 to see a particularly fascinating story that emerges from it – contact between our ancestors and the Eurasian Neanderthals – but for now we'll restrict ourselves to what the Levant reveals about how our behaviour was evolving within an expanding distribution.

Several caves in Israel and Syria have provided rich evidence of early *Homo sapiens*, dating to around 120,000 years ago and younger. They contain the largest number of human fossils from the period anywhere, and many have substantial archaeological layers that represent human activity at specific points in time over tens of thousands of years. Their inhabitants used small hearths on the cave floors, made stone tools, butchered, cooked and ate animals, and wore marine shells as jewelry. On occasion they left small lumps of red ochre scattered around, marks of some kind of decoration or art that is currently lost to us. At times, the caves also contain evidence of Neanderthal presence.

The striking thing about the Levantine evidence is its variability, but as the evidence spans a period from as much as 200,000 years ago (at Misliya Cave, as we saw in Chapter 3) to the end of the Pleistocene and beyond, and the region also forms the only land connection between Africa and Eurasia, this is perhaps not surprising. Two caves, Skhul, one of several on Mount Carmel, and Qafzeh near Nazareth, have yielded a rich sample of early *Homo sapiens* fossils, including near-complete skeletons that have survived the ravages of erosion because they were deliberately buried in shallow graves. Some specialists see burial as indicating some kind of belief in an afterlife and a concern to preserve the body, and the inclusion of 'grave goods' to accompany the burial as assisting in the individual's continued existence in another realm. Until the last few thousand years of the Ice Age, however, burials are so rare that they cannot have been the usual way of disposing of the dead. Where we find them, they seem almost incidental. Furthermore, we have no convincing examples of grave goods until much later either. Perhaps most Ice Age burials reflect only passing moments; brief cultural traditions that rose and died out with their practitioners. We'll return to the Qafzeh burial in Chapter 16 when we come to look at treatment of the dead and explore these problems further.

Physically, the Skhul and Qafzeh human remains are highly variable. Earlier examples such as those from Skhul, dated to around 120,000 years ago, appear more archaic and share some cranial traits with the Neanderthals, yet later examples such as those from Qafzeh, around 90,000 years old, show traits more characteristic of later *Homo sapiens.* We'll look in Chapter 5 at what this reveals about human interbreeding in this porous geographical corridor.

The animal bones from the caves of Mount Carmel reveal a lot about survival strategies. The most numerous are from the fast antelope gazelle, a Middle Eastern equivalent of fallow deer, and the now-extinct wild bovid aurochs, but other large herbivores and smaller animals such as hares and hyraxes are also present. Some

The caves of Mount Carmel in Israel have a long history of excavation which continues to the present day. They have provided rich evidence of Ice Age activity by both *Homo sapiens* and Neanderthals. Neanderthal remains were found in Tabun; several early burials of *Homo sapiens* were found in Skhul Cave (out of shot); and a late Ice Age (Natufian) campsite was found in el-Wad.

bones bear the marks of carnivore gnawing and crunching, showing that humans had to compete with hyenas for meat, but most of the caves' bones carry traces of scraping, smashing and cutting by stone tools and burning by fire, revealing that humans were the dominant force. The location of marks left by cutting tools show that the animals were skinned and dismembered before their meat was removed from the bones and cooked. Long bones were often smashed open to obtain the fatty marrow. In some cases humans exploited caves that acted as natural traps for animals which had fallen into them, but in others they were successfully hunting even the largest adult individuals of these species, probably within an hour or two's walk of the caves.

We should see the Israeli material as part of the complex African situation of near-modern humans. In fact, as Robin Dennell has noted, an early dispersal as far east as India's Thar Desert, via southern Iran and Pakistan, did not require adaptation to any new environment,

Dispersal: from Africa to Asia 61

A Nubian core from Aybut al Auwal, Oman (marked on
the map opposite), dated to around 106,000 years ago.
Note the visible scars where a triangular point has been
removed to serve as a sharp spear or knife point.

and in effect this earliest dispersal didn't leave Africa but rather came
along with it. Until recently, virtually nothing was known about our
earliest presence in the Arabian Peninsula, but its scorching sands
hide a dynamic past, and new archaeological surveys have brought
to life the remarkable rivers, lakes and marshes that flourished in
that vast region during warm periods, fed, as were their Saharan
counterparts, by the rains of the summer monsoon. Hippos swam
in Arabian waters and Asian wild asses (onagers), gazelles and oryx
grazed on the semi-arid grasslands. Small human groups also knapped
stone tools on the lush green banks of rivers at a number of sites,
including the open-air Al Wusta in Saudi Arabia's Nefud desert,
where a 90,000-year-old human fingerbone confirms that it was
Homo sapiens who was present in the region from this time.

Thankfully there are some toolmaking methods that are specific
to Africa, and they can be traced eastwards from there. One is the

Chapter 4

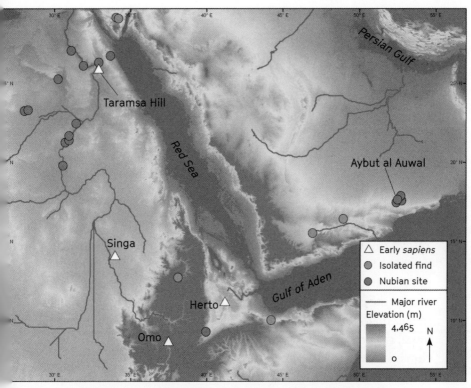

Northeast Africa, the Horn of Africa and Arabia, showing the distribution of surface finds and stratified and dated locations of Nubian stone tool technology (and also the burial of a *Homo sapiens* child at Taramsa in Egypt, as well as other early *Homo sapiens* remains).

so-called Nubian Levallois method, which is known in northeast Africa between 120,000 and 75,000 years ago, and reflects a very specific way of shaping a block of stone (core) to produce a standardized triangular spear and knife point. The sharp and V-sectioned points required by the manufacturers of the Nubian points are specific enough to warrant treating them as the product of *Homo sapiens* across 'Green Sahara' and 'Green Arabia'.

The Levantine and Arabian archaeology can also be tied into climate records from offshore marine cores drilled through the seabed. Computer modelling has also revolutionized our understanding of how climate change facilitated the early dispersals of *Homo sapiens*. Richard Jennings, an Ice Age climate specialist at Liverpool John Moores University, has modelled Ice Age climate for the Arabian Peninsula, and correlated this with periods in which humans were present in the region. I had the pleasure of working with Richard in the caves of Gibraltar in the 1990s, where he continues to excavate. Given that the presence of water would have been critical to the survival of human groups, Richard and his team sensibly used a series of sophisticated climate and topographic data to model the fluctuating amounts of rainfall in the region during the late Ice Age, and the results show African monsoonal rains reaching up to northern Arabia during summers and central Arabia at other times, a pattern that has recurred on numerous occasions over the last 130,000 years. Richard and his team were able to show that the well-dated Ice Age sites of the area correspond nicely with the identified periods of increased precipitation.

Further east, the evidence is as yet very sparse. Similar material is known from Iran and Pakistan but it is poorly dated. As with Arabia there has been much survey activity in the region in recent years, and the distribution of Ice Age sites reveals the potential dispersal routes around the edge of the Iranian Plateau. Further east in northwest India's Thar Desert, archaeological sites with Nubian Levallois tools reveal the presence of *Homo sapiens* during several periods of moist climate, around 96,000, 77,000, 60,000 and 45,000 years ago.

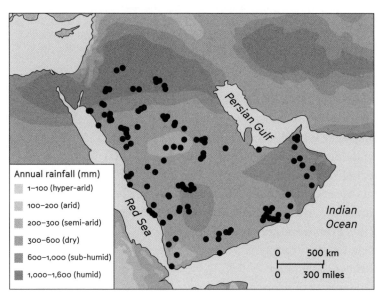

The Arabian Peninsula (note its size relative to the Levant) showing annual rainfall during an Ice Age warm period. The black dots show Ice Age archaeological sites: note how most fall into dry to sub-humid zones. Although they are not shown here, most of the sites are located along now-extinct watercourses.

Chapter 4

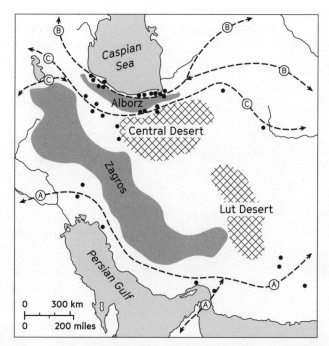

Potential dispersal routes of *Homo sapiens* around the Iranian plateau, inferred from archaeological sites. Two followed the coast, exploiting the rich resources available from land and beach on the Persian Gulf and on into Pakistan and beyond (Route A) and along the plains of the Caspian Sea up into southwest Turkmenistan, southwest Pakistan and beyond (Route B). Route C exploited lowland passes around the edge of the Central desert connecting Azerbaijan in the northwest and Afghanistan to the east.

East Asia

China effectively straddles the boundary between the Palaearctic and Oriental zones, with today's boundary running roughly west–east across the country's centre. During cold periods the Palaearctic zone expanded southwards and its tundra animals, such as mammoths, moved into China from Mongolia and Siberia; in warm periods the Oriental zone expanded northwards, and its warmth-loving animals, such as elephants, expanded their range. But human groups weren't just in the south, dispersing north when mild conditions allowed. A northern dispersal route from the Levant probably took them to Siberia by at least 42,000 years ago, from where they would disperse southwards as part of a Palaearctic community. The Oriental zone could well have supported a continuous human presence once established. It is remarkably rich in plants and animals and winter

Fuyan Cave in southern China provides the earliest securely dated evidence of *Homo sapiens* in the country. Forty-seven human teeth were found in Layer 2 alongside the remains of animals, including hyenas and wild boar. Fragments of stalactites uranium-thorium dated to 80,000 years ago provide a minimum age for the teeth. In terms of morphology and dimensions they are clearly in the range of later *Homo sapiens* and outside the range for archaic humans.

temperatures don't drop below freezing, so it's relatively easy to survive in localized regions. Because of this, once *Homo sapiens* had dispersed into the region, it would be an excellent place to ride out subsequent cold periods by staying put.

Archaeological sites that demonstrate the earliest presence of *Homo sapiens* in southern China are still scarce, or poorly dated. Ironically, there are better examples in the north. Teeth attributable to *Homo sapiens* have been found in several caves, of which the most securely dated demonstrate a presence 80,000 years ago south of the Yangtze River at Fuyan Cave (see PL. VII). The teeth excavated from the cave are very similar in shape to even modern Chinese populations, and dissimilar to those from fossil archaic humans like the Neanderthals or Chinese *Homo erectus*. A more complex picture exists around the same time in northern China, which will be revealed in Chapter 6. But first, there are novelties to deal with. Like other humans.

Contact: Neanderthals and Denisovans

Over 50 per cent of Westerners believe that alien life is out there somewhere, and many of those people believe that aliens have visited Earth or are already 'with us'.[1] Belief in the existence of 'wild men' such as North America's Bigfoot (and the older Sasquatch of indigenous Americans), the Himalayan Yeti, and the Yowie of the Australian outback[2] is remarkably widespread; and although most of us dismiss so-called evidence of 'lost civilizations' such as Atlantis (actually a fictitious island used as an allegory on the overconfident arrogance of nations by Plato), they are still a best-selling trope in fiction and film. Why do these beliefs persist? Like religion, they are cultural phenomena par excellence. They allow us to conceive of simpler lives spent closer to nature; they instil a sense of humility by suggesting that greater powers than ours may be out there; and, perhaps most useful of all, they cannot be *disproven*, and hence form a useful way to challenge the authority of science or 'the establishment' through 'what if?' ways of thinking.

After their discovery in the 19th century, Neanderthals were caricatured as 'wild men'. The first decently complete Neanderthal skeleton to be found – protected by a shallow grave in the little cave of La Chapelle-aux-Saints in southwest France – was of a thirty-year-old male who suffered from arthritis. Two mistakes were made in the anatomist Marcelin Boule's reconstruction of his posture and gait: first, that he had an ape-like stoop (he didn't); and secondly that his gait and locomotion were characteristic of Neanderthals in general (they weren't). We can't blame early comparative anatomists for this; after all, they had no comparable material to work from. We also have to remember that at the time of the Neanderthals' rediscovery by science the notion that the world was *really* old was new. If there really had been primitive humans around in the infancy of the world, as the likes of Mr Darwin were seeming to imply, scientists had little idea what these would look like. They therefore turned to classical depictions of Hercules and the biblical imagination of the rocky world into which Adam and Eve were expelled to dress these shambling archaics. Enter the furs, lion-skins, clubs and bones-through-the-nose immortalized by *The Flintstones*, and which have never quite gone away in media perceptions of 'cave men'. Neanderthals could be called the 'first human outsiders', but the question of exactly how 'outside' the *Homo sapiens* species they were is a matter of considerable debate.

Neanderthals are best seen as a specific biological adaptation of a large-brained human to the northern steppe environments of Eurasia. Their stocky bodies conserved heat (by minimizing the surface area off which it was convected), yet heavy musculature and a high frequency of healed bone fractures reveal a physically demanding life. This was probably the result of the heightened importance of meat in their northern diet; although they exploited the berries, roots and tubers that were available seasonally, isotope analysis reveals that they were highly dependent on meat, which they obtained by hunting and scavenging from a variety of herbivores up to the size of mammoths.

We were not alone

There is broad consensus that the ancestors of *Homo sapiens* diverged from the ancestors of the Neanderthals and Denisovans somewhere between 500,000 and 700,000 years ago. After that, a complex set of changes occurred during the evolution of our own species in Africa from at least 300,000 years ago, in which the results of numerous regional evolutionary processes were mixed around the African continent, ultimately resulting in our own genetic makeup. Then, during subsequent eastward dispersals out of Africa our ancestors came into infrequent contact with other human groups from which we had diverged early in these processes and who had to a degree evolved themselves during the intervening period. This contact led to some genetic mixture between us and the populations of Europe and the Near East (Neanderthals) and Central Asia (Denisovans) and to interaction between these two groups.

Much ink has been spilled as to whether we should regard Neanderthals as a distinct species and how 'Neanderthal-like' some of the anatomical traits of the earliest Eurasian *Homo sapiens* were. To some specialists Neanderthals are too different anatomically to be the same species as us, particularly cranio-dentally. To others they are too similar genetically to be a distinct species. It's an important issue of course, and cuts to the heart of a major problem in palaeontology: exactly what level of anatomical dissimilarity should be taken to represent a distinct species? But it's open to sensationalism too. A perennially popular 'what if' question is whether our *Homo sapiens* ancestors played a role in the extinction of another human species.

I must admit I'm not particularly interested in the species question. As an archaeologist it is behaviour and belief that are important to me, whether we are dealing with one, two or three species in Eurasia. The survival of a number of Neanderthal genes in us all reveals that interbreeding occurred, producing fertile offspring capable of breeding themselves. This is the commonly accepted definition of a biological species. But the dividing line between species is not clear cut. Biological groups that scientists classify as distinct species can and do interbreed (wolves, coyotes and dogs, for example), so the debates continue across what can often seem semantic lines.

As we have seen, humans exhibit considerable diversity in body size, skin and hair colour, facial characteristics and relative limb dimensions across the world, but these are no barrier to accepting that we are all of the same mind and the same species. They are, in fact, very 'plastic' traits, which can evolve relatively quickly, usually as adaptations to specific environments. In short, they can come and go, and the fact that they may be seen as important – usually to justify pathetic racist views – is a relatively recent phenomenon, and not one that preoccupies other primates. On a purely physical basis we might assume that a dispersing group of tall, dark-skinned *Homo sapiens* saw little of meaning in the stocky muscularity and lighter hair of the Neanderthals or the cosmetic features of the Denisovans whatever they were. Biology was at work, for sure; but with humans culture was at work too, and this can be used to build both barriers and bridges between physically distinct groups. A simple visual culture – such as ornamenting the body with colour or jewelry – or a basic but versatile language in which to talk about each other can achieve much, as can the giving of gifts and the exchange of partners. It might seem like an odd concept today, but it's possible that levels of physical difference that seem pronounced to us wouldn't have bothered our Pleistocene ancestors. As we shall see from their art and imagination they drew no fixed cognitive boundary between themselves and other non-human animals, so whether other humans looked a little different would surely not present any obstacles. For the *Homo sapiens* groups dispersing out of Africa it was a world of opportunity, hinted at through the genetic ghosts and bones of the humans who had established populations in Eurasia long before us.

Ghosts and indigenes

We all have ghosts in our DNA. 'Ghost' populations are those that are as yet archaeologically unseen, but which can be detected through their genetic contribution to later populations. Many of them remain ghosts, but in several cases they have been given a physical presence once more when their DNA has been recovered from Palaeolithic human bones. This grand resurrection is showing just how complex the population genetics of human dispersals was. Early ancestral populations can be teased out of modern genomic DNA from across Europe by clever statistical analysis. The Harvard geneticist David Reich discovered that Northern Europeans such as the French share more ancestry with indigenous North Americans than they do with any other living group. The implication is that both descend from a previous population that inhabited northern Eurasia and dispersed into the Americas, leaving little trace behind except in their ghost DNA. Today, half of the world's population derives between 5 and 40 per cent of their DNA from the ghosts of these Ancient North Eurasians, as Reich and his team call them. It could be that the earliest *Homo sapiens* groups to disperse into Europe are the best contenders for these people. They were far closer to Neanderthals genetically, and shared a number of specific anatomical traits with them.

Europeans derive much more of their genetic makeup from an unknown 37,000-year-old ancestor, whose DNA dispersed itself over a wide geographical area, shrinking into a part of southwest Europe. The DNA was then further modified by incursions from the east as farming and metal-using societies spread. It's exciting to think that our DNA contains not only the ghosts of our mammalian, primate and archaic human ancestry, but also the complex climate-related contractions and expansions of populations over tens of thousands of years.

Eske Willerslev, an adventurer and highly respected evolutionary geneticist at the Universities of Copenhagen and Cambridge, is a larger-than-life character. Many anthropologists have heard firsthand his story of killing a bear with his bare hands in a life-and-death struggle, so it's appropriate that this explorer should pinpoint what might be the physical form of these Northern European ghosts. His team sequenced the genome of a boy who died around 24,500 years ago, from the site of Mal'ta near Lake Baikal in Siberia. Speaking as a fully paid-up member of the U5a1 haplogroup, as I mentioned in Chapter 2, I'm pleased to say that the Mal'ta child contains the basal U5 haplogroup. Reich saw this as an ancient DNA expression of the ghost population that had previously been identified only from modern DNA. But debate is intense in this field, reflecting the immense difficulty of interpreting complex DNA, and as Eske Willerslev warned me, it is just as likely that the similarities between northern European and North American DNA derive from later population movements, very different types of ghosts. Whether or not Mal'ta represents the earliest Eurasian *Homo sapiens*, these 'Basal Eurasians' were teased out of the genetics, and represent a second wave of *Homo sapiens* to emerge out of Africa after the earliest had interbred with Neanderthals in the Near East, with high levels of their DNA found in Israel, Iran and India.

Africa has its own ghosts too. We saw in Chapter 2 the complex African evolution of *Homo sapiens* from at least 300,000 years ago and the diverse regional genetic contributions to our ancestors' DNA. Although that has been swamped subsequently by Iron Age expansions of Bantu farmers, fragments of DNA reveal complex population dynamics that of course didn't stop when *Homo sapiens* expanded out of the continent. The Yoruba agriculturalists of modern Nigeria derive 6–7 per cent of their DNA from an unknown African population which split from the common ancestor of the Neanderthals and *Homo sapiens* some time before 360,000 years ago. It may be that some of the human remains from this period belong to this ghost population, or perhaps we've yet to discover it. Scattered African hunter-gatherers such as the Pygmies[3] of Central Africa, Hadza of Tanzania and San of southern Africa, speakers of the ancient 'click languages' and hence considered to be more closely related to our forager ancestors, have Neanderthal DNA in their genomes which almost certainly derives from *Homo sapiens* populations that had interbred with Neanderthals in Eurasia and back-migrated into Africa. It's a two-way story. In Africa, as with Eurasia, the ghosts reveal that there were probably many of 'us' and many of 'them'.

The invaders?

In a biological sense *Homo sapiens* can certainly be regarded as an invasive species, successfully dispersing further into regions that were previously unoccupied by humans as well as those already occupied by various 'others', whether in Africa or Eurasia. Invasion biology is a somewhat grandiose term and can incorrectly imply planned invasions, but it does nicely encapsulate the notion that some species are aggressive colonizers, as we shall see, perhaps 'shooting first and asking questions later'.

David Reich – whose lab pioneered the identification of the ghost populations discussed above – has described Eurasia as a hothouse of human evolution. He identifies four major stages of genetic evolution over the last 2 million years. First, early members of African *Homo* dispersed across Europe and Asia around 2.1 million years ago, leading as far as *Homo erectus* in Asia. Then, after 1.4 million years ago, one *Homo* lineage split off, giving rise to the 'superarchaics', as geneticists have christened them. Among these was the ancestor to the Neanderthals, Denisovans and *Homo sapiens*. Robin Dennell has persuasively argued that humans were continuously present in Eurasia from this time, and however contracted and shifting their populations may at times have been, we should not underemphasize the contribution of superarchaic Eurasians to our evolutionary genetics. Our own ancestors then separated from the Neanderthals and Denisovans between 500,000 and 700,000 years ago, and finally, around 600,000 years ago, Neanderthal and Denisovan populations were themselves separated.

What followed is only being unravelled now. The three lineages continued to evolve, and far from being separate branches of the evolutionary tree, a degree of occasional interbreeding kept their genes modestly connected, until by 40,000 years ago Neanderthals and Denisovans had disappeared, leaving some of their DNA in the *Homo sapiens* populations that survived. Around 45,000 years ago up to 6 per cent of our genome was derived from Neanderthals, but over the course of the Pleistocene this proportion decreased to the 2 per cent level it is at today. Clearly, whatever the Neanderthal DNA did, it was being selected against.

Both Neanderthals and *Homo sapiens* were apex predators dependent on hunting and gathering an omnivorous but animal-protein-rich diet. We can probably include Denisovans in this guild too, although we have little evidence of their behaviour as yet. The further north humans dispersed the more they became dependent on the hunting of meat, the only nutritional package capable of sustaining a large-bodied and large-brained social primate in the steppe-tundra. It's probable that these two or three human lineages converged on a small peak of the ecological pyramid.

Ecological competition can be complex and indirect. Pat Shipman, a Penn State anthropologist and expert on human–animal interactions in the Pleistocene, used a striking analogue to competing predators in the form of the re-introduction of thirty-one grey wolves into Yellowstone National Park in the 1990s (they had been eliminated by human settlers in 1915). The wolves immediately set about killing their closest competitors, the coyotes, the park's erstwhile apex predator. This allowed a rise in number of the coyote's prey, pronghorn antelopes; by contrast, populations of elk, which the wolves began hunting, fell. The elk stopped eating new shoots of aspen and willow, so the woodlands now expanded, and where they prospered at the edge of rivers various species of birds and small animals appeared. The carcasses left over from wolf kills attracted scavengers like ravens, eagles and bears, and the whole ecosystem was completely remodelled in a handful of years. All because of wolves. Now just imagine if an apex predator arrived with a lethal weapon system and an attitude to match. It needn't involve anything as direct as a deliberate policy of wiping out the indigenes (an indigenous person), or even much direct contact between them. Could the precarious ecology of Pleistocene Eurasia have been similarly impacted with the arrival of *Homo sapiens* as competition for the apex predator top billing? For the Neanderthal indigenes, Shipman thinks so.

First contact (before 50,000 years ago)

Archaeologists have known for some time that the Neanderthals disappeared, but it's only thanks to the efforts of geneticists over the course of a little over a decade that we know that they managed to share several genes with *Homo sapiens* and Denisovans before they did so. We saw in Chapter 2 how the entire Neanderthal genome was published in 2010. Sequences of mtDNA were available for a decade prior to this, but as mtDNA is inherited only through the female line it could only inform on interbreeding between Neanderthal females and *Homo sapiens* males (as the mtDNA would need to derive from a Neanderthal female, who would of course need to breed with a male). No wonder unequivocal evidence of admixture only appeared with full genomic sequencing. In fact, there seems to have been a three-way mix of genes between Neanderthals, Denisovans and *Homo sapiens*, the results of which live on inside us all. At around 2 per cent, Neanderthal genes in modern humans have low diversity, suggesting that admixture between the two was rare, although the proportion varies: East Asians, for example, have some 20 per cent more Neanderthal DNA than Europeans, which also suggests that the patterns of interbreeding were not simple. But as we have seen the 2 per cent is a remnant of a greater shared ancestry of up to 6 per cent, much of which has been lost over time.

Neanderthal DNA has now been recovered from a wide range of early *Homo sapiens* specimens from Europe to Siberia, some of which have stretches of it up to seven times larger than those in living humans, reinforcing the view that interbreeding was still occurring as late as 50,000 years ago and in places perhaps much later, with many Early and Mid Upper Palaeolithic humans carrying DNA from Neanderthal admixture that occurred between a few thousand and a few hundred years before their deaths.

The Near East is perhaps the most likely area where the two populations occasionally met. The Levant was a 'Goldilocks Zone' for both Neanderthals, expanding from the north, and *Homo sapiens*, expanding from the south. Such population extensions and contractions were probably bringing the two groups into the same regions of the eastern Mediterranean and Levant from at least 200,000 years ago.

Neanderthals occupied the Levant between 300,000 and 120,000 years ago and again between 80,000 and 50,000 years ago, interspersed with the presence of *Homo sapiens*. In the bones from the early burials in Skhul and Qafzeh caves in Israel, some have seen traits shared with the Neanderthals. Whether this is correct or not, the porous corridor of the Levant seems the most likely region where the two met and exchanged genes, probably at discrete periods over tens of thousands of years. Perhaps the sensible view is that these human groups rarely met, but when they did obstacles to interbreeding rarely occurred, producing both infertile and occasionally fertile offspring.

This would require each group to recognize each other as potential mates, which is a question about how they might recognize similarities. In our historical haste to look for differences between the two, we've neglected the many behavioural similarities shared between Neanderthals and *Homo sapiens*, at least prior to 50,000 years ago. The Levantine stone tool technologies of the two share a number of technical traits, even if there is some evidence for different scales of land use. As my colleagues Nigel Goring-Morris and Anna Belfer-Cohen have argued, when technology did take a major turn around 50,000 years ago this could well have resulted from some of the last interactions between the two, rather than the traditional view that our own solely innovative species was replacing the old things. Levantine Neanderthals were far from one-trick ponies; their stone tools reflect a flexible technology, one that was by no means less sophisticated than that of their nearby African contemporaries.

In the survival game information counts, of course. But so do genes. As Robin Dennell notes, indigenous genes can be exceptionally important, particularly if they provide immunity from local diseases or an ability to digest newly available foodstuffs. Perhaps Denisovan genes passed on an ability to avoid hypoxia (lowered blood oxygen levels caused at altitude). As long as the two groups made little distinction between themselves a degree of cautious interaction may have been sensible. But competition needn't be direct or even intentional. Neanderthals may have been losing a demographic arms race even if they weren't losing a technical one. We know that Neanderthal groups were small, and if the number of archaeological sites on the ground is anything to go by, their populations had probably been shrinking from a peak around 100,000 years ago. Possibly their fragile web of interconnections was already under threat, constantly remodelled by an unstable climate. A number of other large mammals became extinct in Europe around the same time, including another social carnivore, the hyena, so perhaps we should be thinking of the gradual loss of significant components of a northern ecosystem. If two top carnivores couldn't survive it suggests that their subsistence strategies were lacking. If Neanderthals were running around the landscape hunting large dangerous animals in a highly successful but relatively unselective way, where would they be able to go when competition arrived on the scene?

Low populations would be particularly vulnerable to competition. Regional extinctions occur when the population of a species in an area is reduced below the minimum numbers necessary to keep reproducing it; in other words, when the dead are no longer being matched one-for-one by the newborn. If this occurs across the entirety of a species' distribution then the result is absolute extinction. We can model the approximate population numbers of the Neanderthals based on modern data for hunter-gatherer population densities in similar environments to those at specific points in the Pleistocene. These models suggest that the population of Neanderthals in the Levant probably numbered around 2,000. This is remarkably low, but we will see even lower populations when we get into northern latitudes. To put it in perspective, that is 2,000 Neanderthals scattered across Lebanon, Israel, Sinai, Syria and Jordan: a tiny fraction of the 126,742 people that attended a concert given by The Rolling Stones in 1995.[4]

This is where diet is important too. My colleagues Mike Richards, Erik Trinkaus and I obtained some of the first stable isotope measurements on Neanderthal bones, allowing a direct measure of where they derived their dietary protein from. We've long known from the animal bones on their campsites that meat was of great importance to their survival, but to know *how* important it was requires the nitrogen and carbon from their bones. Our results showed that 80–90 per cent of their dietary protein derived from terrestrial herbivores, a finding that has now been reproduced for many Neanderthals across their range. They clearly occupied a top predatory niche successfully for tens of thousands of years – like hyenas – but it may well have been precarious. The heavier and more muscle-bound Neanderthals needed to obtain around 10 per cent more calories than their *Homo sapiens* counterparts. This was particularly the case for pregnant or lactating females, who probably required as much as 5,500 kcal daily, more than male athletes today (5,000 kcal/day) and way more than average females (2,000 kcal/day). It was of course impossible to ensure that amount of calories daily, and Neanderthal teeth often bear developmental hypoplasias – lines resulting from impoverished development during periods of malnourishment – but their evolutionary longevity indicates that *on average* they managed to obtain it. As the only package of calories and nutrients rich enough to provide sufficient calories in most of the environments the Neanderthals occupied, meat and fat was crucial to survival. This itself may have presented problems; a meat- and fat-rich diet can lead to an overdose of vitamins and minerals and deficiency of calcium, which can prove fatal to pregnant women and their foetuses. Berries, roots and other wild plants would supplement the meat to a small degree, but perhaps the Neanderthal's top predatory niche was increasingly running on a (butcher's) knife edge. If they had over-specialized in meat eating, where was their ecological escape route if the availability of that meat came under threat?

Second contact (after 50,000 years ago): shoot first, ask questions later

Archaeology reveals that something important was happening to human technology after 50,000 years ago. The various Levallois methods among both Neanderthals and *Homo sapiens* groups inside and outside Africa were replaced with a technique of striking long, narrow blades off prism-shaped cores, and a number of new tool forms were shaped on the new blades. At the same time, well-made weapon tips and other tools carved out of bone appear. But what exactly did these new weapons signify? John Shea of New York State's Stony Brook University, an expert in Palaeolithic hunting technology, has studied the complexity of these changes. He characterizes them as a 'turnover event', in which the changes reflect the final replacement of the region's Neanderthals by the invader species *Homo sapiens*.

We saw in Chapter 4 one of the earliest periods in which *Homo sapiens* expanded out of northern Africa during mild and wet conditions. Climatic deterioration brought this situation to an end sometime after 80,000 years ago, when the Palaearctic zone expanded southwards, bringing Neanderthals down into the Levant. They were probably the region's main human inhabitant between 75,000 and 45,000 years ago. Once again, around 45,000 years ago, climate deteriorated, bringing about Neanderthal extinction in the region and far more widely. From that time, the region's sole human occupants were *Homo sapiens*. Shea has cleverly teased out the subtle indications that the change in archaeology reflects a new population of *Homo sapiens*, one which now had mastery of crucially important innovations in weaponry in the form of a complex projectile technology that combined a light, penetrating weapon with high-velocity delivery systems. The bow and arrow, which may have been used in Japan as early as 38,000 years ago, was otherwise introduced only towards the end of the Pleistocene. Instead, it seems that the revolutionary new killing technology was the light spear thrown with the assistance of a spearthrower (or *atlatl*).

The heavier spears used previously could be effectively thrown at very close range but were largely hand-delivered weapons, used like bayonets. The new javelins (let's call them that to distinguish them from hand-thrust spears) had a longer effective range and were fast, and hence could be used on large and dangerous as well as small and fast prey. We cannot underestimate the game-changing importance of this innovation; as Shea has noted, light projectile weapons open up a new set of potential resources and are a niche-expanding technology. He is not exaggerating when he says that this change made *Homo sapiens* the quintessential generalists, and that in evolutionary competition the generalists always outcompete the specialists. Shea has meticulously analysed the characteristics of African and Levantine stone points, showing that between 50,000 and 100,000 years ago a number of African points fall into the size and weight range of projectiles, suggesting that African *Homo sapiens* were using these in addition to their heavier spears, probably as a means of expanding their ecological range. This certainly explains how they were capable of occupying arid areas of North Africa and expanding even into arid parts of the Levant in the process. And to use a modern analogy, who would you back: the one running with a bayonet or the one taking careful aim with a pistol?

The simplistic view that the Neanderthals were simply outwitted in the evolution game by a more 'intelligent' adversary potentially rears its head here, but it's very wrong. After all, we wouldn't argue that grey squirrels are 'brighter' than reds or that Japanese knotweed has embarked on a deliberate programme of annihilation. It could simply be that as populations shrank and animals became fewer, viable breeding populations just couldn't be maintained. An archaeologist 40,000 years from now would be mistaken if they were to infer that the sack of Rome was considerably helped by the possession of rifles on the part of the barbarian hordes. You may think this a facile example, but consider that barely 1,000 years separates the fall of the Western Empire in the fifth century AD and the earliest firearms, easily enough to be lost in the error margin of a radiocarbon date measured 40,000 years in the future.

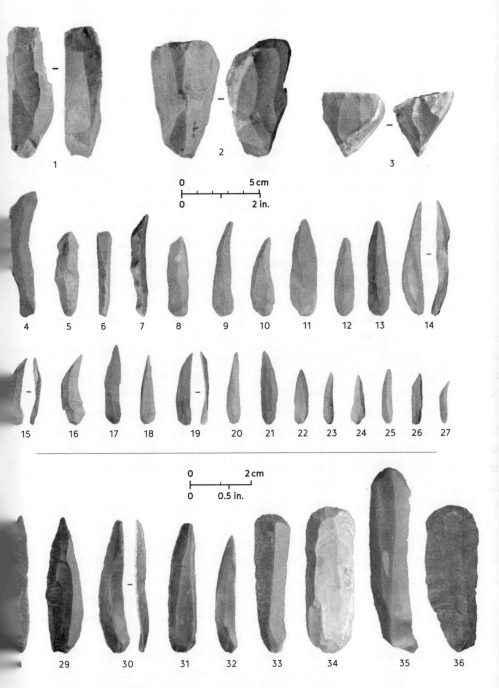

The new killing technology: a selection of stone objects from Emireh Cave, Galilee, Israel. Prismatic cores showing where long, narrow blades have been struck off (1–2); smaller, pyramidal core for removing bladelets (3); typical blades (4–21) and bladelets (22–27) produced on these cores; light javelin points of 'el-Wad' type (28–32). Endscrapers (33–36), also produced on slim blades, were used to work hides.

Imprecision is something I've been taxed with since my days in the Oxford Radiocarbon Accelerator Unit. The results produced by laboratory dating techniques express the methodical uncertainty (imprecision) that comes with any date. There is always some error in our measurements and calculations. Here's a real radiocarbon date, which happens to date a sample drilled from a *Homo sapiens* mandible from Oase Cave in Romania: 34,290 +970/-870 years ago. As we saw in Chapter 2, this raw radiocarbon measurement needs to be calibrated into real calendar years, taking those plus and minus errors (imprecision) into account. The result shows that this particular *Homo sapiens* individual lived and died between 35,000 and 39,000 years ago. It could be anywhere in that range. Now let's compare this to another real date, on a Neanderthal fingerbone from Spy Cave in Belgium: 33,940 +220/-210 years ago, calibrating to a life and death somewhere between 36,000 and 37,500 years ago.[5] These age ranges overlap, and may be described as 'statistically the same age', and indeed the results could reflect *Homo sapiens* living in Romania at the same time as Neanderthals were in Belgium. But equally, the Neanderthals could have been living around 37,500 years ago and the *Homo sapiens* 35,000 years ago, two-and-a-half millennia apart. Unless we are dealing with ideal sedimentary conditions on the same site, where we might infer that populations from higher up in the sequence must have lived later than ones lower down, we simply can't tell what is correct. We can model sets of dates like this all we like – and many people do – but at the end of the day our modelling depends very much on what assumptions we decide to make in our organization of the models.

In caves where we have evidence of the two groups, the archaeological remains that are unambiguous signs of Neanderthals *always* underlie those that are unambiguous signs of *Homo sapiens.* In Europe, we have not a single case of the mixing (interstratification) of the two that might otherwise suggest a degree of coexistence in any given area, and in a number of cases a decently thick archaeologically sterile sediment separates the layers, suggesting that perhaps several millennia passed between the extinction of the last Neanderthals, say, in southwest Germany, and the arrival of the region's first *Homo sapiens.* At best, the archaeology on the ground suggests that if the two groups overlapped anywhere in Europe it was very brief. That may not matter: as we saw above, new apex predators can dramatically remodel ecosystems in a handful of years, but it is one thing to remodel Yellowstone, and quite another to bring an entire apex predator to extinction across the vastness of Eurasia.

So why did things change, and why did Neanderthals become extinct as part of this change? There are similarities between the visual culture of Neanderthals and *Homo sapiens* in the period between 50,000 and 40,000 years ago, particularly in their use of coloured pigments and jewelry. Although Neanderthals seem to have favoured pendants made from very specific parts of animals and our ancestors were more drawn to shells, it may be that these adornments of the body formed a common visual language between the two. The archaeology left by *Homo sapiens* groups in Europe only really changed after the Neanderthals had become extinct. Perhaps the two things were in some way connected? Perhaps our ancestors now thought of themselves as more culturally distinct from others, a more exclusivist view in which 'they' were different from 'us'? But they weren't the only ones.

The Denisovans

Denisova Cave in the foothills of the Altai Mountains overlooks a point where the Anui River narrows, and where prey could be monitored and ambushed (see PL. VIII). It's a very useful site for hunter-gatherers, and so it's no surprise that excavations by the Russian Academy of Sciences over four decades have unearthed huge amounts of archaeological remains in the cave's three chambers. It's gained most fame for a few scrappy human remains, and specifically for the human genome they contain, which has revolutionized our understanding of human dispersals in the region. Its sediments are 6 m (20 ft) deep, and Zenobia Jacobs of the University of Wollongong in Australia led a team that used thermoluminescence dating to tease out the time and tempo of how they accumulated. With fits and starts broken up by periods of erosion that scoured some deposits out, the sediments span the period between 300,000 and 20,000 years ago, during which time the environment varied from tundra and steppe to coniferous woodland.

The cave was almost continuously occupied by denning carnivores such as cave hyenas, wolves and bears over this time. By contrast human visitors were infrequent, but over the millennia plenty of evidence of their activities, such as lighting hearths, butchering prey and knapping stone, accumulated. But they also left their DNA behind, in the few teeth and bones that came to rest in the cave in various periods and also in minuscule amounts adhering to grains of the sediment itself. This is remarkably lucky: perhaps the region's severe cold helped to preserve it. By 2010 the science of ancient DNA sequencing had advanced so much that techniques were available (and affordable) to extract, replicate and understand incredibly tiny remnants. And so, like Proust's world of memories that flowed from a madeleine, a long-forgotten world came tumbling out of minuscule scraps of genes.

The identifiable human material from Denisova is meagre: three molars and a distal phalanx from different individuals at different times. We saw in Chapter 2 how Katerina Douka and Tom Higham used the ZooMS technique to work through the scrappy fragments of bone from Denisova Cave that were too small to identify to any particular taxon. Their efforts paid off, identifying more human bone material. It's still not much – fragments of a long bone and cranium – but it allowed further sequencing that gave some surprising results. Overall, the cave has so far given up the remains of at least four Denisovans, two Neanderthals and, most unexpectedly and remarkably, a hybrid daughter of a Denisovan and Neanderthal. There isn't enough material yet to define the Denisovans formally, since we define species on the basis of skeletal morphology. While entire genomes have been sequenced from the few pieces of bone we have, there isn't enough skeletal material yet, so we still use the informal name Denisovans. Perhaps the name *Homo altaiensis* will be used once enough material has accumulated.

A genome was first sequenced from the fingerbone and a tooth in 2010. Analysis revealed that far from being the remains of the Neanderthals, as the excavators had assumed, these individuals belonged to a sister group. Comparison of genomes revealed that the ancestors of Neanderthals and Denisovans had separated around 500,000–700,000 years ago from a common ancestor with *Homo sapiens*, and that Denisovans had separated from their Neanderthal relatives around 600,000 years ago. While we still don't have enough skeletal material to say what they looked like (aside from the fact that their fingertips were like ours and their molars more similar to earlier *Homo erectus* than to Neanderthals or *Homo sapiens*), the relatively short evolutionary separation didn't stop interbreeding on the few occasions that first Neanderthals and then *Homo sapiens* temporarily expanded into the Denisovan homelands.

Further genetic sequences followed, allowing a reconstruction of which humans were in the cave in different periods. Overall, a conservative estimate is that the cave was frequented by Denisovans between 200,000 and 50,000 years ago, with some use of it by Neanderthals somewhere between 100,000 and 180,000 years ago, but both disappearing with the appearance of Upper Palaeolithic *Homo sapiens* sometime after 45,000 years ago with their new-fangled eyed needles, awls and pendants. It's a similar time-share situation to that between Neanderthals and *Homo sapiens* in the Levantine caves, and one of those regions where the range of one group of humans meets another, in this case at the extreme eastern end of Neanderthal

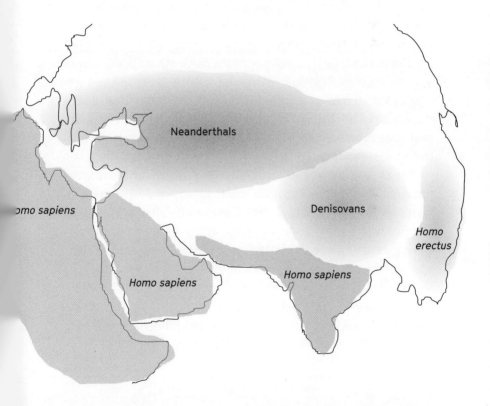

Opportunities for contact: the distribution of human groups in Eurasia between 110,000 and 50,000 years ago. *Homo sapiens* dispersed from Africa during this period; to the north, Neanderthals ranged from western Europe to southwest Siberia. The Denisovan range spread to the east of the Neanderthals, and *Homo erectus* persisted as late as 100,000 years ago further east.

distribution and perhaps at the time the northern end of the *Homo sapiens* dispersal. The cave's archaeology is very complicated and the sedimentary dates imprecise, so it is as yet impossible to establish how close in time any of these groups came to each other in the vicinity of the cave. But they must have met, as their genes reveal admixture both with Neanderthals and *Homo sapiens*. Denisovan genes have been found in modern Asians, Australians and Melanesians, but not in Europeans, and in one sense they can be seen as the Asian equivalents of Neanderthals: two contemporary indigenes in the east and west of Eurasia respectively. Neanderthals contributed their DNA to living humans across the entire continent, however, whereas the Denisovan DNA contribution was more limited, presumably because their population was smaller and more isolated, as indicated by its low genetic diversity.

The discovery of the Denisovans took the issue of interbreeding and hybridization to another level. This newly discovered group had interbred with Neanderthals and *Homo sapiens*, who had themselves interbred. Not only that, but one of the fragmentary bones belonged to a Denisovan female who lived around 118,000 years ago, and who had a Neanderthal mother and Denisovan father. Of course we don't know the nature of the liaisons that led to such hybrids – they may have been violent rather than loving – but there was certainly no biological barrier to reproduction.

The Denisovans are still painfully slow to step further into the limelight. ZooMS was used recently to identify a 160,000-year-old mandible found in Baishiya Karst Cave on the Tibetan Plateau as Denisovan. It's some 3,000 km (1,850 miles) southeast of Denisova Cave, giving us some idea of the range of the Denisovans, which spanned the tough environments of the high altitudes of the Altai and Tibetan Plateau. We've only made first contact. Much excitement surely lies ahead in the field and in the laboratory, and whatever they turn out to look like, the Denisovans are probably the nearest we will ever come to spotting a Yeti. Not so different after all.

Chapter 6

Diversity

Our ancestors managed to colonize regions of Europe and Asia that were already inhabited by indigenous humans, and to inhabit other areas for the first time. They also managed to outcompete all other human groups that they came into contact with, even if that did result in some genetic exchange, as we saw in the last chapter. Archaic humans – and we might include the earliest *Homo sapiens* outside Africa here – adapted only to specific environments, dispersing and contracting as these environments waxed and waned in response to climate. But now, things were about to change.

Biogeographically, *Homo sapiens* entered a very different world from Africa when they dispersed into the Indian subcontinent. Robin Dennell, with characteristic astuteness, summarizes the new landscapes of India, Myanmar, Bangladesh and Sri Lanka that *Homo sapiens* needed to adapt to as an area the size of the European Union with considerable diversity: the Himalayan mountains; wide floodplains of rivers such as the Ganges; the upland Deccan; the forested slopes of the Ghats; and on into rainforest country. Before this we can't really say that our ancestors had truly left Africa; it's just that the Africa that we know was environmentally much larger and its animal life had expanded with it. Dispersals had been relatively rapid due to the similar environmental affordances that took people from the Nile Valley and Arabian Peninsula around the Iranian Plateau to Pakistan and the gates of India. But the spread now slowed as they adapted to increasingly diverse environments, paving the way for dispersal into much of Asia and ultimately into the Americas. This part of the story is all about diversity. In the modern world humans display considerable environmentally related variability, from the short and stocky Inuit (average male height 163 cm or 5 ft 4 in.), who are adapted to the cold conditions of the circumpolar realm, to the tall thin Dinka of the Nile (average male height 176 cm or 5 ft 9 in.), adapted to African warmth. Human variability originates in the expansion into novel habitats.

The discovery of Levallois-style technologies similar to those that the Dinka's ancestors used in the Nile Valley suggests that the Great Indian Desert had been reached as early as 74,000 years ago as the easternmost point of a dispersal at this time. It is possible that our presence goes back much earlier but evidence for this is questionable. It is only from around 45,000 years ago that more widespread, unambiguous evidence of *Homo sapiens* is recorded in India. This comes in the form of microblades: small blades and bladelets which were hafted onto tools and weapons with a mastic, which appeared in Africa by 65,000 years ago. These are first found in South Asia between 48,000 and 35,000 years ago, although to the specialist many differences underlie a superficial similarity and rather than being carried eastwards it is more likely that we are looking at independent innovations made by human groups in South Asia who by now had considerable ingenuity and flexibility. By 45,000 (perhaps even 65,000) years ago people were able to live year-round in rainforests, meaning that they could disperse as far as the Eurasian shores of the Pacific.

These were not the first humans in the region. Until recently it was thought that *Homo erectus* persisted as late as 40,000 years ago, at least on Java, but refinements in the dating of deposits show that they more likely became extinct by around 125,000 years ago. It's possible that they were the earliest human inhabitants of the Philippines, arriving by drifting rather than intentional voyaging; around 700,000 years ago, humans were butchering rhino there with simple stone flakes, but we don't know who they were. Neither do we know if they were continually present in the region from these archaic populations to the time that the small-bodied human *Homo luzonensis* was living there around 66,000 years ago. So far, only several teeth, finger and toe bones and part of a femur are known from Callao Cave in northern Luzon – from perhaps three individuals assigned to this fascinating new species – but their morphology is intriguing. The curvature of their phalanges suggest that these may have been tree climbers, little different from the African gracile australopithecines of some 2 million years earlier. Analysis of the mtDNA of modern populations from the Philippines reveals that *Homo sapiens* arrived before 60,000 years ago, making it a distinct possibility that they encountered *Homo luzonensis*. Further excavations will no doubt add to this exciting story.

Much more is known about *Homo floresiensis*, which persisted on the Indonesian island of Flores from at least 150,000 years ago until its extinction around 50,000 years ago. This human stood only 1 m

A selection of 48,000-year-old microblades and microblade cores from Unit 2 at Mehtakheri on the banks of the Narmada River, India. Top row and second row: cores from which microblades have been removed; on the far right of the second row is a small point, fashioned for boring or perforating softer materials. Third row: hammerstones of varying sizes used for knapping. Bottom row: bladelets and blades from earlier stages of working, showing how much larger the cores initially were.

(3 ft) in height – hence the nickname 'hobbit'[1] – and had a brain the size of a chimpanzee, yet made stone tools. It lived alongside the dwarf stegodon (of the elephant family), giant rats and storks, and vultures, all of which (bar the rats, who clearly didn't desert a sinking ship) had become extinct by 50,000 years ago. As yet we don't know whether this was a broader extinction event perhaps related to climate change, or whether incomers were responsible. In Liang Bua Cave, where much of the evidence of *Homo floresiensis* derives from, a novel stone material for working – red chert – and the use of fire appeared by 46,000 years ago after all traces of its former inhabitant disappeared. These almost certainly mark the arrival of *Homo sapiens* on the island. Archaeologically, this is a similar pattern to the disappearance of the Neanderthals and the arrival of *Homo sapiens* on the fringes of Europe; one disappears, to be succeeded by the next. But whether this means that the predecessors were wiped out by their successors, or whether the latter were simply dispersing into an ecological niche that the human indigenes had already vacated, remains to be established. Both *Homo luzonensis* and *Homo floresiensis* may have been easy prey for a larger competitor they had no experience of before its sudden arrival.

Since my student days, a number of new human species have been added to the already speciose list of fossil hominins: new variants of australopithecines, paranthropines, and the small-bodied *Homo naledi* in Africa; *Homo antecessor* in Spain; and in Asia the Denisovans and the small-bodied species just described. That's just the unambiguous ones. It may be that other suggested new species, such as the Chinese 'Dragon Man', turn out to be genuine as more data emerge from the ground and from genetic sequences. Whatever the case, the world was certainly still rich in human diversity as *Homo sapiens* began its dispersals out of its African homeland, and more human species and groups will inevitably come to light in the future.

But now the story takes a different turn: by 30,000 years ago these diverse human species had all disappeared. Erik Trinkaus, a renowned specialist in the anatomy of early *Homo sapiens*, sees the period between 50,000 and 35,000 years ago as the final phase of the establishment of our species, during which modern human biology became the dominant form of humanity. We can sample the increasing behavioural flexibility of our ancestors by making four brief stops: southwards to the rainforests of Sunda land, the islands of Wallacea and the tremendously varied environments of Sahul land, and northwards into the Siberian cold.

Sunda: archipelagos and tropical rainforests

During the lower sea levels of the Pleistocene the major islands of Southeast Asia – Sumatra, Java and Borneo – were joined to the mainland across the shallow (and now-submerged) Sunda Shelf. When climate was relatively cool, forests and grasslands and their faunal communities expanded without difficulty across this huge landmass. When it was warm and wet, tropical rainforests replaced them. In the former, large animals such as bovids, pigs and deer would have provided conventional prey, but the rainforest was really something else. Imagine a familiar environment: grasslands with small stands of woodland around sources of water where a variety of large herd animals could be predictably found in large numbers. They provide meat, fat, hide, sinew and bone, and smaller animals that offer fur, as well as a variety of seasonally gatherable plants that complement the carnivorous element of the diet and provide fibres for textiles. Now imagine entering something very new, where these things are lacking. The small animals are often inaccessible, hidden high up in the dense tree canopy; and unlike the gregarious grazers and browsers of more open environments, larger animals cannot be found in any number in one place, which means that the effort of hunting them is often not repaid by the amount of nutrients they return to their predators. Many rainforest plants are poisonous unless they can be processed by leaching, cooking or other ways to remove their toxins, and they may only be available in the canopy or underground at certain times of the year. Rainforest landscapes cannot simply be occupied; they must be learned, and it takes a lot of thought, exploration and generations of indigenous knowledge to survive.

But survive they did. By 50,000 years ago evidence of human presence appears in Borneo, and by 45,000 years ago people were producing microliths in Sri Lanka. Sunda seems to have provided a refugium from more extreme climate change, and it's possible that as its environments spread northwards into adjacent areas of southern China then *Homo sapiens* made its initial forays into that country. Demography was probably complex: a 45,000- to 63,000-year-old cranium and a mandible from a second individual found in the cave of Tam Pa Ling on Laos, although clearly belonging to *Homo sapiens*, display anatomical traits shared with archaic humans. In Borneo's Niah Cave, cutmarked and burnt bones reveal that its earliest *Homo sapiens* inhabitants were eating wild pigs, monitor lizards, pangolins, monkeys, tortoises and turtles; and microscopic starch grains show that they were processing yams and sago palms and detoxifying other plants. This wasn't simply survival either. Very recently, exciting examples of culture have been emerging, a glimpse into the minds of these hunter-gatherers. Hand stencils created on the walls of Lubang Jeriji Saléh Cave in Borneo have been dated to at least 51,000 years ago on the basis of uranium-thorium dating of overlying calcite crusts; these are almost certainly connected to similar examples further east in Wallacea.

Wallacea: coasts

Alfred Russel Wallace, as we saw in Chapter 4, was the first scientist to divide the world up into biogeographical regions, and his discovery in 1859 of one of these was celebrated by naming it after him. The 2,000 or so islands of Wallacea, as it is still known, form a transitional zone between Asia (and Sunda) to the west and Australia to the east. The babirusas ('pig-deer') and rats of Sunda could still be found there, but so could the most westerly marsupials, as well as a rich set of its own endemic flora and fauna. It's a vast biogeographical zone in its own right, and those human species new to science such as *Homo floresiensis* had adapted to it long before the arrival of *Homo sapiens*. Three teeth excavated in the Lida Ajer Cave on Sumatra show that somewhere between 63,000 and 73,000 years ago *Homo sapiens* was living in the rainforests of Wallacea, so far the earliest evidence of any form of human adapted to this highly specific environment.

But one is never far from the sea in Wallacea, and seafood is the key to survival there. In addition to gatherable shellfish, fishing was clearly part of the adaptation to Wallacea at least as early as 42,000 years ago. Some 39,000 fish bones were recovered by fine sieving sediments excavated at Jerimalai on Timor-Leste; these derived from several coastal and pelagic (open sea) species and included mackerel and juvenile tuna, which were probably caught by line and hook. Fish bones are fragile, and can disappear in acidic soils, or can be missed unless care is taken to sieve the sediments from archaeological sites such as Jerimalai. Such approaches are a relatively recent development, but it's not just the small foods that we're only now beginning to see: other aspects of a rich culture are coming to light with new fieldwork and laboratory dating methods.

Excavations in Niah Cave in Borneo have revealed the presence
of *Homo sapiens* as early as 50,000 years ago, in a variety of
environments including mangroves, lowland swamps and upland forests.
Its 'Deep Skull' – the partial cranium of an adult human female – was
carried around the landscape before it was buried in the cave.

A hand stencil in Leang Timpuseng Cave on Sulawesi has been
dated to at least 40,000 years ago. It's not that far from Borneo, and even
though getting there did require a sea crossing we should see this as
evidence of a widespread visual culture of *Homo sapiens* in the region.
Add to this nearby depictions of babirusas dated to at least 35,000 years
ago, and it becomes clear that non-figurative art had emerged in Sunda
before 40,000 years ago, and figurative art not much later. As we will
see, this is a remarkably similar picture to that at the western extreme
of Eurasia, suggesting that similar developments in visual culture were
shared by early *Homo sapiens* across their entire range. Add to the cave
art the presence of many ochre-stained shells drilled and ground to be
strung like necklaces, that are at least 41,000 years old, excavated from
several caves in Timor-Leste, and all this evidence of human culture
across the Old World means that the focus on Europe is falling away
a little. Let's not forget too the abundance of perishable materials with
potential for creative transformation, such as woods, plant fibres and
the like, none of which survive archaeologically.

We should see Wallacea as a series of coasts separated by stretches of open water. As Robin Dennell notes, to successfully disperse across it, as Pleistocene *Homo sapiens* undeniably did, requires the ability to construct seaworthy sailing craft; to be able to navigate and steer them by day and night; to store drinkable water for consumption while at sea; and to be able to fish. True, most of the islands of Wallacea would have been visible from land; the lowered sea levels of the period would have resulted in relatively high islands, with improved visibility between them. But seas still needed crossing, and that required boats.

Sahul

Rather ingeniously, by using the bathymetry of Wallacea and known sea levels in the period between 65,000 and 50,000 years ago, we can model how visible its islands were from each other. From this, the relative costs of potential routes across to Sahul land (Australia, Tasmania, Papua New Guinea and other islands) can be calculated based on how easily (or not) the voyages could be worked out prior to departure, and what distances of sea would need to be navigated. The resulting 'seascape cost surface' reveals that a particularly good window of opportunity presented itself around 65,000 years ago, when sea levels were at their lowest. At this time, the least-cost route would have taken pioneer *Homo sapiens* sailors east from Sulawesi across the Molucca and Ceram Seas to the Bird's Head Peninsula on the western side of Papua New Guinea.[2] Of course this doesn't rule out other crossings by a more costly southern route from Bali and Timor-Leste to northern Australia. Perhaps several dispersals occurred at distinct times, with enough contact maintained between these pioneer groups to keep their culture and biology similar. This hypothesis is supported by the analysis of mtDNA from Papuans, which suggests that Sahul was settled by two groups arriving in the north and south between 50,000 and 65,000 years ago, who were then isolated for 20,000 years.

If marine resources were already important parts of the diet of humans in Wallacea, then they would already be boating, and that implies fibre lashings and nettings that are archaeologically invisible but no less sophisticated than well-made stone tools. We are an inquisitive species and it might be imagined that humans were simply curious to check out that island on the horizon, perhaps driven too by the constant search for new fishing, gathering and hunting grounds. There is no need to assume that one day, someone sat down and said 'let's colonize Sahul'. Modelling shows that it wouldn't have required a huge number of people to establish a viable human population on Sahul either: perhaps one or two thousand to avoid the highest likelihood of extinction in the conditions of the period. We shouldn't see this as one fleet of a number of boats, but probably a number of voyages of as few as 100–200 people over the course of the best part of a millennium. This is a very different picture from an earlier proposal that the job could have been done by a single pregnant woman swept out to sea on a log. But it does give us a feel for the tempo of a successful dispersal into a vast continent, and for the presumably large source populations in Wallacea. Far from being a deliberate and mass exodus, it perhaps resulted through the search for new resources as traditional hunting grounds in lagoons and estuaries became depleted.

After Greenland, Papua New Guinea is the world's second largest island; Australia is only discounted from this line-up as it's usually classed as the smallest continent instead. Whatever the case, Sahul land is vast. Yet by 55,000 years ago *Homo sapiens* had established populations across the entire region; they may have dispersed into the north as early as 65,000 years ago. Thousands of stone tools as well as evidence of ochre grinding have been found in the oldest levels of Madjedbebe, a rockshelter in the Northern Territory, and plant residues and macrofossils show that its inhabitants were eating a range of seeds, tubers and nuts. The problem here is not with the obvious human presence but with its dating: dates for the sediments in which the archaeology accumulated were very imprecise, and while they could have been as old as 65,000 years they could also have been much younger.

Let's say that Madjedbebe reveals a human presence in the north by 59,000 years ago. We're on safer ground around 55,000 years ago, by which time a number of archaeological sites show our species was inhabiting high-altitude tropical forest-grasslands, savannahs, semi-arid grasslands and woodlands as well as temperate forests. It's clear that a variety of resources were hunted and gathered from these inland environments, yet one issue has pervaded the question of the impact of the arrival of our ancestors in the region. From an ecological point of view, the most obvious legacy of our dispersals is the spate of extinctions that followed them,[3] and shortly after the arrival of *Homo sapiens* in Sahul some seventy species of animals both large and small became extinct. As we will see, similar processes were at work in the Americas, and debate continues as to whether our species played a role in any of them. For Sahul, however, this seems unlikely. There is no smoking gun in terms of direct evidence of human involvement, and various processes of extinction were occurring before humans arrived, suggesting very strongly that – at worst – they tipped a balance that was already precarious and in many cases played no role at all.

The problem is an old one for archaeologists; just because dates for the arrival of one species and the disappearance of another coincide broadly in time, how can we demonstrate the two events were causally linked rather than two distinct processes unrelated to each other or coincidentally contemporary? Three of Sahul's megafauna ('big animals') that became extinct around 43,000 years ago are the giant bird *Genyornis* and the giant marsupials *Diprotodon* and *Procoptodon* (the latter a very frightening kangaroo), but was it the arrival of *Homo sapiens*, the gradual decline in climate conditions, or a very cold snap that was the cause? We'll revisit this question when we follow our early ancestors into the Americas in Chapter 17. Certainly a variety of animals were hunted and trapped, such as kangaroo, platypus, wallaby, emu and a number of birds, but this didn't lead to their extinction.

As excavations continue, the evidence for a rich and regionally varying culture is emerging. The earliest convincingly dated rock art is 28,000 years old, but a case has been made for its appearance as early as 40,000 years ago and this estimation will almost certainly be pushed back in time as more examples and dates emerge. It's interesting that red ochre hand and arm stencils in at least five caves of southern Tasmania appear to be some of the oldest rock art traditions of Sahul, given the great age of similar art in Borneo, Sulawesi and, as we will see in Chapter 13, Europe. Pigments were certainly being processed on Sahul from perhaps 45,000 years ago, and beads were drilled from *Dentalium* shells by 42,000 years ago. Not long after, one can recognize regional traditions of jewelry based on different shells where perhaps groups were distinguishing between themselves and others. The world's earliest known cremation burial from the shores of Lake Mungo in the southeast has been dated to 40,000 years ago, at which time shell beads and ochre were being carried to the site over distances of 200–300 km (125–185 miles).

Siberia and the Palaearctic: short summers, long cold winters

And now to another extreme and to the edge of the Americas. The ability to adapt to diverse environments was crucial in our dispersal into the Palaearctic realm. This is characterized by prolonged, frigid winters with temperatures below freezing in some regions for nine months of the year. It gets colder from west to east: compare the annual lows of the Iranian Plateau (-5°C or 23°F), Kazakhstan (-20°C or -4°F), Siberia (-30°C or -22°F) and Mongolia (-45°C or -49°F). Rain and particularly snow are ubiquitous throughout the Palaearctic, and it should be obvious that warm tailored clothing of hide and fur, as well as fire, shelter and the storage of food are essentials in this wilderness. I've often flown over Siberia on my way to Japan. As with Canada I can barely grasp just how many hours pass by above a vast land of mountains, rivers, lakes and snow cover. It's no wonder that human dispersals into this region occurred later than those that took *Homo sapiens* across the grasslands into the Asian rainforests (PL. X).

We saw in Chapter 4 how during the particularly cold periods of the Pleistocene the Palaearctic zone expanded southwards into China and Mongolia. It's into this expanded steppe-tundra that *Homo sapiens* dispersed, first into the Zagros Mountains of Iraq and Iran by 45,000 years ago, displacing the Neanderthals, and on into the Altai and the Palaearctic regions of northern China and Mongolia by 42,000 years ago, probably displacing the Denisovans in this land of mammoths and woolly rhinos. Continue eastwards from here and the Korean Peninsula can be entered from the north, as populations did by 40,000 years ago, and from there the islands of Japan, reaching Palaeo-Honshu (the connected southern islands of Honshu, Shikoku and Kyushu) by 38,000 years ago and, via the Amur River, Palaeo-Sakalin (including Hokkaido) by 30,000 years ago. Here, animals were trapped in communal drives along hillsides defined by fencing and pit traps, and humans exchanged obsidian (a volcanic glass sharper than a steel scalpel) over long distances.

To the north of Mongolia, some 1,500 km (950 miles) east of the Altai, lies the world's largest lake by volume, Baikal. This was where shrubby tundra steppes met pine, larch and birch taiga. In this region the mighty rivers Yenesei, Angara and Lena rise, flowing 2,000 km (1,250 miles) north to the Arctic Ocean. It's easy to spot the Lena and its huge estuary from a plane, and I've often philosophized to myself

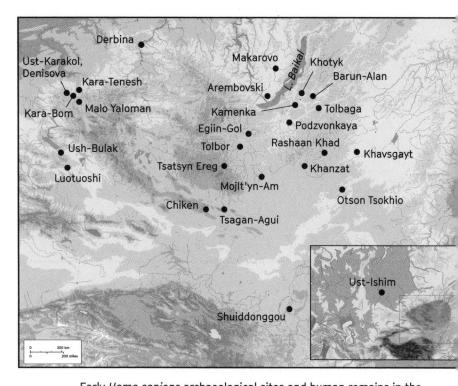

Early *Homo sapiens* archaeological sites and human remains in the vastness of Central Asia and Siberia: Kara-Bom provides the earliest dates for the arrival of Upper Palaeolithic blade technology (and thus *Homo sapiens*) in Central Asia, between 45,000 and 50,000 years ago; situated at the confluence of the Karakol and Anui Rivers, the seasonal hunting camp of Ust-Karakol was occupied at least 38,000 years ago, when microblade production had also appeared (the Denisova Cave is nearby); the seven sites in the Lake Baikal area all demonstrate the presence of *Homo sapiens* between 45,000 and 40,000 years ago; Upper Palaeolithic blades and beads of carved ostrich eggshell were being made around 43,000 years ago at Shuiddonggou in northern China; and at Yana in far northeastern Siberia (not shown on this map) a true mammoth-based economy had developed by 40,000 years ago. The genome sequenced from a *Homo sapiens* fossil from Ust-Ishim contributed very little to the modern Eurasian gene pool, evidence of the 'ghost population' that shared some of its DNA with both northern Eurasians and native North Americans.

about our dispersals into these harsh places, looking down on the vast blanket of snow, and how difficult survival would be here. But our ancestors were surviving in the area by 45,000 years ago, having brought with them a ubiquitous culture in the form of jewelry, flutes and tools very similar to those back in the Altai and, for that matter, to those of early *Homo sapiens* arrivals in Europe around the same time. We might ask why hunter-gatherers should bother with a land

Chapter 6

Brain evolution as it happens: fMRI and DTI scans showing areas of the brain that are active during toolmaking. The 'hot' (red) scale on A–C shows areas where the volume of the active areas increased during intense training, and the 'cold' (blue) where volume subsequently decreased. The more intense the training the greater the demand on these areas of the brain. D combines fMRI and DTI scans for specific technologies and expertise.

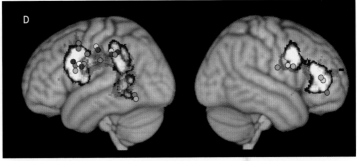

subjects with above-threshold connectivity　3 ▰▰▰▰ 6

——— VBM increase from T1 to T2
——— VBM decrease from T2 to T3

D

Toolmaking (FDG-PET)
● Pre-practice
● Post-practice
● Pre- & post-practice

Toolmaking (FDG-PET)
● Oldowan (simple method)
○ Acheulean (complex method)
○ Oldowan & Acheulean

Toolmaking observation (fMRI)
● Trained only
● Naive only
● Trained & naive

One of several dozen ochre (haematite) blocks from the Middle Stone Age of Blombos Cave, South Africa. These were ground to produce a red pigment and also bear fine engravings made with a bone tool; some of the earliest evidence of our ancestors' visual culture.

iii Over 300,000 years ago at Jebel Irhoud in Morocco these caves filled with sediments containing the remains of a number of early members of our own species and the stone tools they used.

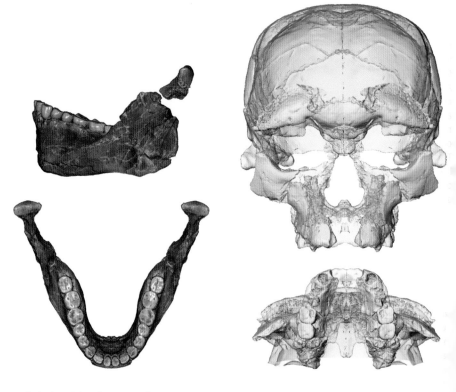

iv Jebel Irhoud fossil 11, one of the earliest known remains of *Homo sapiens*, has been reconstructed digitally, allowing for distortions caused by the weight of sediments to be corrected. By doing this it can be compared to other early fossils of our own species and to those of the Neanderthals and other human groups.

v Three-dimensional scans of the Irhoud 1 cranium (blue) and Irhoud 10 facial remains (beige) are combined here after correcting distortions to approximate what an entire s of one our earliest African ancestors looked In almost all ways the Jebel Irhoud skulls we more similar to modern *Homo sapiens* than other humans such as the Neanderthals.

vi Around 100,000 years ago in Blombos Cave our Middle Stone Age ancestors used a cobble as a pestle and an abalone shell as a mortar for grinding ochre into a powder. This could be mixed with liquid to form a paint for decoration and perhaps symbolism.

ii At least forty-seven human teeth found in Fuyan Cave, China, have been dated to at least 80,000 years old, providing the earliest securely dated evidence of *Homo sapiens* in the country. The morphology and dimensions of the teeth fall clearly into the ranges of modern *Homo sapiens* and outside those of archaic humans.

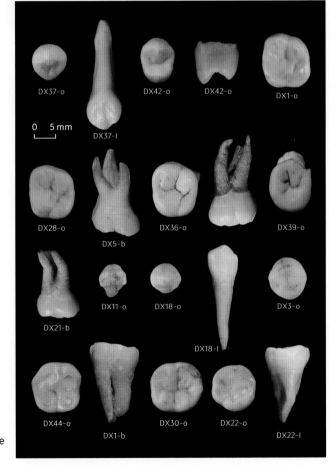

VIII Long-term excavations in Denisova Cave in Russia's Altai Mountains give us a shadowy glimpse of a new human group, the Denisovans.

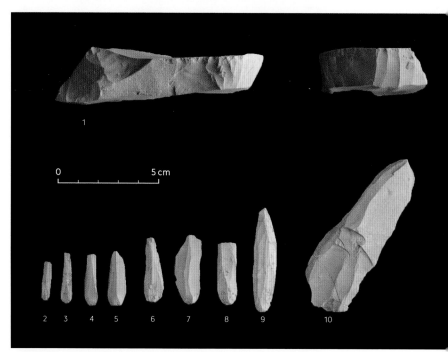

IX 40,000-year-old stone blades, bladelets and their cores from Labeko Koba (Pays Basque) reveal the technological diversity that accompanied the earliest dispersals of *Homo sapiens* in Europe.

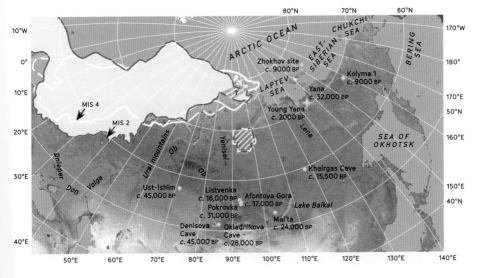

x Securely dated Palaeolithic sites representing the earliest appearance of *Homo sapiens* in the vastness of Siberia, between 50,000 and 38,000 years ago. These are characterized by stone blade technology. The maximum extent of the ice sheets in the cold Marine Isotope Stages (MIS) 4 and 2, around 65,000 and 20,000 years ago respectively, are also shown.

xi (right) Heat maps of isotropic voxels – pixels of between 89 and 144 micrograms (millionths of a gram) in mass – represent the precise thickness of bone in millimetres. Here, fragmentary remains of a human femur from Cro-Magnon (France) can be digitally refitted, showing that they derive from a single individual and allowing the reconstruction of stature and musculature.

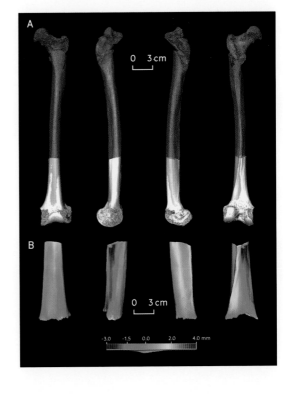

xii (overleaf) Reconstruction of a group of Cro-Magnons – early European *Homo sapiens* – with hide and fur clothing as well as jewelry of shell, teeth and mammoth ivory, all typical of the European Upper Palaeolithic.

XIII Hand stencils in the cave of El Castillo in northern Spain were made by spitting ochre a[?] hand placed on the cave wall. Several dozen were produced here at least 40,000 years ago[?]

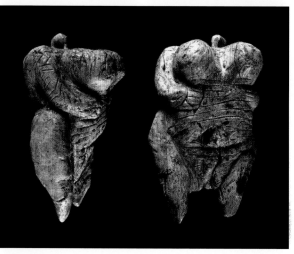

XIV Three female images from the European Early and Mid Upper Palaeolithic dated to between 31,000 and 25,000 years ago. Top left: serpentine carving from the Galgenberg Hill, Austria (Aurignacian). Top right: limestone carving from Willendorf, Austria. Bottom: mammoth ivory carving from Hohle Fels, Germany.

that was brutally cold and saw virtually no daylight in winter? The answer is probably because it was so rich in nutrients on the hoof; its steppe teemed with a variety of large herbivorous prey, but nothing so impressive as the huge mammoths which we shall meet at a location far to the west in Chapter 9. With such an abundant source of meat, fat, hide and tusk, it's no wonder that, as Robin Dennell puns, Palaeolithic hunters of the Arctic ran a mammoth economy! They were doing so inside the Arctic Circle by 40,000 years ago, and it was probably mammoths that were the main draw.

This northern dispersal had taken *Homo sapiens* groups into a biogeographical zone that was distinctly different from the one they had evolved in, but they had diversified and adapted, and we must leave them temporarily at the western edge of Beringia, the continuous mammoth steppe that is now riven in two by the Bering Strait.

Chapter 7

Catastrophe: the Coming of *Homo sapiens* in Europe

It is 1826, and *The Deluge*, nearing completion, rests on its easel in the London studio of the artist John Martin (1789–1854); the painting will shortly be viewed in the rarefied light of the Royal Institution and later the French Exhibition, where it will establish his fame. A knock at the door: Martin's son Leopold, the house's only inhabitant today, answers. A dapper Frenchman stands at the door, bright flower in his lapel. He apologizes; he is in town briefly, and asks humbly for an audience with this English painter who he has heard so much about, a true successor to Turner, who manages to evoke the biblical, classical and (as we would now say) prehistoric worlds so powerfully. He's not here, Leopold explains. Ah, but what a shame! Might I at least glimpse his latest work? As the visitor is ushered into the house he drops a calling card on the little tray in the hall. He is taken to the studio, where he is effusive in his praise of this magnificent evocation of the Flood. After offering thanks the dapper man takes his leave. Leopold, excited to learn exactly who this impressive visitor is, takes up the card. It reads *Jean Léopold Nicolas Frédéric, Baron Cuvier.*[1] On his return, Martin's disappointment at missing the great naturalist is greater than Cuvier's.

Cuvier: catastrophes natural and intellectual

As an undergraduate on a tour of French Palaeolithic sites, I took a detour to visit Cuvier's grave in Paris's Père Lachaise cemetery. He keeps august company: Bizet, Chopin, Champollion (decoder of the Rosetta Stone) and many other great and good rest here. Cuvier is rightly celebrated as the founder of comparative anatomy and palaeontology and a major contributor to the discipline of geology through his development of biostratigraphy (the use of specific animal fossils to hang geological deposits in relative time). In 1819, in recognition of his immense contribution to science, he was created a life peer, and his name is one of only seventy-two inscribed on the Eiffel Tower.[2]

Cuvier compared many animal fossils to those of living species, including the elephant. It had long been known that the remains of 'elephants' were occasionally unearthed in northern latitudes, but it was assumed that these were indeed elephants that must have been carried north by that great catastrophe, the biblical Flood. Cuvier made a careful comparison of the anatomy of such finds to that of living elephants, concluding that these 'mammoths' were in fact an extinct animal closely related to elephants but distinctly different. Mammoths were among the very first extinct animals to be recognized, among which was also *Megatherium* (another Cuvier name), the American giant sloth. Cuvier even coined the formal term *Mastodon* for an extinct elephant-like animal found in Ohio. He very clearly demonstrated that a great number of animal species present in the fossil record – like mammoths and mastodons – were not around in the modern world. Clearly, whole species must have disappeared, or as we would say today, become extinct. Yet it was patently obvious that floral and faunal biodiversity remained remarkably high. Surely one would expect a far lower number of species in the world if these extinctions were the rule? The conclusion was inescapable: species must be *coming into existence*. Cuvier's demonstration set up one of the great questions of nineteenth-century science: if it wasn't the work of God, through what mechanism were species coming into and disappearing from the world?

Cuvier had noted that the change of fossil species over time in rocks around Paris and elsewhere appeared to have been relatively abrupt rather than gradual. Life on Earth, it seemed to him, was not gradually changing, but was from time to time abruptly remodelled in striking events. In his 1813 *Essay on the Theory of the Earth*, he developed his theory of catastrophism, in which he suggested that the course of natural history had been interrupted several times by catastrophic events that had brought about (as we would call them today) mass extinctions of life. This recognition has rightly been seen as one of the foundations of modern geology, and catastrophes of various kinds form the backdrop to evolution and diversity. It's easy to misunderstand catastrophism as it is often caricatured; catastrophes are useful ways of explaining major events that we can't otherwise understand, and as a result form some of the earliest 'just-so' stories. The earliest recorded catastrophic theory is that of the Sumerian and Babylonian flood, which in the form of the Noah's Ark[3] story sailed into the Iron Age Hebrew Bible and from there all the way to John Martin's easel.

Catastrophist thinking and 'environmental determinism' may be unfashionable in archaeology and the social sciences today, where human ingenuity is celebrated and *Homo sapiens* seen as the authors of their own evolutionary destiny. But Cuvier knew better, as do today's palaeoanthropologists. In Earth history, ecological catastrophes were very real, very frequent and very dangerous. It's difficult for an intellectually fashionable academic, ensconced in the warmth of their metropolitan study, to imagine just how precarious life was for early *Homo sapiens* out there, *in the wild*.

Volcanoes

A visitor to the Ice Age gallery in the State Museum of Koblenz in Germany would be forgiven for walking over several grey, glass-covered patches on the floor without noticing that far from being up lights, the squares of stone beneath are riddled with indentations, prints left by animals, humans and possibly dogs in an ash layer as they walked over the Late Glacial landscape. The ash and pumice – glassy rock that solidified after it was spewed out of a volcanic eruption – preserves evidence of life dating to shortly after the Laacher See volcano eruption started towards the end of the Pleistocene in what is now Germany. This was already a lake, formed when a previous volcano blew its top. The new volcanic blast created a huge crater that filled with water, enlarging the lake, and left its ashy calling card widely across Central Europe. The prints impressed into the Laacher See ashes and the archaeology below have been excavated at several locations, providing a glimpse into the landscape 13,000 ± 9 years ago. Evidence of the eruption has been found in lake sediments all over the northern half of Europe, and has proven important to attempts to understand the timing of the onset of the last cold millennium of the Ice Age – the Younger Dryas – prior to the Holocene warming which began around 11,500 years ago.

The most powerful volcanic eruption in recorded history was that of Tambora in Indonesia in 1815; it caused the 'year without a summer' and crop failures and famine across the world. It is ranked as a 6 on the Volcanic Explosivity Index (VEI), which rates recorded eruptions

A track of Ice Age horse hooves in the ashes of the Laacher See volcano at Mertloch (Eifel, Germany), precisely dated to 13,000 ± 9 years ago.

according to the amount of material thrown out, to what height, and for how long. Although Tambora may have been recognized by sulphite peaks in Greenland cores, from the perspective of human evolution it was a comparative lightweight. As volcanism has played a major role in the shaping of the Earth and the evolution of life upon it, it's no surprise that it had enormous effects on our evolution and subsequently on human society down to the present day.

As Cuvier was well aware, there are evolutionary winners and losers in the great global remodelling that catastrophes – volcanic or otherwise – have brought about. Each remodel set up the living ingredients on which natural selection works, redirecting the course of evolution and, in turn, the way that constituent parts of the ecosystem interact. Even events way back in life's infancy affected subsequent evolution, like the eruption of the Deicke volcano on the Laurentian core of what is now North America, one of the largest explosions of the last 550 million years. It probably caused or played a leading role in the Ordovician-Silurian extinction, the second deadliest of five mass extinctions in Earth's history (a sixth extinction of wildlife is probably occurring now, a global catastrophe caused largely by *Homo sapiens*). The eruption and its long-lived aftermath destroyed over 85 per cent of living species (these being restricted to the oceans at the time). Scientific opinion differs as to exactly how the eruption may have caused the catastrophe.

Continental drift is tearing the African and Eurasian plates apart, ripping East Africa's Rift Valley out of the landscape. This is why the Rift Valley is full of volcanoes such as Ngorongoro and Kilimanjaro. These volcanoes would have at times closed down the environments of the australopithecines and early *Homo* we met in Chapter 1. But their loss is to an extent the palaeontologists gain. The solidified ash and magma (tuffs) these volcanoes ejected out onto the landscape covered the findspots of human and animal fossils and stone tools, giving us the chance to explore some very early human sites which otherwise would have been lost.

74,000 years ago: Toba and the early dispersals of *Homo sapiens*

The Toba volcano is located on Sumatra, where the Indo-Australian plate grinds across the edge of the Sunda plate at a rate of 6 cm (2.4 in.) per year. For this reason, Southeast Asia is one of the most seismically active places in the world, earthquake prone, and at risk from tsunamis (such as the Boxing Day Tsunami of 2004, which killed some 280,000 people, untold numbers of animals, and caused devastating environmental impacts which will last decades). Toba has erupted only four times in more than a million years. The most recent of these eruptions occurred around 74,000 years ago, with an explosion that reduced the height of the volcano by around 2,000 m (6,500 ft) and ultimately turned it into the largest crater lake on Earth. This was an 'ultra-Plinian' eruption in the language of vulcanologists,[4] pumping out a plume over 20 km (12 miles) in height and with a subsequent ash fall area of some 40 million sq. km (15 million sq. miles), up to 100 times greater than Tambora.

When an eruption pumps that amount of material into the air it increases Earth's albedo (its reflectivity, and hence the proportion of sunlight and radioactivity that the atmosphere and biosphere reflect back into space). Less sunlight means that global temperatures will fall, which in turn affects plant growth and the animal populations dependent on vegetation for food. In the oceans, the volume of ice will rise, and on land the colder temperatures will mean more snow, its shiny surface increasing planetary albedo even further. Toba's last eruption alone probably cooled the Earth by 5°C (9°F), perhaps up to 10°C (18°F) in summer. Its 1–3 m- (3–10 ft-) thick layer of pumice and ash – the YTT or Younger Toba Tuff – has been found in India and the Indian Ocean over 2,500 km (1,500 miles) to the west and northwest, over 1,500 km (900 miles) to the northeast in the South China Sea, in Lake Malawi in Tanzania and at several sites on the Cape coast of South Africa, the latter nearly 9,000 km (5,600 miles) to the southeast. It mantled an area of at least 4 million sq. km (1.5 million sq. miles) with a volume of about 800 cu. km (192 cu. miles) of dense rock. To put this in perspective, the devastating eruptions of Tambora produced no more than 33 cu. km (7.9 cu. miles) of ejecta and the famous Krakatoa eruption of 1883 only 20 cu. km (4.8 cu. miles).

Various samples taken from Toba's slopes and nearby have been dated by the potassium-argon and laser-ablation argon-argon techniques, producing an estimated age of 73.8 ± 3 ka BP (that is, between 76,800 and 70,800 years before present when we take dating imprecision into account). By this time small groups of *Homo sapiens* were distributed in patches from Africa across to East Asia, and from time to time where their ranges overlapped in Central Asia they met and interacted with Eurasian indigenes such as the Neanderthals and Denisovans. This was a precarious situation: small groups dispersed over vast areas dependent entirely on wild resources for survival in a harsh landscape. Whether in the savannahs of Africa or the Eurasian tundras, life was difficult enough without the disastrous effects of a VEI 8 super-eruption to deal with.

But exactly how disruptive was the Toba eruption? Palaeo-climatologists can model this using sophisticated computing based on data collected on the effects of modern recorded eruptions on climate and environment, but it's a difficult task. Just look at the imprecision of modern weather forecasts. Here, there are many more variables to consider: prevailing wind systems, land topography and sea surface temperatures will affect the volume and distribution of the ejecta and the extent to which it stays up in the air, and the composition of its particles will have differing effects on albedo (sulphate particles are particularly reflective). Add to that the ongoing effects of the Pleistocene climate, particularly the glacial loess (wind-blown sediment) flying around in the air, and one can understand why there is a healthy amount of debate over Toba's effects. But even with this uncertainty, its impact on human groups can be detected: genetics reveal that a considerable bottleneck – a dangerous crash in the levels of genetic diversity – occurred in *Homo sapiens* at roughly this time. Genetically, most of us descend from the ancestors carrying this reduced gene pool that dispersed out of Africa from around this point, rather than from those brief and ultimately failed dispersals we saw earlier.

Is this bottleneck the mark that Toba had upon our species? My colleague Stan Ambrose, an authority on the Stone Age of Africa, thinks so. The models suggest that it caused a profound deterioration of climate and resulting environmental degradation, as he puts it. It erupted just as climate was changing from cold but relatively mild interstadial conditions into severe cold stadial conditions. Toba did not cause this; the build-up of ice, loess and other indications of climatic decline are present in many ice and marine cores before the occurrence in them of Toba's characteristic isochron (isotope signature), but it certainly made an already tough situation a lot worse. Stan's careful consideration of the climatic, environmental and archaeological evidence suggests that the one or two centuries of volcanic winter that followed the eruption had significant effects on human populations in and outside of Africa.

It's no surprise that the palaeoenvironmental data indicate severe environmental degradation at the time. Given the problems of chronological imprecision, short-term environmental change (year by year) is difficult to detect, but cold megadroughts, deforestation and the growth of grasslands are evident from Africa to India. Conditions would have significantly remodelled the distribution of *Homo sapiens* in Africa. In some regions, populations would wane or disappear, but others where the situation was not so severe could act as refugia. The presence of human footprints in the ash at Mertloch, 16 km (10 miles) to the south of the Laacher See volcanic eruption, for example, shows that some human groups were able to survive in the region's moon-like landscape until the eruption's middle phase.

Critiques of the 'Toba volcanic winter', as it came to be caricatured, followed, largely from archaeologists pointing out that human presence in regions where Toba material has been found appears to continue from before to after the eruption. How, they argued, could one accept that human populations were disrupted? The YTT isochron has been identified at several sites in Africa and the Levant, in some cases interstratified with archaeology. The apparent continuity of archaeology above and below the isochron at Pinnacle Point in South Africa, for example, has been used to suggest that populations remained in place for several millennia either side of the super-eruption – were thriving, no less; similar evidence has been found at Jwalapuram in India. But this is where our imprecise picture of how long it takes sediments containing archaeology to accumulate over time, and the imprecision in our dating of them, can lead to a false impression that populations were continuously present. Although stone tools have been found stratified a few centimetres above and below the YTT isochron, this could still accommodate a gap of centuries between the events; it is impossible to establish whether human groups genuinely stayed put. In fact, at Pinnacle Point, much of the sediment seems to have accumulated through airborne deposition, with no evidence of human activity such as the burning of hearths. As Stan Ambrose points out, the evidence suggests rare rather than intense human occupation, and a similar situation is indicated at Klasies some 260 km (160 miles) to the east. It's this sort of population reduction, rather than complete destruction, that creates genetic bottlenecks.

It would be no surprise if the relatively rich southern coastal region of our African homeland acted as a refugium in which humans were able to survive; it's just that the evidence doesn't point that way at Klasies and Pinnacle Point. Perhaps the humans were nearby. Stan suggests an alternative: data from lake cores in the region of the Zambesi show that it remained wet and stable while surrounding areas were dry and cold, exactly the sort of refugium – possibly one of a few across the continent – where *Homo sapiens* could survive, albeit in smaller numbers.

In very broad perspective we can see how Toba affected all humans on the planet in one way or another. Neanderthal populations had been at their peak during this time (more sites and wider distribution), but their population then saw a gradual decline. As new excavations improve our currently poor understanding of the Denisovans, I suspect we will find that they were similarly affected, as, perhaps, were *Homo floresiensis* and *Homo luzonensis*. The emerging picture is that the several human species or sub-species distributed across Europe and Asia were severely challenged between 70,000 and 55,000 years ago, as the ancient DNA data implies. There would be evolutionary winners and losers. The memory of the Neanderthals and Denisovans would fade, retreating to a handful of genes preserved in the *Homo sapiens* genome. Others would disappear completely. With hindsight, the winner was *Homo sapiens*. The important point is that African *Homo sapiens* groups responded with staggering organizational changes which are evident when the number of sites begins to pick up again from around 71,000 years ago, with stone tools revealing that groups were far more mobile over longer distances in the landscape. As global conditions improved, populations expanded out of their refugia yet again, and there is fresh evidence of human presence at South African sites. As Stan Ambrose plausibly suggests, this could reflect a change from the defence of relatively small, resource-rich territories to far more widespread strategies in which far-flung groups cooperated with each other. *Homo sapiens* dispersed across and out of Africa once more, to far greater distances, and far more permanently than before, carrying with them the genetic homogeneity brought about by the severe conditions. African *Homo sapiens* groups were building a larger, more connected society, and although their distribution would continue to wax and wane in response to climate change, their presence across much of Africa, Europe and Asia was assured by 70,000 years ago. After populations consolidated, the next step was up into the north and west.

45,000 years ago: first steps northwards into Europe

The Labeko-Koba Cave in the Spanish Basque Country and the Siuren I rockshelter in Crimea may be over 3,000 km (1,850 miles) apart, but they are two of a small set of sites that preserve the evidence of the first tentative dispersal of *Homo sapiens* into Europe (see PL. IX). The evidence is mainly – but not entirely – technical. Knapping waste and discarded tools reveal that a very new way of working stone had arrived in Europe and the few associations we have of these with fossil human material reveal that they were made by the earliest arrivals of *Homo sapiens*. They were organized around the repeated and systematic production of long and thin blades and in particular smaller bladelets, which were removed with considerable skill from fist-sized prism- and pyramid-shaped cores. While Neanderthal knapping was pretty good, this is nevertheless a marked change in the control of material, and characteristic waste products from making these tools as well as the bladelets themselves are unmistakable evidence that *Homo sapiens* has been at work.

These are examples of archaeological proxies, which we use to infer the presence of *Homo sapiens* in the absence of more direct indications. It's a bit like inferring that an electrician has been in one's home based on the screwdriver and snippets of wire they have left behind. If we can be sure that certain tools and technologies were exclusively produced by a specific human group, then we can safely use these to build up a picture of their dispersal. We need to do this because actual human remains from the period are remarkably rare. This is nothing exceptional; humans were far less common than the herbivores that they hunted, and as they were probably not yet burying their dead (one way to protect the skeleton from the vicissitudes of erosion) their physical remains were probably reduced to dust in most cases. We do have a few examples of relatively late Neanderthal and early *Homo sapiens* remains; in my reading of the available chronology for these no reliably dated Neanderthal remains are younger than 41,000 years old. The earliest directly dated *Homo sapiens* remains in Europe constitute a molar and several scraps of bone probably from the same individual, which were found in Bacho Kiro Cave in Bulgaria, in deposits dating to somewhere between 45,800 and 43,600 years ago. This suggests that our species had dispersed to the southeastern Balkans by 43,000 years ago, perhaps in the first of a sequence of distinct dispersals. The few other early *Homo sapiens* remains we have, like the cranial remains from the Oase Cave in Romania, are no more than 42,000 years old. But with so few examples this could present a very misleading picture, which is why we need the much more numerous archaeological proxies.

It's possible that blade technologies found in southern Moravia serve as such a proxy; they appear in Hungary's Szeleta Cave as early as 45,000 years ago. If correct this would place *Homo sapiens* in the Bükk Mountains of northern Hungary at a time when Neanderthals still existed further to the north. In my opinion it's best to see this as the earliest, geographically restricted dispersal through the Balkans, perhaps in part following the Danube and coming to an end at the edge of the Hungarian Plain. It's only after this time that we see a far wider spread of the next proxy: bladelet-producing technologies from the Russian Plain to Spain in the period broadly dated to 45,000–40,000 years ago.

These small bladelets were finely shaped with a blunted, haftable edge so they could be used as elements in multi-part knives and weapon tips. This Protoaurignacian technology, as it is called (after the site of Aurignac in southwestern France), already shows a degree of diversity in the specific techniques to produce the bladelets – presumably a behavioural 'drift' as small populations spread and began to diversify. This is some of the earliest evidence of cultural change in *Homo sapiens*, and marks the appearance of some of the most distinctive traits of the Upper Palaeolithic, as specialists call the whole period from roughly 50,000 to 12,000 years ago.

Dating imprecision is once again important. If the range of dates we have for the Protoaurignacian truly indicate that *Homo sapiens* was present in southern Europe as early as 45,000 years ago, this would suggest a possible overlap of up to 4,000 years with Neanderthals, if the youngest dates of around 41,000 years ago for their last presence

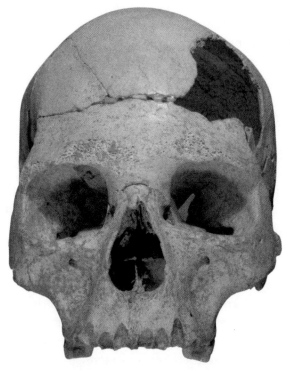

At around 40,500 years old, Oase 2, the cranium of a fifteen year old from Oase Cave in Romania, is from one of the earliest *Homo sapiens* groups in Europe. It shows the degree of anatomical variability characteristic of the earliest Upper Palaeolithic in Europe, in some respects derived from earlier populations of Northern Africa and the Near East, and in others distinctly European.

The deposits in Fumane Cave in northeastern Italy preserve evidence of both some of the latest Neanderthals and the earliest *Homo sapiens* in Europe.

are correct. The problem is that these age ranges are dependent on modelling of available dates, and what we are seeing are the tail ends of probability distributions. A more cautious reading sees Neanderthals gone from all but the western peripheries of Europe by 43,000 years ago, and *Homo sapiens* dispersing briefly around 45,000 years ago and again after 43,000 years ago. This is the simplest way to explain the total absence of any cultural evidence of the two interacting in Europe and the simple observation that the earliest *Homo sapiens* sites always lie above (and not mixed with) the last Neanderthal ones – as at Fumane Cave in Italy, for example. As we've seen, we need to look to the east, in the vastness of Central Asia, to find the regions where the two (and three with Denisovans) occasionally swapped genes. But recall the Ancient North Eurasian ghost population discussed in Chapter 5; our Protoaurignacians are perhaps the best European candidates for these.

Another way that the Protoaurignacian stands out from the earlier sites left by the Neanderthals is a relative explosion in the number and variety of wearable ornaments. These were certainly used by Neanderthals, but examples are rare and suggest that a visual culture including jewelry of symbolic value was not widespread among them, or at least didn't have universal currency. With the arrival of *Homo sapiens*, carefully pierced marine shells and deer incisors became relatively commonplace. Until everything changed.

Another catastrophe... or two

The first explosion disgorged a column of hot gas and volcanic rock at least 40 km (25 miles) into the sky. The power of the eruption was great enough to thrust the surrounding area up by 1,000 m (3,250 ft), the volcanic mountain itself collapsing inwards into a caldera that would later fill with Mediterranean water to form the bay it is today. Then a brief lull, rumblings, and the main event: a vast eruption sending some 200 cu. km (48 cu. miles) of material at least 1,500 sq. km (580 sq. miles) from the source. It was one of the most powerful eruptions of the Pleistocene – on the standard scale reckoned to be VEI 7 – and its ashes fell across much of the area of Europe that *Homo sapiens* had occupied. It is no surprise that much later the whole area of the Phlegraean Fields near Naples – which continued to periodically lay incendiary waste to the surrounding landscape – came to be thought of as the home of Vulcan, the Roman god of fire.

Argon-argon dates at its source show that the volcano blew around 40,000 years ago (39.28 ± 0.11 ka BP). The vast amount of sulphate aerosols it disgorged spread so far that they are traceable in Greenland ice cores. The so-called CI Y2 isochron provides an important marker for the eruption, which coincided with the onset of very cold and dry conditions precipitated by what palaeoclimatologists call a Heinrich Event. These are massive discharges (calving) of ice from the polar ice caps into the ocean, drifting southwards. From a European perspective, this shuts down the circulation of warm, saline waters in the Atlantic, leading to significant cooling.

Heinrich Events occurred repeatedly over the course of the Pleistocene and are marked in marine cores, where they are numbered back from the most recent. As if the CI Y2 eruption wasn't disruptive enough, it coincided with the beginning of Heinrich Event (HE) 4. The two seem to have triggered a feedback cycle, causing an extreme climatic deterioration that lasted for several centuries. Recall from Chapter 6 the extinction of Australian megafauna such as *Diprotodon* and *Genyornis* around this time and we begin to appreciate the global effects of such events.

There are more direct deleterious effects of eruptions, too. Inhaling microscopic glass can cause respiratory diseases such as asthma and silicosis, and high fluoride levels could have poisoned not only humans but also the herbivores on which they depended for much of their nutrition, leading to a host of different bone

The deep sediments in the Crvena Stijena rockshelter, Montenegro, preserve evidence from over 150,000 years ago through to the Bronze Age. Some 5–8 m (15–25 ft) down lies evidence of the last Neanderthals to use the shelter, overlain by the first *Homo sapiens* arrivals. The 7–8 cm (2.8–3.1 in.) thick CI Y2 tephra pictured here overlies sediments containing evidence of the last Neanderthals at the site. The Y2 tephra is up to 1 m (3 ft) thick in Romania.

deformations. Increased sulphur in the air and correspondingly decreased environmental productivity would have affected nutritional intake, accompanied by numerous health problems. No wonder the Protoaurignacian dispersal came to an end at this time.

Perhaps because of these events, it's likely that human populations simply shrank back to their core distribution in and around Africa. Some humans back-migrated into Africa, bringing with them a Eurasian DNA signal, which may be one sign of this contraction. But humans were just one part of much wider ecological communities who were all affected by the volcanic winter. For several thousand years, cold-adapted animals disappeared from the north – hyenas never to return – and mammoth, woolly rhino, reindeer and arctic fox contracted back to a surprisingly southern distribution: in Iberia their remains have been found as far south as Granada (37°N). The Neanderthals were already extinct, the Denisovans possibly so, and *Homo sapiens* disappeared from a cold Europe for several centuries. Like so many Pleistocene dispersals, the first foray into Europe was merely a temporary success.

Chapter 8

Stress, Disease and Inbreeding

It's time to get more intimately acquainted with our Ice Age forebears, and where better to start than with their very bones? Set aside the mental picture you probably have of them: it will almost certainly be wrong. The black skin and hair of tall males and broad females points to their African origins. Both sexes are muscular, although aches and pains and broken bones indicate a tough, mobile life.

Meet the Cro-Magnons: introducing Alpha, Beta, Gamma and Delta

For my doctoral research at Cambridge I spent weeks measuring stone tools at the National Museum of Prehistory in the pretty village of Les Eyzies-de-Tayac in the Dordogne. I was interested in what we could infer about Neanderthal intelligence by the way they were thinking as they knapped flint. The museum would kick me out for two hours every day while the staff took lunch, and I'd wander the limestone valley of the Vézère River, taking in its classic Ice Age sites that justify its claim to being the French capital of prehistory. The sides of the valley are riddled with caves and rockshelters, under which our forebears camped, and whose archaeology has been excavated since the 1860s. One of these shelters is Cro-Magnon, where I often sat to eat my lunchtime baguette. Under the shelter, the partial remains of at least four adults and four infants came to rest on a rock shelf against its rear wall (see PL. XII). Their bodies had probably been exposed to the elements while the soft tissues decayed, and eventually some of the bones were tucked away at the back of the shelter, where they were to lie until they were excavated around 31,000 years later in 1868. They were some of the first human remains dating to the Ice Age recovered by science, and as a result the name Cro-Magnon came to be used as an informal term for Ice

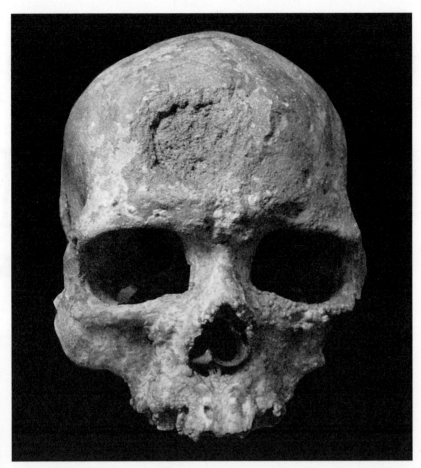

Cro-Magnon 1, the cranium of an old male, almost certainly belonging to 'Alpha' in the new terminology given to the four adults and four infants known from partial remains in the rockshelter. Around 31,000 years old, they were apparently tucked away at the rear of the shelter.

Age specimens of our own species. The remains are fragmentary and eroded, and while it seemed clear from the number of some skeletal elements that three or four adults were represented, it may be that bits of several other individuals lurk among the fragments. How does one tell? And which bones belong to which individuals?[1]

In traditional osteoarchaeology, the articular surfaces of bones (their ends, where they come to form joints with others) and a number of landmarks where muscles attach are matched by eye. This is very time consuming, but works well when the bones of the same side of the body are available, when all of the matching articulated parts are present and the bone is in good condition. In situations like Cro-Magnon,

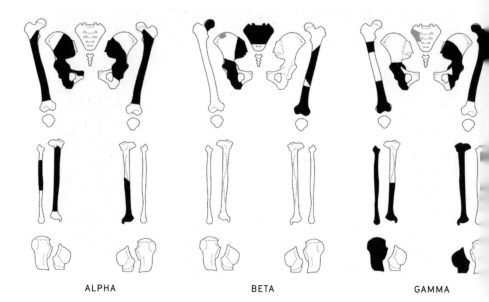

ALPHA   BETA   GAMMA

Remains of the lower limbs of three adults from the Cro-Magnon
rockshelter (Dordogne, France), reunited on the basis of traditional
osteoarchaeology and three-dimensional virtual modelling.

however, where they are damaged and missing, it requires a bit more
technology. This is where three-dimensional virtual modelling of bone
comes in handy. A micro CT scanner is used to reconstruct with great
precision the bone's thickness, density and growth patterns, invisible to
the naked eye, which can then be used to match bone fragments. If we
think of the process as a three-dimensional jigsaw in which a number
of pieces are missing and the edges of others are broken, it is a way of
finding other links between pieces. In this way it is possible to see how
many bones can be associated to different individuals (see PL. XI).

This was exactly the method applied to the Cro-Magnon bones by
French osteoarchaeologists Adrien Thibeault and Sébastien Villotte,
who were able to associate the bones of the legs to three individuals:
Alpha, a particularly tall and elderly male; Beta, an old woman; and
Gamma, another old male. Once the material was reunited, the health
status of the three in life could be assessed. In addition to the wear and
tear expected of an elderly individual in the Ice Age, Alpha exhibited
signs on his cranium and legs of a rare disease, possibly cell cancer.
Beta's upper body was very robust and muscular, a trait found in many
Ice Age females. She had moderate levels of degenerative joint disease
including osteochondritis (a painful joint condition) of the elbow.

Small, isolated populations, mating and inbreeding

Hunter-gatherers, past and present, are often called 'small-scale societies', referring to very small populations organized like small villages, but lacking permanent settlements. Their populations are small in comparison even to agricultural villages. This is because their size is limited by the ecological carrying capacity of the wild resources they are dependent upon hunting and gathering for survival. Carrying capacity is the size of the population that an environment can sustain (carry) without depletion. Hunter-gatherers usually live well below this, at populations typically between 0.1 and 0.001 individuals per sq. km or, to put it another way, no more than an average of one person per 10 sq. km (or 4 sq. miles). Let's put this in perspective: the mean world population density today (total global population divided by landmass minus Antarctica) is about 55 per sq. km (or 142 per sq. mile). The mean masks considerable variation; England's is 432 per sq. km (or 1,119 per sq. mile) and Monaco's over 18,000 per sq. km (or 48,000 per sq. mile), population densities that would be inconceivable to a hunter-gatherer.[2] Estimating Ice Age populations is notoriously difficult; we can assume densities similar to those we know for hunter-gatherers of the recent past who were living in broadly similar environments, although we saw in Chapter 7 that there are no identical tundras or herds of mammoth today. The rising sea levels of the last 10,000 years have significantly remodelled coastlines, flooding vast swathes of low-lying land, so estimating available landmass at any given time in the Ice Age is approximate only. Our vague estimate would be between 2,000 and 30,000 people spread across the continent of Eurasia, rising to 70,000 in the last 10,000 years of the Ice Age. That's one third of the population of Portsmouth, my home town.

No wonder hunter-gatherers have evolved a number of ways to ensure that populations are maintained with acceptable levels of inbreeding (to which we'll return below) but remain below the carrying capacity of the environment. No doubt failure was common, and there could be only one result: local extinction. If snows reduced mobility just too long, if reindeer failed to appear during their spring migration, or if valuable gatherers or hunters died young, the result could spell disaster for a local group. To spread risk, hunter-gatherers evolved a system of fission and fusion in order to minimize their depletion of the land. At those times of the year when resources

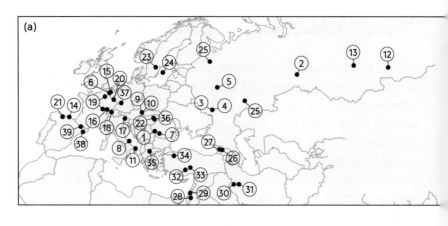

(a)

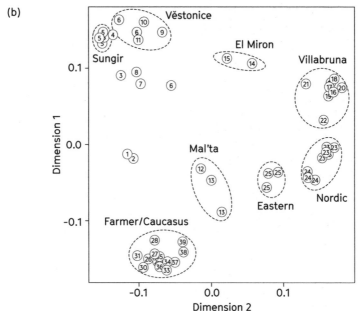

(b)

① Oase (UP)	⑭ El Miron (LP)	㉗ Caucasus (HG, M)
② Ust (UP)	⑮ Goyet (LP)	㉘ Natufian (LP)
③ Kostenki (UP)	⑯ France (HG, LP)	㉙ Levant (EN)
④ Kostenki 12 (UP)	⑰ Villabruna (LP)	㉚ Zagros (EN)
⑤ Sungir (UP)	⑱ Bichon (LP)	㉛ Iran (EN)
⑥ Goyet (UP)	⑲ France (HG, M)	㉜ Boncuklu (EN)
⑦ Romania (UP)	⑳ Loschbour (M)	㉝ Tepecic (EN)
⑧ Paglicci (UP)	㉑ Brana (M)	㉞ Barcin (EN)
⑨ Věstonice (UP)	㉒ Hungary (HG, M)	㉟ Greece (EN)
⑩ Pavlov (UP)	㉓ Motala (M)	㊱ Hungary (EN)
⑪ Ostuni (UP)	㉔ Nordic (HG, EN)	㊲ LBK (EN)
⑫ Mal'ta (UP)	㉕ Eastern (HG, M)	㊳ Cardial (EN)
⑬ Afontova Gora (LP)	㉖ Caucasus (HG, LP)	㊴ Iberia (EN)

Key: HG = hunter-gatherer; UP = Upper Palaeolithic; LP = Lower Palaeolithic; M = Mesolithic; EN = Early Neolithic

Chapter 8

(c)

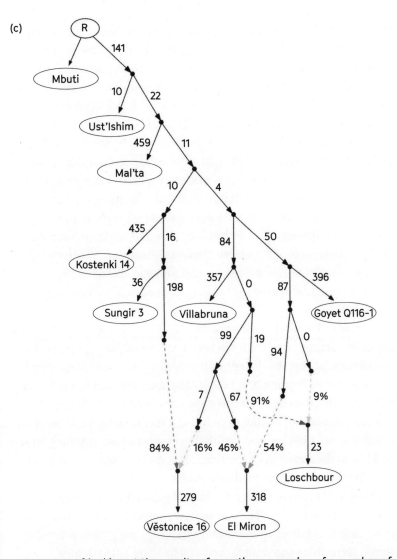

Two ways of looking at the results of genetic sequencing of a number of
Ice Age *Homo sapiens* individuals from the period 50,000–15,000 years ago.
(a) The location of the sites from which genetic samples derive. (b) Genetic
affinities of the sequenced samples; note that the groups form their own
distinct clusters, including Sungir. (c) The same results, expressed as a
genetic family tree, showing not only the distinctive groups of (b) but also
their relationships, including modern Mbuti populations for comparison.
The data reveal the small and relatively isolated groups of Ice Age Europe.
Although individually distinct, Sungir and Kostenki, for example, derive from
an ancestor group, from which, more distantly, the Věstonice population
of the Czech Republic also derives. The numbers on each 'branch' show
the relative amounts of genetic divergence of that branch; the higher
the number, the greater the divergence. Hence, the large amount of
divergence undergone by Kostenki 14 shows that its genetic history was more
complicated than a simple descent from an ancestor shared with Sungir 3.

Stress, Disease and Inbreeding   117 were relatively abundant they could aggregate together in relatively large numbers, and by contrast when resources were few, notably in winter, they split into smaller units, usually comprising a few nuclear families. This determined the structure of their annual cycle.

When we call hunter-gatherers 'small-scale' it doesn't mean that they were simple or backward: far from it. Anthropologists have shown that although they are characterized by small and fluid populations, these were drawn from expansive and complex trans-generational networks, 'multilevel' societies that linked together highly mobile bands – the standard term for a hunter-gatherer social group – into larger societies. Crucially, culture – problem-solving, environmental information, technology, fun, and most importantly, sexual partners – could be shared over vast distances. When the spawning salmon or migrating reindeer allowed, bands came together at seasonal aggregations, sang, danced, told stories and made partnerships.

Modern understanding of ancient DNA gives us a glimpse here and there of the degree of relatedness between several Ice Age individuals. In small populations the danger of inbreeding is ever-present. Small degrees of it are common and biologically tolerable, but too much is a bad thing. Its effects can multiply the expression of a host of bad traits in a population, including reduced fertility, stature and lifespan, and many other physical and health defects that affect anything from breathing to the function of the brain. It certainly explains much of the behaviour of Europe's medieval rulers.

Taboos will actively reduce the risk of inbreeding by prohibition. Today, most countries specifically outlaw mating between first- and second-degree relatives (parents and offspring, and grandparents/children, avuncular and double-first cousins and half-siblings respectively), and hunter-gatherers of the recent past all developed social ways of keeping breeding groups open. We can probably assume that similar mechanisms were practised in the Ice Age – if they weren't we'd probably not be here – but we can use ancient DNA to test whether they were successful.

In order to do this we need the bones of several people from a single site that we know lived about the same time. One such sample is the 33,000- to 34,000-year-old campsite of Sungir in Russia, where four individuals were buried in neighbouring graves, and the fragmentary remains of several others were found scattered nearby. We'll revisit the Sungir burials later, when we come to look at the treatment of the dead, but for now we're interested in the relationship between these people in life. Ancient DNA is able to pinpoint individual relationships to the third degree, that is, it can identify blood relations to the level of first cousins and great-grandparents/ children or closer. The Sungir ancient DNA showed that none of the individuals were closely related, at least to the third degree, a result that is surprising for small groups of Ice Age hunter-gatherers who we might be forgiven for assuming had had relatively restricted access to potential mates. The data reveal that groups preferred to mate within small subgroups, but that they maintained sufficient contact between bands to keep their genes tolerably fresh. They are consistent with modern data suggesting that hunter-gatherers have access to mating groups of at least 200 people, and that in any small band only around 10 per cent of the population are related at the first or second degree. So, by at least 34,000 years ago our Ice Age forebears had recognized that breeding networks needed to be kept open. This is a remarkable discovery, only possible in the age of archaeogenomics. It was also no mean achievement for small-scale groups in harsh Ice Age environments, but there is always a price to pay. Demanding levels of mobility were necessary in order to maintain these networks. The alternative, where mobility and networking were reduced, could bring about extinction in a few generations. Perhaps this was at the heart of Neanderthal demise.

Life

When it comes to reconstructing how frequently Ice Age people gave birth, how likely a child was to survive to adulthood, how tough life was and what adult life expectancy was, we are dependent entirely on the osteological and genetic study of the bones that survive. These range from isolated teeth and bits of bones recovered from campsites to near-complete skeletons protected by shallow graves. Their study gets us some way to understanding the aspects of life that leave a mark on hard tissue or genes, although there is much we'd like to ask that we simply can't investigate. We don't know much about fertility, or the average number of children a woman bore in her lifetime, for example. Infant remains are common among Neanderthal skeletons, suggesting high levels of infant mortality, but with *Homo sapiens* we see evidence of a modest lowering of this, which may be significant, as even a small improvement in the number of infants surviving to reproductive age could allow a population to increase in size. Individuals certainly matured relatively quickly. One way to estimate this is the eruption of the second and third molars, which erupted relatively fast, probably reflecting a generally rapid maturation of the skeleton as a whole.

Rapid maturation, big brains and tough, mobile lives are metabolically expensive. Modern foragers in environments broadly similar to those of the Ice Age, such as the Inuit, expend 3,500–4,000 kcal per day, and estimates for Neanderthals based on their body weights and highly mobile lifestyle suggest a figure as high as 5,000 kcal per day. Based on this, we can assume that the expenditure of *Homo sapiens* was likely at the higher end of the modern forager range, that is around 4,000 kcal per day. This is a lot of dietary protein to replace, and as we've seen, most of this would have had to come from meat and aquatic resources which are mobile themselves. It's clear why Ice Age hunter-gatherers were mobile by necessity, not choice.

For much of the Ice Age, *Homo sapiens* shared characteristics of the long bones of the arms and legs with their archaic *Homo* forebears. These bones were relatively thick-walled, with marked attachment points for developed muscles, characteristics of high levels of biomechanical stress in daily life. Legs were good for walking: the robusticity of Ice Age tibiae (one of the two bones of the lower leg) is comparable to or even greater than that of modern competitive cross-country runners. The length of the femur (thigh bone) is also a very good indicator of mean stature (height). Roughly speaking your height is four times the length of your femur. We can therefore estimate the height of our ancestors based on the femora they have very generously left behind. The picture that emerges is of tall, leggy individuals, a relic of our African ancestry.

Brigitte Holt, an expert in Ice Age human remains, has reconstructed the heights of Ice Age Europeans using the femur/height ratio. She was able to show a decrease in height over time from around 174 cm to 161 cm (5 ft 7 in. to 5 ft 2 in.) in males, and from 162 cm to 153 cm (5 ft 3 in. to 5 ft) in females. These are averages, of course, and we must remember they pertain only to Europeans, but it's clear that there was a sharp reduction in mean height from the time of the Last Glacial Maximum around 20,000 years ago, of up to 10 cm (4 in.) for males and 8 cm (3.1 in.) for females. Prior to this time people were taller and heavier, and their legs were long relative to their trunk.

The reduced mobility brought about by severe climate increased the competition for available nutritional resources from this time, and smaller-bodied humans with lower metabolic and nutritional demands stood a greater chance of surviving to pass on their own genes.

There is a strong relationship between the size and shape of the femur and levels of mobility and body mass. The more mobile an individual, the more bending stress the femur comes under. As a result, more bone wall builds up in order to deal with this stress, leading to a distinct morphology that can be seen in cross-sections of the longbone. If you were to cut through your thigh and through your femur (don't try this at home) it would appear relatively thin walled and round in section, unless you're a top athlete or fitness fanatic. This is because most of us experience relatively minor biomechanical forces in our legs, given that we don't have to walk long distances or carry heavy loads habitually. In highly mobile people, elevated levels of force run through the femur from front to back (anterior-posterior in anatomical terms), resulting in 'crests' of thicker bone at the front and back of the femur's cross-section, particularly in the parts of the bone closest to the knee, where most pressure is felt. Brigitte compared cross-sections of Ice Age and post-Ice Age (Mesolithic) human femurs, finding that the rear crest disappeared over time, a sure indicator of gradually decreasing levels of mobility as climate improved and boreal forests spread, reducing the need for long-distance movement. Her work shows very nicely the physically demanding lifestyle of our Ice Age ancestors. The arms of *Homo sapiens* also became strong relative to legs over the course of the Ice Age; we find this trait among modern Aleuts of Alaska and Kamchatka, as their muscles build due to their extensive paddling of boats. Right arms were particularly robust, almost certainly because of the habitual throwing of javelins.

Pathology

We saw above that some of the adult remains from the Cro-Magnon rockshelter bore the wear and tear of tough lives, and in the case of Alpha, a cancerous disease. Bones often bear the traces of accidents (trauma) and diseases that have caused changes to the surface of the bone. Erik Trinkaus, who is part of the team studying the Cro-Magnon material, arguably has the greatest familiarity with the bones of Ice Age humans of anyone, and he has meticulously documented examples of stress and pathology on many Ice Age skeletons. It was clearly a tough life; Erik found indicators of nutritional stress and breakage on *all* of the specimens he was able to examine, a far higher incidence than one might expect if we were to randomly sample a modern population.

I introduced Erik Trinkaus in Chapter 2. Erik – a world-leading specialist in Ice Age human biology – and his colleagues have shown that trauma-related fractures were relatively common from early in life, many being relatively minor bumps to the head, but including breaks of the legs, arms and ankles and their associated degenerative joint diseases. These were often debilitating, particularly to mobility, but they had healed, which suggests that the unlucky individuals, at least those who were relatively young, were cared for. A young adult found in Manot Cave (Israel) had a healed foot fracture that probably resulted in a painful limp, but he or she (we can't tell which) clearly survived the injury, despite being slow and incapable of hunting, or at least of chasing down prey.

Erik concluded that even individuals who sustained deformities or trauma of the lower limbs continued to be mobile. This makes it likely that older individuals with reduced mobility were left behind to die, their bones consumed by carnivores and not entering the palaeontological record. Mobility then may account for some of the scarcity of older individuals. In short, keep up or drop out.

Given that they live in low population densities, are highly mobile, and do not live in close proximity to disease-bearing domesticated animals, hunter-gatherers typically have a relatively low range of pathogens. Ice Age health was generally fair. With a few exceptions, oral health was relatively good; it's only with the sugar-rich and stone-ground cereals of the new-fangled agriculture that dental standards plummet. Dental caries become more common over time, perhaps indicative of growing levels of dietary stress. Tooth enamel hypoplasias are relatively rare today; these are small lines of pits on the surface of the teeth that result from the interruption of enamel growth caused by calcium or vitamin deficiencies. They are a hard tissue marker of tough times, and occur on a number of Ice Age teeth. Two adolescents buried head-to-head around 34,000 years ago at Sungir in northern Russia bear hypoplasias on their front teeth, deriving from several periods of stress as their teeth were developing between the ages of three and five. As these two children buried together went through this, it is likely that the rest of their band did too.

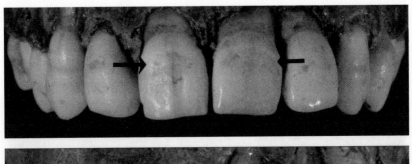
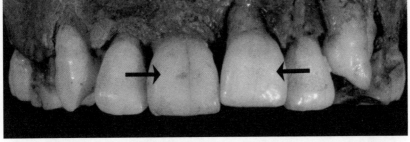

The front upper (maxillary) teeth of the two adolescents buried together at Sungir, Russia (Sungir 2, top; Sungir 3, bottom), showing developmental hypoplasias, some of which (arrowed) indicate severe developmental abnormality. Sungir 2 underwent a period of stress at around three years of age, and Sungir 3 at least three periods between the ages of three and five.

Erik Trinkaus documented seventy-five developmental abnormalities among sixty-six individuals. This is an elevated level, far beyond the incidence in modern societies. These included hypophosphatemia (low levels of phosphates in the blood, leading to breathing trouble and weakness), hydrocephalus (an accumulation of cerebral/spinal fluid in the brain causing headaches, double vision, poor balance, incontinence, mental impairment, seizures, personality disorders and ultimately perhaps brain tumours), systemic dysplasias (genetic disorders affecting the development of the bones, leading to spinal problems, odd limb proportions, breathing problems and obesity), and plenty of dental abnormalities (I said oral hygiene was good, but nothing about how the teeth grew). Several individuals had unnaturally small bodies, some with relatively short legs and often unnaturally bowed femora. Some suffered from an inherited rickets that would certainly have affected walking. One notable example is a very short male individual with chondrodystrophic (malformed cartilage) dwarfism; found with an adult female in Romito Cave in Italy, this man had extremely short forearms, a restricted ability to extend his elbow and marked bosses on his cranium.

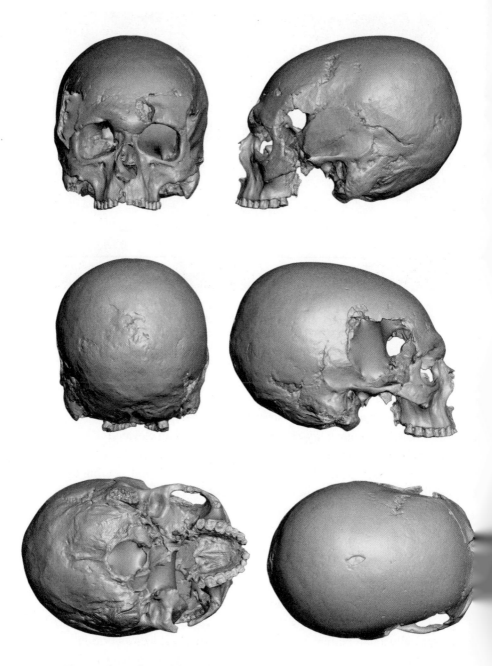

The cranium of an adult male, one of a number buried in the cave of Arene Candide (Liguria, Italy) at the end of the Ice Age. The long and low brain case is probably the result of his sagittal suture fusing too early, prohibiting normal growth. Think of sutures as the anatomical equivalent of interlaced fingers: during development they are open, allowing expansion of the brain case (like hands pulling apart); once they fuse, expansion is no longer possible. As a result, this man's brain expanded occipitally (towards the rear).

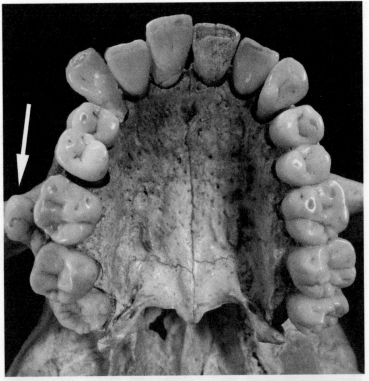

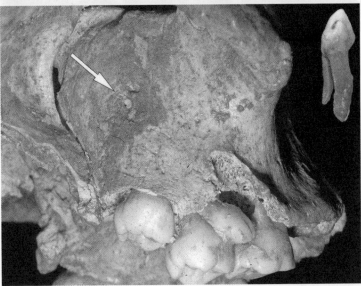

The right side of the upper jaw bone (maxilla) of an adult female from Abri Pataud rockshelter (Dordogne, France) showing supernumerary teeth (i.e. in addition to the normal number). As well as these developmental abnormalities – which are remarkably rare in modern populations – there is considerable evidence of periodontal inflammation (gum disease).

Stress, Disease and Inbreeding

The limb bones of a small-bodied twenty- to twenty-five-year-old male buried at Dolní Věstonice in the Czech Republic. Left: upper arm bones (humeri); both are relatively short and one has an unnatural curvature due to twisting during development. Middle: forearm bones (ulna and radius) of the left arm; a fracture towards the lower (distal) end of the ulna probably caused by a fall resulted in a marked bending of the radius. Right: the thighbones (femora) are short relative to the body, and markedly curved.

Death

Archaeologists understand a lot about the dead, and their bones reveal much about when and how Ice Age people died. If they died before adulthood while their bones were still developing, anatomical landmarks relating to maturation allow us to establish their age at death fairly precisely. These landmarks indicate the way the cranium grows and its sutures fuse, the timing of dental eruption, and the way bones from the neck down grow and their ends fuse. By early adulthood, when the growing is done, it gets more difficult. We're then dependent on tracking accumulated wear on the biting surfaces of teeth, age-related changes in the vertebrae and pelvis, and ageing of the microstructure of the bones themselves. By comparing these to modern standards we can usually estimate how long Ice Age people could expect to live under normal circumstances, as well as in what stages of life death was a particular danger.

Today, global human life expectancy is seventy-two years, but this average masks a lot of variation. Female life expectancy is a little higher (seventy-four) than males (sixty-nine). In Africa average life expectancy is sixty-one, compared to Europe's seventy-seven.[3] Reconstructing Ice Age life expectancy can be done, but it is difficult. Allow me a brief digression. Imagine a village hall filled with the entire local population. Let's say it is Agatha Christie's St Mary Mead; its most famous resident, Miss Marple, would certainly be there, as this is all about death. The whole age spectrum of the villagers is also there: newborns and toddlers, older children and adolescents (the latter loud and difficult, no doubt), adult parents, grandparents and a few great-grandparents.

Let's imagine their deaths; excepting a sudden disaster befalling this sleepy little village, who of the villagers is more likely to die of natural causes? It is the elderly, of course; the older individuals are the more likely they are to die, *on average*. Now let's translate this to archaeology. If all of the dead are buried in the village cemetery, and the villagers most likely to die are in old age, with relatively few dying in their youth or infancy, it should be full of the bones of the relatively old, and those of younger individuals should be relatively rare. If we were to excavate them (or save ourselves the effort and estimate ages at death from inscriptions on their gravestones) we would reconstruct an attritional mortality curve, a profile of the ages of death in which death is more common the older one gets. The ratios of young to old will vary over time, depending on nutrition and the physical demands of life – we all know that infant mortality was relatively high even in the first world until relatively recently – but even so the mortality profile will be dominated by the old. All of this is quite straightforward. Except that's not what we see for the skeletons which survive from the Ice Age.

Erik Trinkaus has calculated mortality profiles for Eurasian humans living between 110,000 and 20,000 years ago, based on available skeletal material, either derived from burials or from scrappy human bones that were lying around on campsites. We should remember that we are looking at *when* individuals died. The skeletal record of Ice Age *Homo sapiens* is dominated not by the elderly, but by adults in the prime of life (aside from the fact that they are dead). The elderly are not as common as they should be.

For comparative purposes, Erik included the same data for various peoples living in the non-industrial world in the last century. They display the expected pattern that Miss Marple would approve of: their sample is dominated by the elderly, who represent over 60 per cent of their dead. By contrast, all of the Ice Age mortality profiles are dominated – quite strikingly in fact – by prime adults. Note that there is relatively little difference between the mortality curves of *Homo sapiens* and Neanderthals; both had low life expectancy and quite unstable population demographics. It seems that Ice Age humans were more likely to die in their adult prime than they were in old age. But no mystery is this simple, and to return to St Mary Mead, what if not all of our village dead ended up buried in the cemetery? What if some died while visiting relatives abroad, or expressed a desire to be left in the nearby forest to decay naturally (why not?) or to be cremated and scattered to the wind? We'd have a very distorted sample of the villagers in the cemetery, that would obscure the real patterns of death in the village.

Understanding the biases that distort our Ice Age picture is a scientific problem that Miss Marple would enjoy. Could the biases be due to the fact that only adults in their prime tended to be buried, and the younger and older individuals were treated in other ways? Erik asked himself this, and could control for it by considering only those bones that derived from burials, rather than the scrappy bones from the campsites. When he did this, the number of elderly specimens actually increased, a sure sign that preferential burial of prime adults wasn't responsible for this pattern. The bones of the elderly he examined were just as well preserved as those of the younger individuals, too; it couldn't be explained by skeletons being more likely to decay the older they are. In short, it's a real pattern, but what does it mean? You'll have to wait until Chapter 18 for a possible answer.

Chapter 9

In Mammoth Country

The wind was freezing, and the sodden coastal cave stank of seaweed and bird droppings. We huddled together, focused on the task at hand, getting the footage we needed. The Goat's Hole Cave at Paviland on Wales' Gower Peninsula is a remote place, accessible only at low tide or via a difficult abseil. It towers above the waters of the Bristol Channel, but during the low sea levels of the Pleistocene a hunter sitting in its mouth would have looked out onto a vast plain rich with horse, bison, reindeer and those icons of the Ice Age, mammoths. Thousands of years ago an Upper Palaeolithic hunter-gatherer had been buried in the cave in his ochre-red parka and leggings, the grave scattered with a number of objects carved from a very magical material. I was there with the science broadcaster and writer, and my old friend, Alice Roberts, filming a piece on the cave's archaeology for a television series.[1]

In 1823 the Oxford geologist William Buckland was the first to publish an account of the burial of the 'Red Lady of Paviland', as its occupant quickly became known. Buckland first identified the body as male but, for reasons lost to us, changed his mind, and as the bones are stained with ochre, the name 'Red Lady' stuck. We now know that this was a young man who died around 34,000 years ago. The body was buried with 'several hands full' of carved items of mammoth tusk: ivory, which Buckland thought were the remains of animals killed in the biblical Flood. Perhaps the unfortunate hunter was part of a small group searching for workable ivory in this northern and inhospitable land, during a summer when conditions were tolerable. We will never know, but Buckland and his colleagues had found the first example of a Palaeolithic burial, associated with the remains of an extinct animal, and his discovery and its legacy is what took Alice and me to the Paviland coast that day. I'd been involved in a major re-analysis of the Red Lady and his associated mammoth ivory objects, some of which seem to have been deliberately broken and scattered in his grave as if they were objects of power that needed special disposal. We'll see.

Mammoths are but one extinct group of a rich and varied order, the elephant-like proboscidians (trunked mammals), which arose in the late Miocene and subsequently diversified into the steppe elephants, mammoths, mastodons, and ultimately the elephants of the modern world. The woolly mammoth, *Mammuthus primigenius*, was by the order's standards a relative latecomer, evolving around 400,000 years ago in Siberia, adapted for cold northern latitudes, and spreading to Europe by 150,000 years ago. Mammoths characterize a Pleistocene ecosystem that has no strict modern analogues, in which animal species today characteristic of the Arctic tundra were mixed with those more characteristic of grassy steppes. In the far north today, harsh snowy winters contrast markedly with lush green summers, and we might expect the same in the Ice Age, but differences in the height of the sun in the sky would have muted this somewhat. As a result, the 'mammoth steppe' ecosystem was particularly rich in nutrients, even if those digestible by humans were found mainly 'on the hoof' in the form of the herbivores of the tundra. As archaeology reveals, it was a particularly rich preying ground for *Homo sapiens*.

A large number of remarkably well-preserved mammoths have been found in the permanently frozen Siberian soil above 60 degrees north. The full age range is represented, even several babies such as Dima, Lyuba and Mascha (see PL. XV). The combination of anaerobic conditions (airless, where organisms that consume bodies cannot live) and refrigerator-like temperatures preserves even the most delicate soft tissues of these animals. Some got trapped in bogs and marshy areas, unable to climb out; others died trying to ford rivers. Some bear signs of old age and infirmity, but the full stomachs of others reveal that they were in good health until their fatal accidents (a CT scan of baby Dima's heart revealed that he was in excellent shape at the time of death around 40,000 years ago, having just begun to wean off his mother's milk). We know now that they died in different accidents in many different periods of the Pleistocene, not in a single catastrophe such as the biblical Flood which Georges Cuvier and his contemporaries had to argue against. The bones of a fairly complete Siberian mammoth were reassembled in St Petersburg in 1808 (some of the flesh having been fed to the local dogs), allowing a view of the creature's size and body shape in detail. Cuvier, who we witnessed admiring John Martin's *The Deluge* in Chapter 7, noted that these giants were found only in northern latitudes and that the ridged structure of their teeth was adapted to grinding tough grasses, concluding, correctly, that they were specifically adapted to cold grasslands and were no longer to be found on Earth.

Comparative anatomists and biologists know a great deal about mammoths. In size and weight they compare closely with African elephants. Adult females stood 2.5–2.75 m (8–9 ft) at the shoulder, males 3–3.4 m (10–11 ft) and weighing up to 6 tons. Despite their bulk they were fast; a body charge, stamp of the legs, or a powerful swipe from their tusks or trunk could maim or kill. But many features derived from their evolutionary heritage set them apart from elephants. An adult mammoth in side view (surely to be preferred, as this means it's not charging at you) has the shape of an asymmetrical upper-case letter M, with a large domed head and a pronounced hump of fat at the shoulder, from which the back tapers away to a lower rear. Their ears were small and their tails short and stubby, the size of each compensated to an extent by the long guard hairs, all ways to minimize the danger of frostbitten extremities. The coats of mammoths, when preserved, are most commonly orange, but this is probably because their natural pigments have been lost over time; they were likely dark brown originally. This no doubt explains

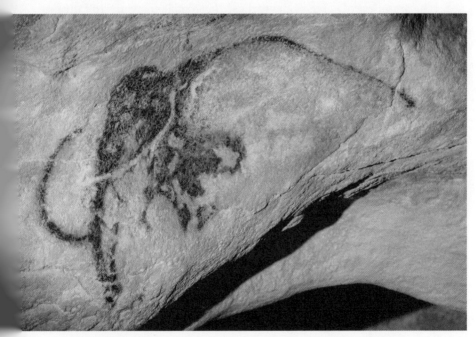

Charcoal drawing of a mammoth in Chauvet Cave (Ardèche, France). Despite debate about the age of the cave's red and black drawings (it is said to be 30,000–35,000 years old; I think it more likely around 20,000 years old), specialists agree it contains some of the most spectacular and lifelike images in the Pleistocene art of *Homo sapiens*.

why most mammoths in cave art were created with dark pigments of manganese or charcoal. A coat of coarse and oily guard hairs up to 1 m (3 ft) long reached down to the toes and protected the body from moisture, and short, thinner and densely packed underwool, in combination with a thick subcutaneous fat layer, provided efficient heat insulation. Like the woolly rhinos (and the subcutaneous fat of the Neanderthals) this was weatherproofing, Pleistocene style.

Mammoths seem to have been flexible within a herbivorous diet, perhaps a little more so than their horse, bison and woolly rhino contemporaries who shared similar grazing. Wear patterns on mammoth tusks show how these could be used to scrape snow cover off food, and two dextrous projections on the tips of their trunks could be used to pluck grasses, buds and flowers up delicately. If modern elephants are useful analogies, mammoths probably organized themselves into social units consisting of adult females and their young, with more isolated males. These would come together for mating and calving in late spring and early summer. As we'll see, it's precisely in these months that mammoths came to the attention of some of the earliest *Homo sapiens* groups in Europe.

Mammoths and humans eye-to-eye

One of the earliest discoveries of what we would now call Upper Palaeolithic art was made by the Édouard Lartet and Henry Christy team at the rockshelter of La Madeleine in 1864. It was and remains a stunning discovery: a 15,000-year-old depiction of an extinct animal carved on the tusk of that extinct animal (see PL. XVI). Here in the heart of southwest France, someone who had actually seen one of these Pleistocene giants sat down and engraved one in accurate detail. The bright whiteness the tusk would have had when freshly carved has faded, but it has lost none of its striking appeal.

Around 500 contemporary depictions of mammoths on cave walls and over 200 on portable objects are known today from northern Spain to Siberia and also from around 11,000 years ago in the Americas. In Europe, with one or two exceptions these beasts were only rarely depicted before 20,000 years ago; perhaps before that the transformation of their tusks into decorative or ornamental objects was thought to be more important. Possibly it was only later, as figurative art grew more common among *Homo sapiens* groups, that more accurate depictions of mammoths became important. Portable models of mammoths were sculpted first in mammoth ivory and later in fired clay; they were engraved onto stone plaquettes or more rarely onto bone and tusk fragments, like the example from La Madeleine. On occasion they were drawn or even sculpted on cave walls by hammering away at the rock. We'll see some examples of these later, but for now I'm concerned with some of the earliest known figurative art of *Homo sapiens*, based not on the use of charcoal and other pigments for drawing, but on the carving of mammoth ivory. Although mammoths were rarely in the Dordogne, we know that ivory was worked there from the abundant waste from carving. In the small caves and rockshelters of the Castelmerle Valley, skilled Aurignacians carefully shaped circular-sectioned rods and broke them into segments, piercing each of these to turn them into beads, and painstakingly carved other shaped beads. Mammoth depictions are known from France in the west, but they are far more common in Central and Eastern Europe, the regions where the great mammoth herds roamed.

The benefits of dung and destruction

Like modern elephants, mammoths would have been keystone herbivores whose rapacious eating habits significantly remodelled their environments both destructively and constructively. The huge amounts of dung they deposited would replenish soil nutrients (when not being eaten by mammoth babies), sustaining the growth of grasses and sedges. Plants could be pulled up by the roots, rare small trees ripped up entirely or stripped of their bark, watersides and paths churned up by the weight of their feet, and stone and tree stumps worn where mammoths rubbed against them to remove parasites and scratch itches. We all love a scratch! Where the mammoth herds grazed we can expect relatively open grasslands marked by trails of dung and destruction, although with elevated numbers of woody plants which spring up from the fertile soil in the wake of destruction – which could be used as fuel. In addition to this, it's difficult to miss the bones of a dead mammoth, at least while it's not covered with snow, and as they tended to die in predictable places such as around water, carcasses and then skeletons would surely form notable landmarks that could be seen from a distance.

For the human hunter, all of these characteristics provided useful clues as to the whereabouts of the animal, enough to get them within sighting distance. Elephants eat huge bulks of food, often indiscriminately swallowing actual food along with clays, sands and even whole birds in their somewhat unrefined mouthfuls. They only digest around half of what they eat, so the resulting dung – carried around the landscape in their stomachs before being redeposited – can offer many clues about the distance and direction of their travel. A knowledgeable tracker can tell from the size, freshness and fragmentation of the dung the size of the animal, how long ago it passed, at what speed, and in what health it is. From that, and by following its rather obvious trail of destruction, a hunting party could locate the animal. Much of mammoth movement was probably repetitive, taking them across well-established tracks between water, mineral licks and forage, and it's easy to see how hunters would build up a complex mental map of the behaviour of the herds. Gary Haynes, a notable mammoth, mastodon and elephant specialist, has indicated how these specific features of the mammoth steppe could well have facilitated rapid human dispersals into new landscapes. Mammoth tracks could be followed on exploratory treks, reducing the chances of getting lost. Learning the landscape in terms of its tracks, hills and watery places where herds aggregated would have sped up the process of dispersal of *Homo sapiens* and improved the chances of success.

A 45,000-year-old example of such a watery place is revealed by rich palaeontological deposits that have come to light from time to time since the 1890s in the peat bogs of Niederweningen, Switzerland. Here, the remains of a half-complete adult mammoth were recovered from a 1-m (3-ft) deep band of peat, along with the bones of woolly rhinoceros, horse, bison, their predators hyena and wolf, and a host of small animals such as voles and shrews. Pollen and small plant macrofossils from the same peat band reveal that these animals died at the edge of a lake, in a cold and swampy tundra dotted with stands of spruce, larch and birch trees. It was not the verdant Alpine Switzerland we know today. The skull and bones of the mammoth's left side were preserved, indicating that it had sunk into the mire and died, and that scavengers – probably those wolves and hyenas – had destroyed the right side of its body that remained above the wet mud. It's possible that Neanderthals were still operating in the area, but there is no evidence of any human presence in the Niederweningen swamp.

As we will see, huge accumulations of mammoth carcasses formed at certain points in the landscape, which attracted *Homo sapiens* groups repeatedly in all regions where the herds and humans could be found together. Whether in Switzerland, Germany, the Czech Republic, Austria and all countries across to Ukraine and Russia, mammoths offered meat, fat, sinew, short wool, long hair and ivory in abundance. Mammoth tusks corkscrew helix-like towards each other, a different shape from elephant tusks, which reveals different ways of fighting, and when mammoth bulls locked tusks their tips could be dug into an opponent's shoulder or upper back with enormous pressure by a turn of the head. Like thirsty elephants they were probably impatient animals and in the rough and tumble of pushing to the water's edge pieces of tusk broke off, fragmenting into sections that would have formed a useful source of raw material for carving.

The Ivory Age in the Swabian Jura

Mammoths link the ivory work from southwest France to the Swabian Jura of southwestern Germany. Travelling eastwards it's really here and in adjacent Switzerland that we begin to see a stronger presence of these great beasts; this was the southwestern edge of true mammoth country. In this remarkable early *Homo sapiens* foothold in Europe, mammoths were an important source of food for at least 10,000 years, a huge span of time. But it's the hard tissue, tusk, that stands out. It's likely that jewelry carved from small ivory beads in the tundra of the Upper Danube basin was well suited to gift exchange, and ultimately circulated as neighbouring groups met around the 900-km (550-mile) curve of the foothills of the Massif Central, Alps and Jura. Here, mammoth ivory working had achieved remarkable levels of technical skill and artistic elaboration that my colleague Nick Conard of Tübingen University, a recognized authority on the region's archaeology, has suggested we could call the Ivory Age. Evidence derives from a series of small caves in the valleys of two tributaries of the Danube. Hohle Fels, Geißenklösterle and Brillenhöhle in the Ach Valley and Vogelherd, Bockstein and Hohlenstein-Stadel in the Lone Valley were used as shelters in fits and starts from at least as early as 40,000 to 31,000 years ago (a period known as the later Aurignacian, defined by developments in tools and personal ornaments derived from the Protoaurignacian).[2] Some of the caves were used only fleetingly, but Hohle Fels, Geißenklösterle and Vogelherd were repeatedly visited over the course of the Aurignacian in a tundra that was rich in mammoth, woolly rhinoceros, wild horse, cave bear, reindeer, red deer, roe deer, and the now-extinct giant deer *Megaloceros*.

Humans were not the exclusive inhabitants of these caves; cave bears denned in them from time to time, and red and arctic foxes were a continuous presence in the area. In fact the foxes tell an interesting story. Although they typically prey on small herbivores, foxes are very adaptable creatures, and can quickly change from hunting rodents to scavenging more variable foods if the situation demands. When they live in close proximity to humans they eat the food the humans discard on their campsites, something we'll see in relation to wolves in Chapter 18. Pleistocene foxes were larger than those of today, and the measurement of isotopes of carbon and nitrogen in the bones of the foxes and their potential prey has been used to reconstruct their ecological niches across Pleistocene time. Nitrogen is informative about the amount of meat from which they were obtaining dietary protein, and carbon as to whether this animal protein was obtained from aquatic or terrestrial prey. Their food sources were wholly terrestrial, typically comprising rodents, such as lemmings and voles, and horse, reindeer and mammoth, and their elevated nitrogen values show that their diet was dominated by large amounts of meat. At some times they ate these animals in roughly equal proportion, but at others raised nitrogen values indicate that they were able to access sustained sources of reindeer and perhaps mammoth meat. Foxes, of course, can't hunt these large animals, but they could scavenge from human kills and butchery sites, perhaps by hanging around the caves known to be frequented by Aurignacians.

Cutmarks on fox bones show that they were an important source of meat and fur for humans, and their canine teeth were pierced for use as jewelry. Mammoths were a big draw to the area: foxes grew in number when they were able to scavenge from human food waste, who in turn hunted (or more probably trapped) them for their products. The Aurignacians wore the trophies of their efforts on their colourful fur and hide clothing in the form of two very different types of modified tooth: fox canines and mammoth tusks.

The Aurignacians took a lot of effort to carry mammoth remains to their caves. The bones and teeth of very young animals are common, probably reflecting the relatively high infant mortality rates or the

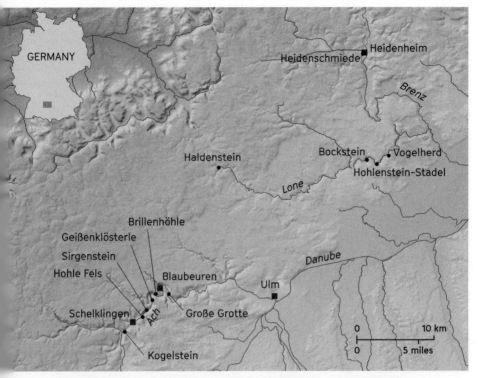

The caves of the Ach and Lone Valleys in Germany's Swabian Jura preserve some of the earliest cultural evidence of *Homo sapiens* in Europe. For over 15,000 years, in a rich mammoth steppe environment, Aurignacians of the early Upper Palaeolithic were able to exploit mammoth bone and ivory for tools, artworks and items of jewelry.

hunters' focus on vulnerable youngsters. Stone tool cutmarks on infant remains show that they were being butchered repeatedly, and if we assume that like other herbivores mammoths calved in spring so as to maximize growth and the chance of survival through their young's first summer, their prevalence suggests that exploiting the vulnerable mammoth infants was a routine spring and early summer activity. Seasonal evidence for horse hunting suggests that this occurred mainly in winter, and cave bear hunting from winter through to spring. The years were perhaps structured by a cycle of horse, bear and mammoth hunting and the activities of making and mending associated with them.

Vogelherd Cave is exceptionally rich in butchered mammoth remains: bones, teeth and tusks of at least twenty-eight have been recovered. The amount of bulky body parts of relatively poor nutritional value such as crania, teeth and tusks is surprising, but perhaps reflects the importance of brain fat. There would be no sense carrying these heavy objects uphill into the cave unless they had a use; one pile of several tusks, teeth, and bones of the head and shoulders in one of its entrances was perhaps brought there as a 'dry bone wall' to provide some shelter within, and at the same time a stockpile of workable raw materials. Tusks and ribs are by far the most common bones, and in places had been piled up deliberately. Tusks are actually incisors that have evolved into a massively enlarged form, and like other teeth they grow in sockets – alveoli – in dense jawbone. They were carefully removed from their cranial alveoli, as well as collected in fragmentary form, fresh or weathered, and in all states transported to the caves for use.

Much of the tusk had been worked. From Vogelherd alone over two dozen figurines and fragments of portable art, 353 rod-shaped blanks from which beads could be carved, and 345 finished beads and pendants have been excavated. Even without the other caves this looks like industrial levels of production. Perhaps spring was really the time that the Swabian Aurignacians almost *became* mammoths in their minds, observing the calving events, killing the vulnerable, butchering and consuming them, sewing soft tissues into clothing and tenting, and transforming their magical ivory into powerful artworks and jewelry. It's difficult to escape the notion that the spirit of these magnificent giants literally suffused the lives of the Aurignacians here.

It's hard to establish whether the mammoths were scavenged or directly hunted. Individuals of all ages are represented among the bones in the caves, but the highest amount are of the very young and very old. Try to imagine going up against a charging adult elephant armed only with a spear and you'll understand why the hunting of the largest mammoths was probably not a common event, or at least one that hunters tended to survive. The impression from the age profile of dead mammoths is that their presence resulted from isolated deaths or relatively safer hunting of vulnerable individuals (who could also have died from a number of natural causes). Monitoring mineral oases and waterholes could result in the odd fresh carcass, and perhaps the infants could be killed shortly after birth and the old when they were bogged down in marshy riversides. It's not a pleasant thought, but that's survival in the wild.

Fresh tusk contains up to 10 per cent water, but when a mammoth died and it began to desiccate, the ivory often fractured into pieces. Tusks grow outwards as a series of conical rings – like a stack of cups

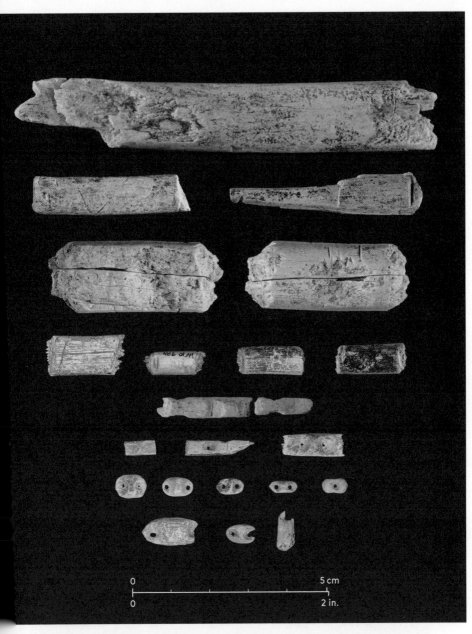

Different stages of the production of beads in the Aurignacian of the Swabian Jura between 37,000 and 32,000 years ago. A long splinter or rod of ivory was ground into a curved outline (top). These could then be cut into cylindrical sections (second row from top), shaped further and drilled with fine perforations (third to sixth rows) before sectioning into double-perforated beads which could be sewn onto clothing and other items (bottom two rows). The cylindrical blanks were also crafted into a small range of beads of other shapes, perforated or grooved for suspension, and some bear traces of red ochre colouring.

Swabian Aurignacian sculptures on mammoth ivory and bone evoking the animal and imaginary landscape of 37,000 years ago: horse head (top left); human or human-animal hybrid (top right); lion (middle left); mammoth (middle right); and water bird (bottom). With one exception (the lion-man illustrated on p. 146), all such items are no more than 7 cm (2.8 in.) long.

in a coffee machine – and because of this they will naturally fracture into long thin blades, a bit like the stone tools *Homo sapiens* preferred for toolmaking. In the lowered temperatures of the Pleistocene the process is arrested somewhat, and large segments of tusks could survive intact for tens of millennia after they were gently covered over by sediment. Over time, however, frosts would break them up and spring melts could re-expose sources of usable ivory, which in many cases could be easier to procure for ivory working than fresh from the animal. I know which I'd prefer to gather. Perhaps meaning was given to the colours that sediments would stain otherwise white ivory with over time – beige and yellow to dark maroon and black, colours which appear among a number of worked pieces. What stories might people have spun to explain these transformations?

The caves of the Swabian Jura preserve evidence of the use of mammoth ivory and ribs for javelin points and tools such as lollystick-like 'smoothers' used to clean hides and borers to pierce them. Tusks were certainly the preferred materials for working into objects of display, while bones could be used for hearth fuel. In Hohle Fels and Vogelherd in particular ivory beads characteristic of the region's Aurignacian culture were found in abundance, as was the waste from their production, and as they are found throughout the Aurignacian deposits from bottom to top it's clear that they remained popular over perhaps several millennia. Nick Conard and his Tübingen colleague Sybille Wolf were able was able to reconstruct the entire beadmaking process, a 37,000-year-old industry in which a skilled craftsperson could produce a single bead in perhaps two hours.

We must pause to consider the caves' exquisite sculpted figurines, which as the world's oldest examples of sculpture, and some of the earliest figurative art in general, are of global significance for our understanding of the cultural evolution of *Homo sapiens*. In most cases barely 5 cm (2 in.) in size, examples have been found in all the major caves. They give us an intimate glimpse of the Swabian landscape from the perspective of Aurignacian artists. About two dozen figurines are complete enough to identify. They are dominated by mammoths and cave lions, but the wider animal landscape is also invoked, in the form of bison, horse, cave bear, fish, a water bird captured in flight, as well as more imaginative pieces we'll scrutinize below.

The Swabian Aurignacians didn't just innovate in visual culture, but also in the audial realm. The fragmentary remains of at least eight flutes carved from mammoth ivory and the thin, hollow bones of swans and vultures have been excavated from three of the caves and in several cases painstakingly reconstructed. In one example two halves were carved separately out of ivory before being bound and glued together with a mastic to form an instrument at least 18 cm (7 in.) long with three finger holes. Another from Hohle Fels, carefully crafted from a wing bone, survives to 21 cm (8.3 in.) in length but originally could have been up to 34 cm (13.5 in.) long. Five finger holes survive, and it bears finely engraved lines near the holes, which were probably carefully measured markings to indicate exactly where the holes should be bored into the bones. Several reproductions have been played by musicians. A small example made from a swan wing bone could be played by blowing obliquely into its end directly from the mouth, producing four notes and tones that could be varied by adjusting the strength of breath. Others have tapered ends like modern clarinets, which suggests that they were mouthed with a reed, perhaps of birch bark, and are perhaps better thought of as 'proto-clarinets' sounding like medieval shawms or bagpipes.[3] We cannot conclude, however, that these features indicate the use of melodic music as we know it. That may have been the case, but it is also possible that the flutes were used to replicate the sounds of various birds and other animals, as lures, or perhaps in rituals. Music, dance, song and ritual are usually connected in pre-urban societies.

One of the Tübingen team, Harald Floss, an expert on Aurignacian art who has studied the Swabian material in detail, notes how these artistic and musical objects represent the appearance of a new human society, a new way of living. Groups from distinct regions were already marking out their differences. For me, this was not necessarily more sophisticated than the preceding Neanderthals but differed mainly because now, *Homo sapiens* had grasped the idea that animals – and creatures of the imagination – could be depicted figuratively, and the circulation of such depictions constituted a major way that society was held together.

The same can be said for music and, we might suppose, dance, song and storytelling. This is not to say that the Neanderthals didn't enjoy a little rhythm and dance once in a while, but my impression of the tangible remains of their art – which was non-figurative – is that it related to the ornamentation of the individual and their expression of themselves in the immediate environment. Some of the Swabian Jura figurines are pierced for suspension, perhaps to be worn around the

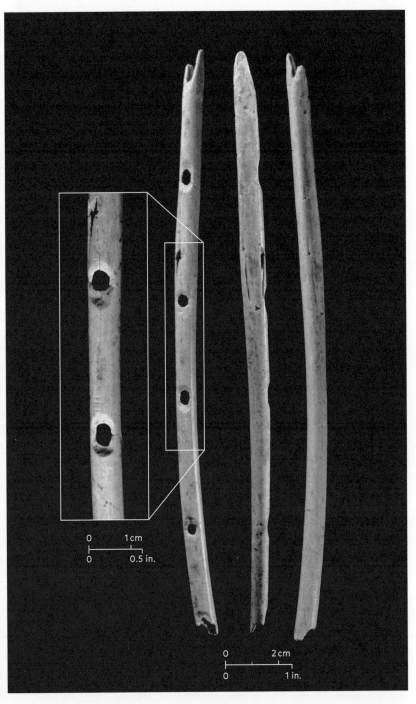

0   1 cm

0   0.5 in.

0   2 cm

0   1 in.

One of several 'flutes' from the Swabian caves, in this case an adapted vulture bone from Hohle Fels. It bears the remains of five carefully placed finger holes; note also the tapered end, where a bark reed may have been attached with mastic for playing like a 'proto-clarinet'.

neck, sewn onto clothing, or attached to other items of display such as staffs or handles. *Homo sapiens* was constructing a culture rich in observations and allusions, displayed on the body and around the campsite, shared widely and reinforced among neighbouring groups by exchangeable objects. Harald perceptively calls this an *artification* of the landscape, the filling of an otherwise natural world with works of human art and ornamentation. We don't understand what specific meaning or functions the carvings had. Some colleagues speculate that they were used in a form of 'shamanism' as practised by some circumpolar groups in the last few centuries, but this is tired old guesswork and we'll probably never be able to test this theory. What we can say is that the carvings are representative of the earliest artistic cultural groups. At this stage, I would say, this impressive culture did not involve the creation of art in deep caves. A fist-sized painted stone was found in Geißenklösterle – certainly evidence for the use of colour on a wider selection of objects – but this was not art on cave walls. Whether this existed in any other Aurignacian region is a debatable point. But visual culture had begun to incorporate elements that may have been lacking in the Neanderthals, such as imaginary beings and supernatural beliefs about the subterranean world. We can now examine a particularly impressive Swabian carving that seems to incorporate both these things.

The lion-man

Approaching 1,000 fragments of worked ivory were found in a little chamber in the back of Hohlenstein-Stadel, and these have been painstakingly refitted into a remarkable figurine carved from a 31-cm (12.2-in.) long fragment from near the tip of a young mammoth's tusk. The front of the cave was used as a campsite, but there is little evidence that ivory was worked there: it seems that the figurine was manufactured elsewhere and brought into the cave for some unknown reason, there to be tucked away in the dark. Thousands of years in the cold, wet ground fragmented it into pieces and eroded the deliberate polish of its surface, but it is still one of the most evocative objects surviving from the Palaeolithic. It is difficult to establish its precise age – many of the fragments were discovered just before the excavation was abandoned hurriedly in 1939 and only generally recorded to a broad level or 'spit' – but it undeniably belongs to the Swabian Aurignacian. Further pieces of the jigsaw were recovered in meticulous excavations in 2012–13 by my German colleague Claus-Joachim Kind and his associates from a layer dating to at least 36,000 and perhaps as much as 41,000 years old.

The carving retains some of the natural curve of the tusk, its arms are carved from the remains of the outer cementum (root), and the position and form of its groin and legs are determined by the pulp cavity. The features of the particular section of tusk from which the object was made may even have suggested to the carver that it could be formed into a human-like sculpture. The head and forelegs/arms are those of a cave lion, its expression calm and almost smiling, as my German colleagues have noted. The shape of its groin reveals that it is male, the lack of mane characteristic of cave lions. The figure stands passively, arms hanging by its side, yet the shape of its muscular shoulders, contracted together, reveals that it is poised for action. It's alert, too; its ears are erect, and its distinctively human legs stand on tiptoe. This powerful and frightening hybrid is ready to pounce.

We will never know the true meaning of the lion-man, but we can get a sense of what it could have conveyed to its creators. The use of a broken tip from a tusk might evoke the impressive fights between bull mammoths, the figurine the process of transformation of this mysterious material into something cultural, its form further emphasizing another transformation between two other powerful animals, the lion and the human. A further comment on transformation might be signified by differences in style and completion: the head and limbs are highly detailed, but the groin and feet stylized; its left side carefully worked but its right only roughly hewn. It seems to me that it is a work of the imagination, alive with the power of creation. We glimpse it only part way into its birth out of the transformed tip of a mammoth's weapon: some of its elements have taken on detailed form but others are still rough, in development; it is in confused state, in some senses relaxed yet bearing the alert instincts of the predator; and it's not yet clear whether the creature will become a man or a lion, or remain a fusion of the two. Unnatural parallel lines were engraved on its left ear, arm and foot; do they represent something more cultural, more human, perhaps tattoos, pigment markings or ritual scars? And let's not forget where the intact figurine came to rest; was it planted (along with pendants of fox, wolf and red deer teeth) in a chamber where cave bears had hibernated? Claus-Joachim Kind suggests it may have functioned as a little sanctuary

The 'lion-man' of Hohlenstein-stadel reborn. Excavated in the 1930s, this figurine was found broken into many pieces towards the rear wall of the cave. Painstakingly reconstructed from many hundreds of fragments, the complete figurine was sculpted from a 31-cm (12.2-in.) section of the tip of a mammoth tusk at least 36,000 years ago.

focused on the lion-man. Or perhaps the object was left there in the dark, in peace, to complete its frightening birthing into the world?

The lion-like shape of its head and the pronounced 'elbows' that resemble the projecting ulna of a lion make it very clear that it is not a fusion of a human with any other animal such as a bear (whose muzzles are much thinner). Yet its upright stance with outstretched legs and human-like feet suggest a bipedal rather than quadrupedal stance. This combination has led to the belief that this is a representation of a human-lion hybrid, underpinning the idea that transformation between humans and animals was part of the belief systems of early *Homo sapiens*. Or does the carving depict a human wearing a complete pelt of a lion? This would explain the upright stance, lion-like shape of the 'arms', and perhaps fur or skin folds indicated by the striped lines on one of them. We do have evidence of the use of lion pelts in the Upper Palaeolithic but they are few, and this would not explain the transformational aspect of the lion-man.

Then this little mammoth-centred phenomenon was gone. Cutting-edge geoarchaeological research outside the Swabian caves, using coring, sediment micromorphology and Fourier Transform Infrared (FTIR) spectroscopy,[4] has revealed that from around 32,000 years ago deteriorating climate caused significant erosion in the river valleys, shattering away the sediment that had accumulated on the valley slopes, collapsing sections of valley side and choking up the rivers. Changes in the regional ecosystem followed as it fragmented. The population of classic cave bears, *Ursus spelaeus*, already in decline, gave way to a newcomer, *Ursus ingressus*. The rich mammoth steppe gave way to an impoverished one in which only reindeer and red deer remained in any number. There may even have been a period in which humans were absent from the region, although there are sporadic indications of human presence between 31,000 and 27,000 years ago. But the sites of this succeeding Gravettian period are not as rich as those of the great Ivory Age of the Aurignacian, and probably reflect smaller numbers of people on the ground. Mammoths didn't quite disappear, but their remains decline significantly, and their tusk jewelry was replaced by pendants of animal teeth. But we can follow the herds eastwards into Gravettian territory, first into the Czech Republic and Poland, then on towards Russia, via Romania and Moldova.

Chapter 10

Cold

'Fly!' the farmer shouts to the horse as he shakes the reins, or so my translator Alex tells me in his heavily accented but impeccable English. Our little cart bounces along the rough track that skirts the valley side as the horse picks up speed on a gentle slope. It does feel like flying, and the three of us are jostled together as the cart leaps over muddy rubble. The wide river far below is perfectly still, but the rolling hills rattle by at speed. Brief glimpses of lapis blue punctuate the greenery here and there, farmhouses and wells hooded with bright canopies nestled in forest glades, woodsmoke curling skywards from the little hamlets. I'm new here, and deliberately out of my comfort zone. I'd gladly accepted the man's offer of a ride back to the village in his cart. We'd met earlier when I'd gone walking through the fields. We couldn't understand a word each other said, but friendship came easily here with the traditional welcome of Moldovan countryfolk, and when he'd been told I was a visiting archaeologist – well that was due a warm welcome!

The village of Climauți nestles on the banks of the River Dniester in northern Moldova, not far from the border with Ukraine. Climauți is one of a number of localities where the spreading Mid Upper Palaeolithic culture constructed shelters out of mammoth bones, a practice that links Central and Eastern Europe from 31,000 to 15,000 years ago. Excavations in the grounds of the village school revealed two circular structures, and judging by the small survey trenches I've excavated with Moldovan colleagues the archaeology is rich along the banks of the Dniester, where mammoth ivory was carved into jewelry and the long slender stone blades and bladelets of the period were made with consummate skill.

This is perfect hunting territory, with mammoth herds on the lowlands and bison, horse and reindeer in the adjacent uplands. My colleague Elena-Cristina Nițu of Romania's Princely Court Museum in Târgoviște took me to her excavation at the campsite of Poiana Cireșului overlooking Romania's Bistriça River. Between 31,000 and 22,000 years ago the region was repeatedly visited by highly mobile groups who were part of a widespread network; some of the shell jewelry they left behind derived from sources in the Mediterranean, around 900 km (550 miles) away. It's what archaeologists such as Clive Gamble of Southampton University call an open network; essentially a welcoming society that used a shared visual culture to emphasize inclusion and connectiveness. It was kept together by long-distance movements and gift exchange, facilitating the spread of a recognizable culture across Europe at the time. But a shift in the population was occurring: as conditions declined, groups from Central Europe were drawn eastwards towards the hunting grounds of the great Russian Plain. We can repeat this journey now, but remember that the weather is often sub-arctic, so wrap up well in your parkas and furs.

Europe 32,000–21,000 years ago

During the Mid Upper Palaeolithic, *Homo sapiens* could be found from France to Siberia. We shouldn't think of this as a uniform spread. We can recognize distinct cultural peaks here and there, reflecting how groups migrated from region to region as ecosystems fluctuated in response to a gradual decline in conditions as the height of the last

One of the iconic sites of the Upper Palaeolithic, the Abri Pataud in the side of the valley of the Vézère River lies today within the village of Les Eyzies-de-Tayac (Dordogne, France). It contains deposits over 9 m (30 ft) deep with abundant archaeology of the Aurignacian, Gravettian and Solutrean occupations.

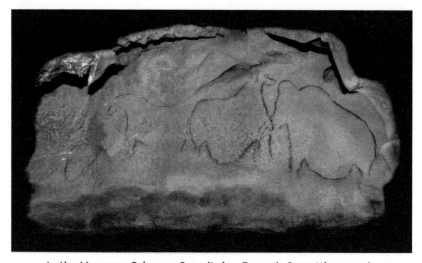

In the Mayenne-Sciences Cave (Loire, France), Gravettians made charcoal drawings including these two horses and a mammoth in the depths of the cave well away from daylight. The images, each around 0.5 m (2 ft) in length, are highly naturalistic, although they follow a convention in which horse heads are drawn too small for their body size.

glacial peak of the Pleistocene approached. At any one time large parts of the continent were probably unoccupied, but enough long-distance contacts were maintained so as to keep culture broadly similar. The recognizable stone technology and visual culture of the period probably originated in the central Danube Basin around 32,000 years ago, spreading first to Belgium, France and Austria, and perhaps emerging separately in the basins of the Prut and Dniester rivers. The tools were a technical response to living as hunter-gatherers in increasingly severe conditions, in which mammoths played a crucial role as providers of meat and fat as well as bones for use in the construction of living structures. But we can also see striking changes in other aspects of society, which included occasional burial of the dead, cave art and a widespread tradition of figurine manufacture. One cultural peak centres on the Dordogne, where caves and rockshelters were repeatedly used for camps, and deep caves were used for creating art and for depositing the dead. As we will see in Chapter 13, I think that the practice of creating figurative art deep in the underground darkness originated first in this period, and alongside the carving of animal and human-like figurines suggests that by now a widespread set of spiritual beliefs had arisen, perhaps serving to unite far-flung people around shared myths and codes of behaviour. Their striking artistic legacy can be seen as a celebration of nature, and their treatment of the dead reveals that very odd things were happening. We can pick up the story where the mammoth herds were abundant: in Central Europe.

Central Europe: the Pavlovian

On 31 December 1853 a peculiar event occurred, recorded in the *Illustrated London News*, when nineteen 'scientific and literary men' dined inside a life-size model of an Iguanodon. The model was so large that a scaffolding had to be constructed around it so the diners could be waited upon.

Dining inside an Iguanodon was an enjoyable gimmick for sure, but in Palaeolithic terms it's not that odd, as a way of life took off in the Pavlovian period which was to spread eastwards and persist for some 15,000 years. It was based on the location of mammoth carcasses at places where they accumulated in high numbers, and the use of their large and heavy bones to create structures for living in. As my colleague Marcel Otte has noted, the dwellings themselves were something akin to gigantic animals, perhaps seen as offering protection from the wild to the inhabitants within.

Mammoths were central to the lives of the Pavlovians, an early Gravettian culture centred on the Czech Republic and adjacent parts of Austria and Slovakia between 31,000 and 26,000 years ago. This didn't mark the first appearance of *Homo sapiens* in the region: rare Aurignacian sites reveal brief dispersals into Austria, the Czech Republic and Poland following the HE4 climatic deterioration described in Chapter 7. From around 31,000 years ago, settlement became more intense, and succeeding Gravettian groups were attracted to accumulations of mammoth bones on the slopes above the gravelly Dyje, Morava and Bečva rivers that wound through the Moravian Corridor that connects the north and south of the continent. As with the earlier exploitation of mammoth in southwestern Germany covered in the previous chapter, their remains probably accumulated as a result of both natural death and seasonal hunting, particularly of the vulnerable young and old. Many of these accumulations are huge, reflecting repeated visits by human groups over the course of centuries, staying put each time for much of the year. Camps were established on the slopes leading down to the rivers, where the surrounding countryside could be scanned for a herd and the prey ambushed as it passed by.

Pavlovian culture was exceptionally rich. It had a regional identity of its own, although it also enjoyed the benefits of long-distance contacts, as revealed by the presence of high-quality flints sourced from around Krakow some 270 km (165 miles) to the north. High levels of mobility were necessary, not only to ensure access to vital materials but also to maintain connections with other Gravettian groups. This explains why we can see broad similarities in the ways that materials were worked, in the form that weapons and tools took, and in more mysterious objects such as the famous 'venus figurines' that we will examine below. For a culture surviving in sub-arctic conditions the Pavlovian was a remarkable achievement.

At Pavlovian campsites mammoth bones were used to create dwellings of various sizes, probably tepee-like summer tents and more robust yurt-like winter ones, although much of the sorting and piling of mammoth and other bones is rather odd and can't be explained in prosaic ways. Pits are very common, and were usually filled to the brim with mammoth remains, but only some of them were used as natural refrigerators dug down into the frozen ground to store meat. They are usually large and contain non-meat-bearing bones like scapulae and skulls, as well as teeth and tusks. And what do we make of the items of jewelry, such as pendants made of fox canines and red ochre, that were repeatedly placed in the pits? Or of a reindeer skull placed carefully on top of one; a human female buried in another and covered up with a mammoth scapula; or four mammoth skulls surrounded by ochre and parts of wolf skeletons; or even a pair of human hands and feet?[1] Something else was afoot, if you'll forgive the pun.

In addition to the use of high-quality stone transported from sources in southern Poland, Pavlovians had a good line in carved ivory and antler. The pits and sunken foundations for dwellings were probably dug with adzes of reindeer antler that are commonly found scattered across campsites. Items made for display, such as pierced ivory 'diadems', were probably sewn onto hats or the front of hoods, perhaps to help hold them down against the cold winds. These and other objects were heavily decorated with a very characteristic set of engraved geometric and curved lines. Everything was busily expressing Pavlovian identity. Beads as well as human and animal silhouettes were carved out of mammoth ivory, and also sculpted out of loess before firing. Remarkably, stray lumps of this clayey sediment were often fired accidentally as they were thrown into hearths, and in addition to a number of fingerprints bear traces of a variety of textiles that would otherwise be lost to us. Perhaps lumps of clay had fallen onto matting or had been stuck onto the outside of bark containers in order to make them watertight. Either way, they preserve intricate details of a rich and varied technology in which fibres derived from nettles, milkweeds and the bark of alder and yew trees were twined, braided, knotted and woven into cordage, basketry, nets, traps and clothing.

Some objects, such as ivory 'spatulae', modified mammoth foot bones, were probably used in textile production as blanks for weaving and perhaps loom weights. The nets were probably used to trap grouse and other birds whose remains are common on Pavlovian sites. Ravens are often found, but not great eating, their presence reminding us that feathers for decoration and bones for tool manufacture were as important as their meat. I'm surprised at how comfortable the clothing would have been. The archaeologist Olga Soffer, who has worked extensively on Pavlovian textiles, showed me her shawl of nettle

At the large site of Pavlov I (Moravia, Czech Republic), around 31,000 years ago, a mammoth tusk, a fragmentary skull and antlers, vertebrae, ribs, fore- and hind-limbs of a single reindeer, the paw bones of a wolf, a fox jaw and part of a horse leg were deposited in a shallow pit. Were these a ritual deposit of a wolf skin and a reindeer head and skin?

fibre; it was remarkably soft and warm, and I imagine the Pavlovians sitting around the fire on their thick mats, furred and feathered parkas discarded yet warm in their nettle fibre underclothes, sipping hot nettle soup (which, incidentally, tastes delicious).

The hearths were used for one other purpose which, like textiles, was until recently thought to be a later innovation, spreading with agriculture and settled village life. But I'm pleased to credit Pleistocene *Homo sapiens* with the invention of ceramics. This eventually resulted in pottery – containers – in the Late Pleistocene. At this stage its use was restricted to little figurines of animals and humans, which have been found in contemporary sites in Austria and younger ones in Croatia. It was obviously a popular regional phenomenon. Almost all of the figurines are fragmentary, having shattered as they were introduced into the fires. They were sculpted by making elements such as limbs and moulding them to the body, which can result in points of weakness along which they can break, but the fragmentation is so ubiquitous that it must have been deliberate. It seems that the figurines were fired as soon as they were made, before they dried out. The water inside them heats and expands and – bang! – the figurine fractures explosively. It seems that they

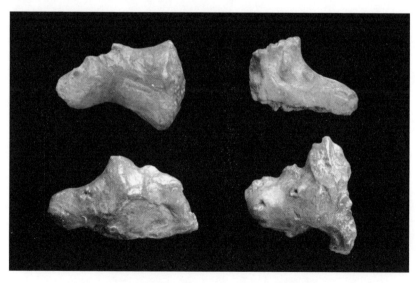

Fragments of small Pavlovian figurines of woolly rhino from the site of Pavlov. Palm-sized figurines of animals and human-like females were sculpted out of clayey loess and fired while still wet, exploding when they were placed within hearths. Almost all examples are fragmentary as a result: this cannot have been accidental, and was a deliberate act.

Chapter 10

were made not as works of art but to be destroyed. An obvious reason would be some form of hunting magic in which prey are ritually 'killed' to ensure success in the hunt, but this wouldn't explain why a number of them depict human (or human-like) females. Unless they too had been sacrificed. It's now time to turn to the 'venuses'.

The world of the venuses

Erik Trinkaus and I were sat at a grand table in the palatial office of the director of Vienna's Natural History Museum. The director had offered to introduce us to a very famous old lady. He removed the little box from the safe, bringing it to us with a degree of reverence, and setting it down on the polished wood. We sat in awe of the little figurine inside. About the size of a human hand, it was exquisitely carved from limestone, which chemical analysis has shown had been carried from a source near Brno around 150 km (90 miles) away from its findspot. The obese lady had been carefully shaped, polished and coloured with red ochre; she wears an elaborately carved hairstyle or headgear and her hands rest above her breasts, the fingers defined by deep incisions. When she was made, between 28,000 and 29,000 years ago, no one could have conceived that she would one day re-emerge in the world and be christened the Venus of Willendorf.

Between 31,500 and 27,000 years ago a widespread phenomenon can be found from the foothills of the Pyrenees in the west to Siberia in the east. These are small 'venus figurines', human-like females carved out of ivory or soft stone, and moulded in loess fired in hearths, that were clearly important to the lives of the Gravettians (see PL. XIV). It's a bit of an unfortunate name, coined by the excavator who found the first example in France in 1864 and who, referring to its exposed genitals, named the figurine the *vénus impudique* (immodest venus). But names stick, and, while archaeologists never assumed these objects represented Palaeolithic examples of the goddess Aphrodite/Venus, this one has proved to be a useful shorthand for a subject that is perennially popular.

We don't know if the figurines represented real women, female-like imaginary beings, or an abstract ideal, but they all possess the same characteristics. They are often obese, which would have been less than ideal for mobile hunter-gatherers and perhaps, as Erik suggests, may have been caused by short-term high calorific intakes, perhaps when groups were sedentary over the course of the long winters. A number appear to be pregnant, too. They typically lack faces – in some cases heads – their bodies tapering to near points from wide midriffs. Arms are lacking or tucked into the body, and feet are absent or rudimentary at best. Breasts, hips and buttocks are often exaggerated and out of proportion, and pubic areas are commonly emphasized. It seems that the sculptors intended to direct the viewer's gaze. We've tested this, albeit with modern subjects. My research student Sam Hirst has undertaken experiments in which he's tracked the eyes of people viewing images of the figurines, revealing that their eyes usually first 'fix' on the breasts and bellies and remain on those areas for longer than they do others. It's worth pointing out that these figurines are exclusively female (we have only one convincing male equivalent, which is more like a mannequin), and that they emphasize those characteristics that identify them very clearly as female to the extent that most of them are almost caricatures of the female form.

The few examples we have from the west, like the *vénus impudique*, were found alone; they are much more common in Central and Eastern Europe, where they can be found singly, in pairs or even in threes. Biologically, they represent a great deal of variability in terms of age, fertility, pregnancy and how and which body parts are emphasized. They are naked, although sometimes ornamented with colour or with incised decorations that might represent clothing and jewelry. The focus on the exaggerated female form across such a large area cannot be random or accidental; clearly they had a widespread meaning, one that focused on some aspect of femininity. Aside from this they are very heterogeneous in form, and several geographical groupings can be recognized that reflect variations on the theme. Some examples are thin and angular with no particularly exaggerated parts; others are obese, with sexual parts accentuated; and some follow the form of the soft stone pebbles they are carved from. Hips were emphasized in the west, breasts and bellies in the east.

We will never know whatever specific meaning or function the venuses had. 'Umbrella theories' purporting to explain them all are unfashionable in archaeology these days; after all, who would try to explain 'art' in a simple theory? All we can do is to remember their form, and where they were found. While they were probably more complex than children's toys or adults' pornography, they may represent ideas about fertility or birth. Perhaps they depicted a human-like protective and nurturing mother goddess, or perhaps they gave

The 'Black Venus' of Dolní Věstonice (Moravia, Czech Republic), 11 cm (4.3 in.) tall, was discovered amid the remains of hearths, close to fragments of figurines of an owl, reindeer and bear. Pavlovian figurines such as this were made from fired loess, essentially a ceramic technology over 30,000 years old. This highly stylized example bears several common characteristics of the European venuses: lack of facial detail (is she wearing an obscuring mask?); arms tapering into the body; pronounced breasts, buttocks and hips; and legs tapering to a point.

Cold

the concept of domesticity and safety a recognizably human form. We don't even know who made them, or who she or he intended them to be seen by. Perhaps the very suggestion that they could be explained in clear terms is an overly modern concept. I certainly think that it's more interesting to examine where they came to lie. In Western Europe they seem to have been tucked away in the depths of caves or against the walls of rockshelters, but in Central and Eastern Europe they are found in hearths and pits, singly and in twos and threes. I find this intriguing, because it mirrors the way burials of the dead are treated in the same period. In France burials are found in caves; further to the east we find shallow graves on campsites. If we think of some venuses as buried not in 'pits' but in graves of their own, it becomes even more interesting that most of the real burials we have are of men. Was there some kind of gendered connection between dead male humans and 'dead' female figurines?

Alexander Verpoorte of Leiden University has conducted a detailed study of the context of Pavlovian anthropomorphic figurines. They are by far the earliest examples known of a true ceramic technology – clay hardened by fire – and have been recovered on large and small campsites in Moravia, Slovakia and Austria. Nearly three dozen are known from the Moravian sites, among a far larger number of animal depictions including mammoths, bears, lions, horses, rhinos, marmots and wolverines. They contrast with a few examples of isolated human heads carved out of mammoth ivory. A mixture of silty loess and water was kneaded into limbs and torsos that were moulded together. Detail was kept to a minimum; incised lines represent folds of fat and some were impressed with bands of herringbone incisions (belts?), but it seems to have been their general shape that was important. We have to remember that, like their makers, they may have been clothed, the miniature hides and furs long since decayed away. At major sites such as Dolní Věstonice and Pavlov, fragmentary anthropomorphic figures were found in small clusters within and adjacent to large accumulations of ash, charcoal and burnt bone, alongside figurines of carnivores and herbivores. Some were found inside the remains of hearths that may have had hoods of clay intended to produce the high temperatures necessary for the firing of loess, effectively little kilns. Some of these were in small pits, and sometimes near to clusters of mammoth bones.

The grey-black colour and hardness of most of the Pavlovian ceramic figurines reveal that they were fired at around 700–800°C

Chapter 10

(1,290–1,470°F) in a reducing (oxygen-poor) heat, probably in the hearths, where they then cooled amidst the ashes. As we have already seen, the figurines had all broken, in many cases due to thermal shock – fired while still wet. They never left the spot where they were moulded and fired. There are no complete examples – why are we lacking a single example of a 'perfect' figurine, one of the 'successes'? There is a change in emphasis over time, too: the human and animal figurines are most common in the earlier part of the period; anthropomorphs are much rarer and animals absent in the succeeding Willendorfian-Kostenkian phase.

It's tempting to see the 'venus' theme as one of nurture and creation, whether or not they represented protective goddesses, or were simply symbols of female nurturing. Ian Hodder, a noted archaeological thinker, suggested that the venuses helped the Pavlovians to 'domesticate' the wild steppes, by controlling the creation of figurines representing the wider environment and perhaps drawing some kind of distinction between it and campsites. For Alexander Verpoorte it's not about drawing boundaries, however; he doesn't feel that the camps were built as islands of culture set aside from the wild, but instead they were orientated towards a focus, the hearth, where people sat, made and mended, and created figurines both animal and humanoid. I likewise don't think that the behaviours that comfort and reassure in the vast, dangerous world need defined boundaries. Turning inwards, focusing on each other and on the acts of creation that reassure – whether they were magical or not – may explain this intimate fireside behaviour. To me, the Pavlovians were temporarily turning their backs to the wild. Just like the figurines with their hands always away from the viewer, keeping their secrets whichever way one turns them, the wild can be hidden – briefly at least – in the warm firelight and familiar faces. But we must remember that the figurines were destroyed and buried too; perhaps a comforting reminder that the power to make and destroy could be harnessed in a wild world.

The herds of the east

Conditions were deteriorating, and around 27,000 years ago the Pavlovian disappeared. Populations were slowly shifting further into the continent, where the environmental effects of the cold turn were less marked, and around this time the Kostenki-Avdeevo culture appeared in the basins of the Don and Dnieper rivers of Russia and Ukraine. It marks the first of several high points of Mid Upper Palaeolithic culture in Eastern Europe, which, with a few absences during very cold periods, last to the end of the Pleistocene. Perhaps the human population shift tracked mammoths, who were themselves dispersing back into a more eastern range: as before it seems to be intimately linked to the locations and exploitation of mammoth carcass accumulations. The bones were used to construct tents on campsites which are riddled with pits and smaller stake holes for drying and storage racks. In these sites, however, the tradition of mammoth architecture turned into something visually striking. As in the Pavlovian, bone, antler and ivory beads, pendants, spatulae, points, figurines, and venuses of ivory are abundant, the latter often found in the pits. Small human and animal figurines very similar to Pavlovian examples were not sculpted out of loess but carved from soft marls. And the ceramics are still highly fragmentary in almost all cases. Were they also made to be broken?

Many Kostenki-Avdeevo camps have a number of circular structures built of mammoth bones and tusks, particularly several camps at Kostenki. At Kostenki Locality 11/1a, one of these was 9 m (30 ft) in diameter, constructed astonishingly from 573 bones from at least forty mammoths (try to imagine a similar amount of elephants and you'll grasp the scale of these sites). Its floor had been dug a little below the surface and flattened, and the excavated loess was probably used to 'plaster' in the gaps between the bones. At Kostenki Locality 1, large semi-subterranean dwelling structures were placed in a huge oval around a line of nine centrally located open-air hearths.

Although they were only occupied for a few months of the year, we can think of such sites as small villages, with central spaces and spatial organization, a feature only thought to appear with the Neolithic of the Near East. They reveal, I think, that if hunter-gatherers are putting a lot of effort into building camps that they will repeatedly visit for several months of the year, then social rules will govern what gets built where. It is village life, however temporary.

There are many odd things in these settlements. At Gagarino in southeastern Kazakhstan, areas can be recognized where mammoth skulls and long bone 'uprights' had been placed around several small pits, all rich in ochre and the scattered ashes from hearths. At Khotylevo 2 in western Russia, three ivory venuses and a carving of two females on a chalk block no more than 6 cm (2.5 in.) in height were found associated with similar structures, and another cluster of mammoth bones contained a circular spread of ochre in its centre, its periphery lined with a number of small pits containing arrangements of mammoth bones. One of these contained two ivory figurines: an obese female in a sitting posture, buried alongside a spindly asexual human. Nearby, a pregnant female figurine in bent posture lay supine on a bed of bright red ochre. My colleague Konstantin Gavrilov of the Russian Academy of Sciences suggests that these are cult areas, set aside from other parts of the camp, where ritual objects were used. He makes a persuasive argument; these were not 'rubbish pits' or foundations for tents. Why sort all of the mammoth bones into types and cluster them in little groups around pits that seem to have had no prosaic purpose? It may be an exaggeration to call this an Ice Age temple, but the site is redolent with mysterious meaning.

When the severe conditions of the Last Glacial Maximum passed, another cultural high point was reached between 18,500 and 17,000 years ago in the basins of the Dnieper and Pripyat rivers. The steppes were still cold and dry, but herbivores were abundant, particularly mammoths, which continued to be the core focus of human groups we now call Mezinian. Impressive residential sites arose around the mammoth herds, and a rich artistic culture developed that linked people scattered across the eastern European plains. The sorting and use of mammoth bones continued in much the same way as before. Mezinians hunted reindeer on their north–south migrations in spring and autumn, when horses were also abundant. But it was mammoths that were most intensively used, as food, fuel and architecture. Fresh mammoth bone – still with its combustible marrow – served well as fuel. It would have been greasy and smoky when first lit, but soon settled down to burn in fires lit outside and inside tents. The fatty epiphyses (articular ends) of mammoth thigh bones were particularly useful as lamps for illuminating what must have been dark and smoky interiors.

A number of open-air camps, such as Gontsy, Dobranichevka, Mejiriche, Ioudinovo and Mezine, reveal that mammoth-bone architecture reached its greatest sophistication at this time and followed some general blueprints. A typical floor area of 25 sq. m (270 sq. ft) seems quite generous compared to the average living room size in the UK today (17 sq. m or 180 sq. ft). Mammoth crania were pushed into the ground in a circular or oval pattern. If they retained their tusks these would curve upwards and inwards to form the superstructure for the walls. Large flat bones and columns

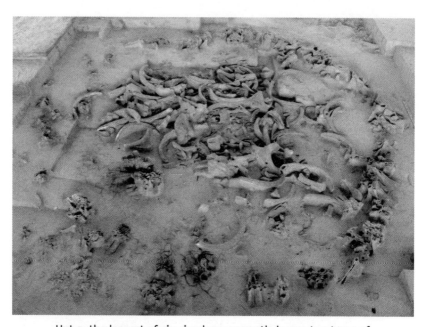

Hut 5, the largest of six circular mammoth-bone structures of different sizes at Gontsy (Ukraine), collapsed inwards around 19,000 years ago. A foundation of thirty-six mammoth crania defined a circle 8 m (26 ft) in diameter, atop and around which were placed at least five mammoth jaws, 125 tusks, sixty scapulae, twenty pelvises and other bones, consolidated by loess excavated from nearby pits.

of vertebrae were used to further construct the walls, stabilized by long-bone uprights, and many of the elements were drilled so they could be lashed together. They probably stood up to 2 m (6 ft) high, presumably covered with hides and lined with hides and mats inside. Triangular-shaped jawbones were either stacked as many as five high to form chevrons, or laid side-by-side with chins alternatively up and down to form zigzags, complemented by 'columns' of upright long bones rooted into the floor. At Mezine and Mejiriche these bear traces of chevrons drawn in red and yellow mineral pigments. Lioudmila Iakovleva has noted that the chevrons and zigzags on mammoth-bone structures were also engraved onto female figurines, and suggests that there was a symbolic code integrating women and mammoths in the context of the dwelling. She also notes that it may be no coincidence that mammoths were probably organized in matriarchal groups; did the Mezinians recognize this, and attribute a similar nurturing and domestic role to their own women, perhaps within the gigantic animal dwellings that they were constructing? It's a very attractive suggestion.

But were the mammoth-bone structures homes in the same sense that we think of them? Konstantin Gavrilov of the Russian Academy of Science believes we've misunderstood some of them. Far from being collapsed tents he points to the fact that they have been little disturbed since being abandoned, and hence that we really see them as they were, rather than as the result of a slow collapse over time. Meticulous excavations by Konstantin's colleague Gennady Khlopachev at the 15,000- to 12,000-year-old campsite of Yudinovo 1 revealed that

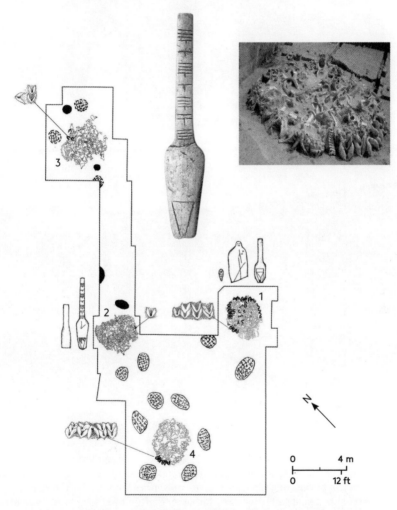

Plan of the Mezinian campsite of Mejiriche (Ukraine), showing four mammoth-bone structures (one illustrated), each surrounded by pits. Details of the chevron and zigzag architecture created by placing mammoth jaws atop or aside each other are shown. A highly stylized female figurine carved from mammoth ivory derived from one of the pits.

Bracelets of mammoth ivory have been found on a number of Mezinian sites from the period 18,500–17,000 years ago. They are usually fragmentary, presumably discarded when they broke, and often bear engraved geometric decorations. Like the Pavlovian earlier, decoration was clearly preferred to blank space. This complete example from Mezine (Ukraine) bears a design of linked lozenges; note the skill with which these have been engraved, and the careful piercings (presumably for a hide or sinew lace). The decoration would not be out of place on Bronze Age goldwork.

five excavated structures were piles of mammoth remains that had been sorted into bone types and placed carefully into circular and arc-shaped low walls, sometimes with pits and larger depressions. They are certainly structures, but as Konstantin argues, cannot be seen simply as shelters to sleep in. We've noted the odd attention to detail in the way bones were stacked and in the pits, which don't seem to have been for storage. It seems instead that whatever their specific function they were erected to stand out as special places. Archaeologists often associate the rise of 'monumentality' – the investment of huge amounts of labour in highly visible structures, such as the 'temples' of the Neolithic Near East – with settled agricultural societies. While the mammoth structures didn't need as much effort as the construction of stone 'temples' such as at Göbekli Tepe in Turkey, we shouldn't underestimate the amount of work they did require. Perhaps they originated in food processing and storage but were transformed into something of a more spiritual nature, with the community sharing in the construction effort and the rituals that presumably took place, providing a continual message that everyone belonged.

Aside from the larger settlements and their mammoth-bone structures, a number of much smaller, transient Mezinian sites lacking tents give us a glimpse of Mezinians as they monitored and hunted game, trapped animals for fur, and collected especially valued flint and other stones of good quality for knapping, pigments for colouring and art, and a magical new material we've not encountered yet: amber. Unlike in the rest of Europe, where the use of this beautiful material was very rare, it was collected from several outcrops in Ukraine and carved into distinctive beads and pendants which are found on the large campsites alongside scraps from carving. At one camp, Dobranichevka, dark brown amber was carved into a 9-cm (3.5-in.) female pendant lacking head and arms in the style of the 'venus figurines'. I wonder whether the unique colour of this striking material was thought to resemble the complexion of human skin (which, remember, was still dark at this time).

Chapter 11

Refuge

I live in York in northern England, which around 25,000 years ago was under glacial ice for several thousand years. Between 26,000 and 19,000 years ago the ice sheets of the Last Glacial Maximum (LGM) advanced southwards across the dry, rolling plains of what is now the North Sea and down the adjacent eastern side of the UK, sludging a rocky, pasty 'till' or 'diamicton' underneath it which can still be seen atop the Jurassic deposits exposed in the sections of the coastal cliffs.

The glaciers extended westwards to Ireland, where they were at least 700 m (2,300 ft) thick, and beyond into the Atlantic. Over Scotland they reached between 1 and 2 km (or around 0.5 to 1.25 miles) in thickness, depressing the land with an unimaginable weight that the country is still rebounding back from. My office in Durham University's Department of Archaeology would have been under perhaps 1,000 m (3,250 ft) of ice. And to the south, beyond the ice sheets, the landscape was subjected to severe periglacial conditions (periglacial meaning at the edges of glaciated areas): sea level was much lower, freezing water shattered rocks into gravel, valley sides collapsed, and the cold winds that blew over the reshaped landscape mantled it with sands and loess. The land was devoid of mammalian life, not even a collared lemming. The winter of the world was coming.

The Last Glacial Maximum

The last great gasp of the Pleistocene epoch was a global phenomenon. As we saw in Chapter 3, the marked climatic oscillations of the 2.6 million years of the period were caused by a complex mixture of changes to the Earth's orbit, axis and precession, which affected in turn the distribution of its ice, water and wind systems and their effects on the environments that humans had to adapt to. Previous glacials had shut down vast migrational tracts, bringing early dispersals to an end. The LGM was the last significant cold period of the Pleistocene and the point at which global ice sheets reached their maximum extent (although further cold snaps occurred right up to the succeeding Holocene, they were nowhere near as severe). For over 7,000 years the Earth's waters were once again locked up at the poles, as ice. The timing of these events varied by a few centuries from one region of the world to another, but overall they seem to have occurred fairly synchronously between the two hemispheres. As the polar ice sheets grew considerably, sea level lowered by as much as 135 m (450 ft), exposing vast new landmasses. These linked otherwise distinct islands, such as Australia, Papua New Guinea and Tasmania, and the British Isles to continental Europe.

The LGM was in fact a complex and unstable climatic period, preceded by a severe cold snap precipitated by a Heinrich Event (HE2) around 24,000 years ago. This was followed by the Last Glacial Maximum itself, which was, however, slightly less severe. Conditions were cold and dry, particularly after HE2. The cold-adapted faunas migrated down the narrow passes to the east and west of the Pyrenees, woolly mammoth and reindeer as far southwest as Asturias in northern Spain, woolly rhinoceros, wolverine and arctic fox to the Spanish Basque Country. Further north, Britain, northern France, northern Germany and Poland were abandoned by herbivores and their carnivorous predators, including *Homo sapiens* – the Gravettians. Even where these animals and humans were able to hold on, they weren't unaffected. Europe's many mountainous regions have also acted as barriers even until the recent past, and in the Pleistocene they more frequently became impenetrable barriers. Mountain glaciers are particularly sensitive to climate change, and in many regions of the world they reached peak growth as early as 30,000 years ago.

Gravettian communities existed against a backdrop of deteriorating climate, and late Gravettian groups across Europe became increasingly isolated from each other as conditions worsened. Barriers to movement expanded, and the tundra environments available to them correspondingly fragmented and shrank. Undisturbed sites in the period 26,000–24,000 years ago are few in number, and dwindle further as the Last Glacial Maximum took hold. As animal populations disappeared or became more sedentary, their human predators did the same, fragmenting into distinct regional groups of the Solutrean in southwestern Europe and the Epigravettian in the Balkans and adjacent parts of Italy, Hungary, Romania, Moldova and Ukraine. Their stone tool technology shifted in focus away from the production of large blades towards the production of little bladelets from small cores, perhaps because fewer sources of good material were being accessed.

Humans survived in refugia, regions that could still be occupied by hunter-gatherers even in times of maximum environmental stress. Without refugia, groups would become locally extinct. Within them, constrained population sizes often resulted in genetic bottlenecks – reduced variation – which would spread new haplotypes if and when surviving populations were able to expand their range once conditions improved. Too much genetic reduction – inbreeding – can of course have deleterious effects and, I'm sure, must have done for some *Homo sapiens* populations. As the effects of climate became more pronounced closest to the poles, refugia were available in milder areas to the south where herbivores were relatively abundant, such as southern Europe, the Levant, the southern Caspian foreshores, the Ganges floodplain, the Yangtze Valley and the Sunda Shelf (which joined the islands of Southeast Asia into a vast landmass during low sea levels). In southern Europe, group mobility and contact within the scattered local territories remained relatively high, enough to keep groups alive, breeding and culturally similar. For the expert craftspeople it was a technological baptism not of fire, but of ice.

The Solutrean

By 25,000 years ago the Gravettian had disappeared, abruptly replaced, it seems, by the Solutrean. This was to last over 3,000 years, from before 25,000 to 22,000 years ago, nearly the same amount of time which separates us from the pyramids of Old Kingdom Egypt. It takes its name from the Roc de Solutré in east-central France, where hunters were trapping and butchering horses repeatedly from Gravettian times until well beyond the Solutrean. Its earliest manifestations, however, are found in southern Portugal and Spain as early as 26,000 years ago, where a new type of stone weapon tip was produced, based on a blade that naturally converged towards a point and thinned at its base to aid hafting. Over the course of the Solutrean the shaping of leaf-shaped points progressed through increasingly intensive knapping and thinning from early to late stages. During the HE2 event – around 24,000 years ago – laurel-leaf-shaped points represented the zenith of the weaponsmith's knapping skill. There are widespread similarities in this Middle Solutrean phase, probably due

The Roc de Solutré near the French city of Mâcon (Saône-et-Loire) provided the opportunity for Upper Palaeolithic hunters to intercept and kill seasonally migrating horses. During the late Gravettian, Solutrean and Magdalenian, dozens of horses were butchered on the slopes below the rock. The site's name was given to the Solutrean during the infancy of Palaeolithic archaeology.

to high levels of group mobility and efforts to maintain long-distance contact with other groups within the refugia.

The Solutrean concept spread into different landscapes. Degrees of similarity changed over time, too; it was initially homogeneous across its range from northern Iberia to south of the Loire, but variations on shared themes increased as Solutrean populations fluctuated over space and time. Iberian laurel-leaf points were not the same as southwest French ones. When we start to consider the distribution of subtly differing weapon tips we can get to the heart of how *Homo sapiens* survived in their ever-changing world.

My Bordeaux-based colleague William Banks has developed Eco-Cultural Niche Modelling to explore the specific relationship between climate, environment and Palaeolithic groups. Will and his associates use sophisticated biocomputational models to reconstruct the ecosystems that human groups could adapt to. Applying this to the Solutrean groups at the height of the Last Glacial Maximum, Will was able to explore whether weapon tips varied because they each related to ways of adapting to particular ecosystems, and whether the fluctuation of these ecosystems underlies the cultural change that we can observe archaeologically over the span of the Solutrean. As Will asks, were humans 'niche conservative', expanding, dispersing and contracting as they followed traditional lifestyles in the very specific ecosystems they'd adapted to, or were they more fluid and adaptable? His team found that Solutreans were particularly conservative in the ecological niches they tolerated, even when major changes were occurring in the types of weapon systems that were favoured. This is an important discovery, as it contradicts traditional explanations for weapon system change as being the result of technological 'arms races' that occurred as Palaeolithic groups struggled to adapt to new environments. The changes occur over geographical space, not over time, showing that the differences between regional point types were a response to traditional environments that differed from region to region. Middle and Upper Solutrean groups hunted reindeer in the sub-arctic conditions of southwest France, but in Portugal they hunted red deer in pine heathland where not a single reindeer ever roamed, and their points differed accordingly.

Expert weaponsmiths

The need to produce lethal javelins of stone drove Solutrean technology in several ways. The makers used bone tools as pressure flakers, allowing a precise and gentle knapping which could be used to control shape very finely, and where possible they applied their considerable skills to the best quality flints. Where that quality wasn't available they could improve it artificially. Gently heating flints and other silica-rich rocks to 200°C (390°F) removes water trapped in minuscule pores, re-aligning their mechanical structure and hence, strength and uniformity. It makes resulting tools and weapons less likely to break at the wrong moment.

In Spain, small pits have been found next to hearths, in which flint blades were placed, covered and gently baked by fires lit above them for this purpose. It was the alchemy of the period. But Solutrean weaponsmiths were not just thinking of the tip of the weapon but of the whole system. Reindeer antler might have been becoming scarcer, but it must have been highly valued as it formed a crucial component in a new piece of hunting technology that took projectile weaponry to a new level. This is where we find the first examples of an upgraded javelin weapon: the *propulseur* (known in the Americas as

A knapping waste scatter in the upper layer of the Solutrean campsite of Les Maîtreaux (Indre-et-Loire, France). Over 250 waste pieces resulted from the manufacture of shouldered point weapon tips. Areas devoid of waste left and right show where the knapper's knee or foot rested.

the *atlatl* or spearthrower). Missile weapons are dependent on velocity for effectiveness; a faster missile achieves greater penetration. Hand-thrown spears (javelins) derive their velocity mainly from the length of the arm; the longer it is, the greater the weapon's effectiveness. Propulseurs were effectively artificial arm extensions: a length of wood that could be held at one end, with a crook at the other into which the javelin could be socketed. Both could be held in one hand, a finger securing the javelin released at the last second, the swing of the arm transferring velocity to the javelin via the propulseur. Shafts could be of wood, but crook ends – the notches into which the javelin socketed – were carved from tough-wearing antler. In the Solutrean these objects were plain, but as we will see they became ornately carved later, forming some of the most impressive pieces of Palaeolithic art.

A thrown javelin needs a light and lethal tip. At the open-air campsite of Les Maîtreaux north of the French Massif Central we

0   10 cm

0   4 in.

Broken examples of Solutrean laurel-leaf points, and
refitting waste flakes from the production of one, all from
Les Maîtreaux. The refitting flakes allow us to reconstruct a
sequence of knapping; note the presence of a light, chalky
outer skin (cortex) and the darker flint within this.

can see Solutreans at work making just that: exquisitely crafted fine laurel-leaf-shaped points. The camp is one of a number of Late Solutrean sites in the valley of the Creuse River, which drains the Massif Central northwards, cutting through abundant deposits of very high-quality flint, just the sort required by expert craftspeople. It was so good, in fact, that the absence of thermal reddening shows that heat treatment was unnecessary. This fine material could be improved no further.

The artistic world

Solutrean culture wasn't just about flintknapping expertise. The Solutreans left a rich legacy of artistic achievement, having marked their landscapes with drawn, painted, engraved and sculpted art. Many archaeological sites of the period have produced an item or two of portable art, and a number have produced abundant examples of these. Solutreans painted motifs in caves, and hammered and engraved them on cliff sides. They clearly liked to live in a landscape alive with images. Open-air Solutrean sites are relatively rare; caves were important locations for camps, and it may be no coincidence that the regions in which settlement occurred are rich in caves and rockshelters. Some of them were decorated, which like Mezinian chevrons was a way to mark the landscape as their own. They can be found clustering around major rivers, from northern Aquitaine and the lower Rhône Valley through the Basque Country to the Cantabrian coast and as far south as Valencia, southern Andalusia, and the Portuguese Estremadura.

The deep sediments in Parpalló Cave in Gandía, Spain, have produced approaching 6,000 engraved and painted stone plaquettes spanning the course of some 15,000 years from 28,000 to 13,000 years ago. Because of this series of well-dated art objects, Parpalló provides a long-term reference for the development of Upper Palaeolithic art in Western Europe. Solutrean occupation is rich; it's one of the Solutrean sites that reveals the heat-treatment of flint for producing laurel-leaf-shaped points, and around 1,000 of the decorated plaquettes belong to the period. Red deer, aurochs (extinct wild cattle), horse, ibex and variously shaped non-figurative 'signs' were engraved or painted in red and yellow onto the plaquettes' surfaces.

Part of a 13-m (40-ft) Solutrean sculpted frieze in the rockshelter of Roc de Sers (Charente, France). During the severe conditions of the Last Glacial Maximum the wall of the shelter shattered and the panel fell in pieces to the Solutrean archaeological levels beneath. The excavator planned the position of each fragment accurately, and the entire panel can thus be reconstructed.

A remarkable aspect of the Parpalló plaquettes is the longevity of stylistic traits – ways of depicting certain parts of certain animals – which appear in the cave's earliest (Gravettian) levels and persist over its entire 15,000 years. They became ancient traditions, upheld even as other trends came and went. In some periods, like the earliest Solutrean, artists used a shorthand of ears, mouths and tails to depict animals, and in others, like the Middle Solutrean, they were being particularly innovative, creating scenes comprising several highly detailed animals and showing a degree of animation of each of them. The plaquettes are alive with life, given additional meaning through marking with a wide variety of signs that we cannot read. It's tempting to think of each of them telling a vivid story.

The Côa Valley in northeast Portugal reveals that these stories were placed on the landscape itself as well as in miniature on plaquettes, as at Parpalló. Such images have been recovered from the remains of campsites located underneath the rocks on which the same bestiary of animals were pecked and engraved. With over 1,000 images, the Côa has the largest known concentration of Palaeolithic art in the open air. Evidence of campsites that were occupied for several months of the year is found on the valley bottoms, and on the plateaux above are smaller sites where hunters sat at the hearth repairing their gear while waiting for prey. In some cases the archaeological sediments have actually covered the engravings on the valley sides, which is important as it allows the independent dating of the art: at one such site, Fariseu, an engraved panel was covered by a level containing a Solutrean occupation dated to 21,000 years ago, which provides a minimum age for the art underneath. But theme and style provide their own evidence of the evolution of the Côa art over time, just like at Parpalló. In the earliest phase, at least 21,000 years old, aurochs, horse and ibex are the most common themes, depicted with large bellies, round hips, large heads, and little in the way of detail. In the next phase more detail is evident, and rare depictions of humans (or human-like beings) make an appearance. In the third phase, as much as 10,000 years younger than the Solutrean, red deer dominate, and animal bodies become more geometric in shape, with coats depicted by scored lines. These sorts of changes are the stock-in-trade of the Palaeolithic art specialist. There are always surprises, but by and large chronological schemes based on what was depicted and how have proven to be remarkably reliable.

The links between the standing rocks of the landscape and collected portable objects suggest that we shouldn't see the rock art simply as a kind of background decoration, but that to Solutreans the quotidian and the spiritual were perennially blurring together.

Around 23,000 years ago the Solutrean world began to fracture, and the regionalization of groups in western Europe that had begun in the Upper Solutrean increased. By 21,000 years ago it had disappeared even from its most southern peripheries in Mediterranean Spain. Further north it had gone earlier, replaced suddenly it seems by an enigmatic group, the Badegoulians, who had probably dispersed westwards from an origin around Hungary. Badegoulians had an awful line in stone tools, but for reasons we'll explore later, they were pretty good at cave art, at least while they camped at Lascaux.

Chapter 12

Hearth and Home

I'm writing this chapter from my apartment in Monrepos Castle, originally the country home of the Princes of the Wied just north of Stuttgart in Germany, but nowadays housing an Archaeological Research Centre and Museum of Human Behavioural Evolution. I've been coming to this magical place since my student days, and now I'm back after two years of Covid-related confinement, part of a small research team working on a rich collection of depictions of horses, mammoths and other Ice Age animals engraved onto stone plaquettes around 16,000 years ago. These were used as paving, hut foundation stones, seats, work surfaces and hearths of campsites at Gönnersdorf and Andernach, each camp visible to the other across a Rhine that flowed through many small and shallow braids separated by gravel banks rather than the deep and powerful river it is today. These rich sites – particularly their art – are icons of the European Upper Palaeolithic Magdalenian culture, and offer peculiarly intimate glimpses of life over several months of the year once the landscape was again habitable.

During the severe cold of the Last Glacial Maximum, human populations had disappeared from northern Europe, where periglacial desert prevailed. Populations instead shrank back to southerly refugia – in northern Iberia and southern France, Italy and the adjacent parts of the Balkans and the Czech Republic, and the Russian Plain – where the tundra supported reindeer, horse and other herbivores that were vital to survival. Around 19,000 years ago, conditions began to warm once more, and the tundra spread northwards. *Homo sapiens* was part of this rich ecosystem, expanding northwards out of the refugia alongside their herbivorous prey. They took with them a new culture, refined and polished over several millennia in the refugia, which we term the Magdalenian in western and central Europe, and the Mezinian in the east.

The archaeology left by these Late Upper Palaeolithic societies is thankfully unaffected by the severe erosion that the Last Glacial Maximum subjected earlier sites to, and we have a number of sites across Europe for the period 19,000 to 13,000 years ago that are exceptionally well preserved. They reveal in intimate detail a far-flung, highly mobile, technologically versatile and artistically rich society. Portable items such as tools, weapons and works of art circulated over hundreds of kilometres, maintaining a similar cultural message over vast distances of inhospitable tundra.

It is the art which took us to Gönnersdorf. For now, though, we will look at the evidence for domestic space at this and several other sites. The best place to begin is in one of those refugia, southwest France, from where the expanding Magdalenians followed horse and reindeer – and as my colleague Olaf Jöris suggests perhaps saiga antelope – into new lands, ultimately spreading to the Vistula river in Poland. We can follow them in this major biogeographical recolonization of northern Europe.

Hard rock: the classic rockshelters of the Dordogne

As a student in the late 1980s, returning home from a summer job in field archaeology, I glanced through the window of a junk shop, where several old books stood out in the dusty mess. Among them was John Lubbock's *Prehistoric Times* of 1865. Lubbock (later Lord Avebury) had been Darwin's friend, and is mainly known in Britain for inventing the bank holiday, but even then I knew of his importance to prehistorians, for publishing the first synthesis of what came to be called the Upper Palaeolithic. He drew upon a rich emerging seam of stunning archaeological discoveries, and was the first to coin the terms Palaeolithic and Neolithic to refer to the Old and New Stone Age periods, respectively. The book was a first edition and is worth much more than the £8 I paid for it, but I like to think it was a portent. I couldn't have imagined then, muddy little digger that I was, that I would be invited to the Royal Society in 2013 to talk on his contribution to archaeology for the hundredth anniversary of his death. As I write this I fondly remember standing next to the microscope Darwin gave Lubbock as his protégé, sipping a glass of wine inside the Wellington Arch in London.

The framework of how we understand Ice Age archaeology came together in the 1860s. Natural scientists – amateurs and professionals alike – had realized the value of the remains that had accumulated under the great rockshelters and in the caves of the Vézère Valley in southwest France and in other regions of Europe. Deep sediments in these preserve evidence of human occupation over remarkable spans of time, and the abundance of art and artifacts in southwest France reveals how important this region was for human survival in northern latitudes during the Ice Age. They also attest to the presence of permanent populations of reindeer, horse and bison in the region even in the height of the glacial cold. Salmon, trout and other fish could be trapped seasonally as they swam up rivers to spawn, and reindeer intercepted as they forded rivers, all within reach of convenient caves and rockshelters in the limestone cliffs that provided easy shelter when that choice was preferred over tents in the open. For a hunter-gatherer the Vézère Valley was a Garden of Eden.

Some shelters in this region, such as Cap Blanc and Laugerie-Haute, preserve evidence of occupations between 22,000 and 15,000 years ago – the Solutrean and early Magdalenian – and others, such as Limeuil and La Madeleine (after which the culture is named), for the later Magdalenian between 15,000 and 13,000 years ago (see PL. XIX). These latter two sites have provided some of the richest archaeology of the period. The material they have provided offers a glimpse of the vast scale of time over which these sites were occupied repeatedly, and many of the activities performed there.

La Madeleine and Limeuil almost certainly acted as aggregation camps, locations where several smaller groups came together from widely distant regions for several months of the year, a situation which as we will see explains the richness of Gönnersdorf around the same time. Although the natural walls of these shelters were not carved into spectacular reliefs as at Cap Blanc, numerous objects of portable art attest to the abundant artistic outpouring of the Magdalenians (see PL. XVIII). La Madeleine's Magdalenian archaeology spans at least fifteen distinct archaeological levels, each a compressed mass of discarded tools and butchery waste several tens of centimetres thick, probably reflecting the activities of relatively large numbers of people for several months of the year, repeated time and time again between 17,000 and 14,000 years ago. To put this vast period into perspective, the same length of time separates the shelter's first and last Magdalenians as separates us from Tutankhamun, and this is just the later Magdalenian! Over time, some parts of the site were kept clear – relatively tidy spaces for working, cooking and resting – whereas others resembled a rubbish dump. In one area, an infant was buried in a small pit, protected by a lining of stones. It would be wrong to describe La Madeleine as a settled village, but we can imagine a number of tents erected under the large rock overhang, and perhaps several dozen inhabitants; a veritable metropolis for the period.

The Vézère Valley seems to have been exceptionally important as a homeland for reindeer. As their winter and summer feeding was available over relatively short distances, long-distance migration was not required, and reindeer were probably in the region year-round, no doubt for much of that time passing along the valley. The distribution of cutmarks left by stone tools on reindeer bones from La Madeleine and Limeuil shows how they were expertly butchered, some fresh from the kill, others apparently in stiff condition judging by the larger number of cuts necessary to do the job. They were brought to the site whole, probably from kill sites close by given their weight, and after careful skinning, their limbs and heads were removed, and the major muscles filleted from the former and tongues from the latter. Like marrow in horse bones, tongues are a fatty delicacy in reindeer whose meat is otherwise low in fat. In some cases the butchery seems to have been wasteful to our modern eyes, probably when more reindeer were taken than were necessary for the group.

After the removal of soft parts, hard animal tissues were also worked into specific tools; reindeer antler could be used as knapping hammers or sectioned into rods and shaped into javelin and harpoon points as well as exquisite needles, and teeth and shells were turned into jewelry that would have been recognized as Magdalenian over great distances.

Expansion into the cold wilderness

The melting glaciers of the Jura and Alps made the Swiss Plateau between them habitable by 17,500 years ago. As plant cover developed, horses and reindeer returned to the region, and by 16,000 years ago remains of over fifty campsites in small caves and in the open between the lakes and mires of the Jura foothills show that Magdalenians had established a viable population year-round, sharing this cold, shrubby and treeless environment with mammoths, woolly rhinos, reindeer, horses, bears and lions.

Objects sourced from far-flung regions such as the Rhineland, Upper Danube, Paris Basin and northern Germany suggest that communities kept close contact across these distances. Ideas and practices travelled, too; one specific example that spread northwards with expanding populations over a century or so around 16,000 years ago was the technique of producing exquisitely small sewing needles – as vital for surviving the cold climate as meat and fat – out of horse metatarsals and metacarpals (foot bones). During butchery the limbs were disarticulated first; the foot bones were left intact. Parallel lines were scored along their length, isolating thin slivers that could be prised out and shaped into needles. After this, the foot bones were smashed open to obtain their fatty marrow. This was one of many routine tasks that would have been familiar to Magdalenians, but perhaps little thought about, rather like turning on our mobile phones and swiping through social media; just one culturally specific way of doing things. The cosmopolitan society was expanding.

Moving homes: reindeer hunters in the Paris Basin

During my time as the resident archaeologist in Oxford University's radiocarbon dating laboratory, I collaborated with colleagues including Clive Gamble and William Davies of Southampton University and the geneticist Martin Richards on a major project aimed at dating the northwards recolonization of northern Europe and its genetic signature. The abundant radiocarbon dates we obtained, and which have been accumulated by many other researchers since, reveal a relatively rapid human expansion north and east. By 16,000 years ago wild horses and reindeer were once more established in the Rhineland, Belgian Ardennes and Paris Basin, and by 14,800 years ago they had even reached England and Wales. In all of these regions they were accompanied by their major predator: Magdalenians. By 16,000 years ago small groups had spread as far as Poland, where the size of the sites suggests only a limited population exploiting a similar set of animal prey to the Swiss groups at the Magdalenians' northern and eastern fringe. Keeping connections with the groups back to the south would have been important for survival, and probably explains why many different materials were circulating over such long distances. A little later, a more northerly route had taken them up to the Paris Basin.

I visited colleagues' fieldwork in the Paris region in 2010. I spent one of the days in a sand quarry with Palaeolithic jewelry specialist Marian Vanhaeren, whose work I discussed in Chapter 4. Marian was working on excavations at Pincevent, one of a number of

Magdalenian campsites in and around the Seine and Yonne valleys, and I spent time there with archaeologist Pierre Bodu and his team, where they were excavating evidence of reindeer butchery. A number of late Magdalenian sites are known in the area, dating to between 15,000 and 14,000 years ago, and due to their remarkable preservation by the gentle covering over by river silts, as well as superb standards of excavation, they offer a rich view of life in the north of the Magdalenian.

Discrete archaeological layers at Pincevent occur over a depth of more than 2 m (6 ft), reflecting repeated visits to the location during the course of a century or so. In one part of the site, activity focused on the mass killing and butchery of reindeer in the autumn. It was still temperate enough to sleep in light tents spread out over this butchery ground and revealed by clusters of refuse, but as a harsh winter set in they refocused activities to a large shelter and hearth, supplementing their preserved reindeer meat with horse. The picture is similar at other sites in the region; some are overwhelmingly dominated by reindeer, others are more balanced between reindeer and horse, reflecting hunting strategies that shifted between mixed hunting when the number of animals was lowest during summer and winter, and an intensive focus on reindeer while they were on the move in spring and autumn and could be killed in large numbers and dried for prolonged use over the difficult winter.

The camps reveal much evidence of working reindeer antler into tools and javelin tips, and knapping of good-quality flints collected from the local area into regular blades for working into knives and weapon tips. Another activity was the teaching of the young. A number of refitting flakes from cores knapped on these sites show truly expert levels of skill, but others reveal a poor or learner level, almost certainly the sign of youngsters practising this critical skill. One particularly important task to be carried out at the fireside was the production and repair of weapons. These were routinely resharpened and repaired, and over the course of more than 5,000 years of the Magdalenian we can observe a steady evolution of antler weapon tips (sagaies), marked by an intensification in the use of reindeer antler and increasing diversity.

In all cases the occupational waste clusters into distinct units, snapshots in time representing the activities of individuals or small work groups engaged in a variety of tasks around hearths in the open air and inside tents.

It is, ironically, the absence of materials that gives the game away in some camps. Outside, there is no reason to clean areas of waste products; there is always somewhere to sit and have a break. But to sit and sleep inside a tent requires that it is kept relatively clear of rubbish. Away from the clear area next to the hearth small amounts of refuse are patterned in an arc shape, probably reflecting where people came to rest against the outer hide wall of a circular tent. The location of the hearth to one side suggests that it was lit in the entrance area, where occupants could benefit from its light and warmth but with less smoke inside. The ash and waste dump to its other side shows that waste was thrown out of the tent over the fire.

There is one tent that we must stop by before we head east. This is structure W11 at Étiolles, where the distribution of large stones used to secure tent poles shows that it was trapezoidal in shape, enclosing about 16 sq. m (170 sq. ft), with a central hearth and a relatively clean interior, and an entrance in the shortest of five sides indicated by the tossing of waste outside. It is one of the larger tents known, but otherwise not exceptional among the Paris Basin sites. Except for the fact that if we now travel over 400 km (250 miles) to the east, we find an identical tent at Gönnersdorf. Why would that be the case?

Gönnersdorf and Andernach: 16,000-year-old campsites on the banks of the Rhine

In a largely treeless tundra, wood from the few birch and pine trees scattered around would have been a valuable resource. Wood rarely survives archaeologically but some spears and other objects do, enough to show that (thrusted) spears, (thrown) javelins and, eventually, arrows would have had elegant shafts onto which stone and bone tips were hafted. The twiggy brushwood of the dwarf trees that were most abundant would not suit this purpose, nor would it do for tent poles, for which longer branches of the few larger trees that survived where they were sheltered in valleys were critical. We can assume that javelin shafts and tent poles would have been carefully looked after and carried around. This probably explains the presence of several identical tent structures found from the Paris Basin to the outskirts of Berlin; tents would be dismantled, hides tied up and suspended from the tent poles as groups moved to their next camp.

We know Magdalenians walked or canoed vast distances, and while we can't be sure that it was the same tent – with the same occupants – erected at Étiolles and Gönnersdorf, we can be sure that, like those horse foot bones, this was a very specifically designed piece of kit that was used across Magdalenian northern Europe. Perhaps the tent poles even served as a simple frame to drag items along like a sled, either by oneself or using dogs.[1]

Thousands of bones, stones, items of jewelry and plaquettes of schist as well as large blocks of quartzite, quartz and basalt collected from around the site are scattered across Gönnersdorf. Hundreds of engravings of prey animals were created on the schist plaquettes, and in terms of art alone, no other Magdalenian site has produced anything like it. The camp was not just used briefly; the bones and teeth of animal prey can reveal evidence of the season in which they were killed. The horse, reindeer and other animals, especially arctic fox and arctic hare, killed at Gönnersdorf show that it was occupied for half the year, perhaps more. This probably explains the abundance of archaeological and artistic objects. In the modern world we are unlikely to invest much effort into decorating a house we rent briefly, and the same goes for hunter-gatherer campsites. A long stay warranted more than a disorganized mess, and Gönnersdorf was more like a modern campsite than a music festival. Objects cluster together in four main concentrations, each comprising many smaller activity zones, showing how space was organized into particular activity areas, some for messy tasks such as butchery and hide working, others for making and mending (which required heat or light and could be done squatting or sitting by the fire), and relatively clean and warm areas in which to sleep.

Across the site, the bones and teeth of at least fifty-seven horses, at least thirty arctic foxes, several reindeer and hares, two wolves and the odd bison, as well as chamois, were recovered from butchery areas, in addition to the bones of raven, ptarmigan/grouse, swan and goose. The Neuwied Basin and adjacent lowlands offered considerable hunting and trapping opportunities, and no wonder small groups would travel 150 km (90 miles) or more from all directions to aggregate together here. High-quality stone used for toolmaking – usually flints, chalcedony and quartzites – reveals this cosmopolitan travel. We can identify the geological sources from which certain visually distinctive stones derived, and when they are identified on campsites in the form of tools and the waste from their manufacture

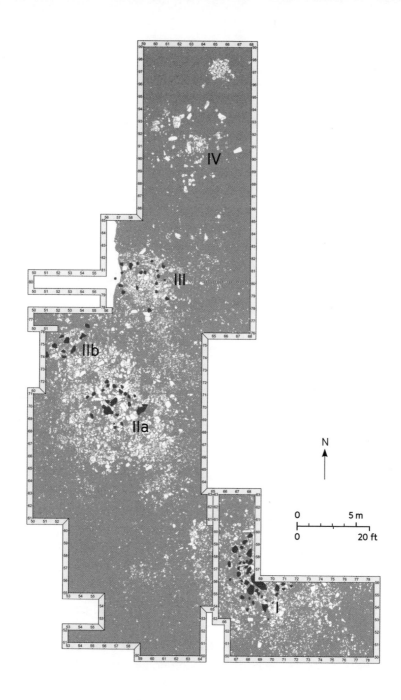

Site plan of the excavations at Gönnersdorf. Meticulous plans such as this are crucial to understanding how Upper Palaeolithic hunter-gatherers organized their camp sites. Each number around the edge of the excavation area relates to one square metre, and the image plots every stone plaquette, tool, animal bone, hearth, pit and other feature, where they were left 16,000 years ago. Four clusters of material are visible, marked I, IIa/IIb, III and IV.

we can easily reconstruct from where, and how far, they have been carried. At Gönnersdorf some were obtained within short walks, but the great majority of materials were carried to the site over long distances, particularly if they were of high quality. Baltic flint came from at least 120 km (75 miles) to the north, flints and quartzites from the Meuse River the same distance to the west, and coarser stones from a similar distance to the east and southeast. Ochre pigments, jewelry and other exotics also attest this far-flung network; a javelin foreshaft made of whale bone was found at Andernach, which has parallels with others from sites in the Pyrenees, and along with jewelry made from the shells of Mediterranean molluscs reveals ultimate access to the coasts of the west and south. It may be significant that these latter were found buried together in a small pit. Were these so mysterious or powerful that they had to be buried out of sight?

This huge procurement area leads my colleague Olaf Jöris to see the site as one where far-flung groups aggregated together for several months of the year. For small groups of hunter-gatherers living in a hard environment, aggregation is necessary in order to cement alliances, obtain partners (avoiding inbreeding) and exchange information, all crucial to survival on the tundra.

Many of the bright and varied stone flakes and bone fragments can be refitted to each other like a three-dimensional jigsaw puzzle, allowing us to reconstruct bones from their fragments or cores of flint that had been knapped to create the tools that were used at the site. My zooarchaeologist colleagues Elaine Turner and Martin Street have painstakingly refitted large numbers of these together. There were often connections between each activity cluster, showing how materials were moved over several metres between different sets of people; a reindeer leg goes one way, a horse head the other, and tools are shared as needed. We can imagine the frosty breath of perhaps a dozen parka-clad workers as they cooperated in small groups.

The interpretation of the four main clusters at Gönnersdorf has changed over the years as methods of analysis have improved. Originally, they were seen as the remnants of four different tent-like structures, but now we know that they represent several highly organized outdoor activity areas and one tent. Palaeolithic archaeologists know their stones and bones, and can reconstruct the activities they represent in great detail thanks to a host of scientific techniques of analysis. At Gönnersdorf a wide variety of tasks were repeatedly undertaken, as we might expect for a site that was occupied for several months of the year. Stone tools often retain microscopic traces of wear that they accumulate in use; these can be compared to microscopic traces created by experimental use of similar items, revealing that they were used alongside tools made of bone and antler to chisel, drill, cut, flay, knap, whittle, scrape, pierce and sew, transforming animal carcasses, rocks and what little vegetation was around into food, clothing, tents and equipment.

The schist blocks were used as seats, work surfaces, ovens, and to stabilize structures such as racks for drying and storing meat and fish. In Concentration IV, some of the largest plaquettes brought to the camp formed the structural frame of a light, rectangular tent, the 16 sq. m (170 sq. ft) interior of which was periodically cleaned; you don't want to sleep on sharp flints after all, do you? It is this arrangement that is virtually identical to the W11 structure at Étiolles: the same dimensions, trapezoidal shape, and with the same central circular hearth and activity area. Now we know a little about how far the Gönnersdorf group's connections spanned, that similarity of tent design doesn't seem so surprising. We know that some carried Meuse flint from the west, and at Andernach another person carried a javelin reinforced with whalebone; why not someone a tent in the latest Parisian style?

Repeated setting of fires in small hearths at Gönnersdorf, as well as the creation of art on the stone plaquettes surrounding the campers, transformed this and other campsites into a little space at least that felt like home. Many of the schist stones have been reddened by heat, and tools and bones which fell into the fires also bear the cracks of such fiery damage. Warmth and light were critical to survival, provided by both stone ovens and small concavities hammered out of the schist stones, used to burn a wick of juniper or pine wood in animal fat. Hearths at Gönnersdorf were assembled time and time again from the ubiquitous schist plaquettes, burned, dismantled, and often reassembled for later use.

Highly detailed images of horses, mammoths, woolly rhinos, birds, seals and other animals were lightly engraved onto many of the plaquettes, whether they were used in hearths or for other purposes. Several hundred are known, which suggests that this activity was frequent and routine: perhaps sitting by the fire and engraving familiar prey animals was the Magdalenian equivalent of knitting in front of the television. Despite the frequency of depictions

Schist plaquettes were used as paving, seats, work surfaces and to protect hearths at the 16,000-year-old campsite of Gönnersdorf on the banks of the Rhine. They were collected locally and carried to the site, where small clusters reveal individual hearths and work places. Note the spread of bones across this outdoor working area; a reindeer antler is visible in the left foreground.

of mammoth and woolly rhino, their bones are almost completely absent from the site, and radiocarbon dating shows that when Gönnersdorf was inhabited these creatures had already become extinct in the region. But their presence to the north is still attested, suggesting that those individuals who travelled from the north with their Baltic flint brought their knowledge – and perhaps tall stories – of these formidable beasts.

For the disparate groups of people who came together here, such images may have helped them share information: this is what a particularly aggressive stallion looks like (it's worth going for weaker prey); as you've not seen one, this is what a mammoth looks like (the one that got away was *this big*, I tell you!). In this sense the plaquettes would be the Ice Age equivalent of a chalkboard. But the functional view of art we have in the West – something which is predominantly decorative and recreational – breaks down in non-industrial societies, where it usually has functions that relate as much to the spiritual realms as to the quotidian. There are several clues on the Gönnersdorf plaquettes that there was something more to them than simply diagrams and sketches. One of these relates to non-animal images, which are also common themes, and the other is how the form of the plaquettes relates to the shape of the images engraved within. These clues suggest there was much more at work during their creation. We will return to the Gönnersdorf plaquettes in Chapter 15.

Chapter 13

The Sightless World
of Palaeolithic Cave Art

Thin beams of torchlight play around the vast rocky chamber. White
stalactites flash brightly as if surprised by our intrusion, until the
light is swiftly swallowed by the shadows. Then they leap out at us,
the bison and horses. Drawn in black they emerge from the shadows
themselves, running, cavorting, mating in the small concavities around
the chamber's sides. We pick up our feet and stamp them down.
Their noise is amplified by the mysterious place and returns to us
thunderously after a split second, as if the herd was stampeding into
the world from somewhere above our heads. It is deafening, unearthly,
and it seems as if our feet have transformed into hoofs, ourselves into
the herd beasts. At this timeless moment, everything else is forgotten.
It is the source of creation, the place where the prey come alive,
and the place where the natural order of things is made. Far from the
light, our world has turned in on itself, and we feel shrunken and
insubstantial, undefinable and insignificant, here in the so-called
Salon Noir in the cave of Niaux.

I came to a place where no light shone at all

If every single person alive in the world 20,000 years ago were to light
an animal fat lamp at the same time, the combined light would be truly
pathetic in comparison to the single shaft of light that is beamed into
the sky from the pinnacle of Las Vegas's Luxor Casino. At full thrust
it has the power of over 40 billion candles. That's a lot of Palaeolithic
lamps, but estimates suggest that there were probably no more than
1 or 2 million people alive around the time that Lascaux's art was
created. Until the introduction of electric light, the pre-modern world
was a very dark place indeed. Even large metropolises such as Paris
and London were places of inky darkness at night, illuminated only
by flickering pools of flame-derived light. In order to appreciate the

earliest art of *Homo sapiens* in a way that approximates how it was seen by its creators, we need to imagine our way back beyond the world of electric light, and into an environment where artificial light was provided only by burning. Back to the world of the fireside, the torch and the lamp.

Imagine the profound darkness and the vast, impressive skies that were nowhere spoiled by light pollution; the way that the distant vistas of the cold steppe-tundra would shrink as night came on, enveloping everything, reducing the world to a tiny circle of flickering light. No wonder, then, that people wanted to turn their backs on the world, reassuring themselves with the firelight playing across familiar faces as the wind blew around them, the wolves howled, and who knows what else wandered out there in the wilderness. Dante's *Inferno* – from where I took the subheading above – captures the emotions that humans experience in the dark. In the world above, night would at least come and go, one of those regularities like the seasons or the migrations of prey that our ancestors would have undoubtedly found reassuring. But there were places of perpetual night, where no natural light shone. They offered little except anxieties and danger. Why on Earth were our Palaeolithic groups drawn into them?

Although in the popular imagination Neanderthals and early *Homo sapiens* are characterized as 'cave men' (and women), there is little evidence of them using the dark zones of caves for their camps. In fact, while the daylit zones of cave mouths were often used as conveniently roofed shelters, there was no practical reason to venture into the darkness beyond other than to check there were no lions, hyenas or bears lurking there ready to pounce on unsuspecting sleepers. There is no food to be had in the darkness, but there are plenty of ways to injure oneself or even die in the frightening depths. Caves are unfamiliar and unexplainable. Strange noises with no discernible source break an otherwise deathly silence. Even the sounds one makes when exploring them are muted in some places, amplified in others. At times one must crawl or stoop, just like a hunter approaching their prey; at others one must ascend or descend using ropes. At one minute one can feel insignificant in the vastness of a seemingly endless chamber; at another oppressed and enveloped in an intimate crawlspace. It's no surprise that where our early ancestors encountered caves, they formed an important arena for the exercise of the human imagination.

The hearths, animal fat and twig lamps and torches available to Palaeolithic *Homo sapiens* issued only a low light that barely penetrated the darkness beyond a couple of metres, throwing shadows around as it constantly flickered. Unlike the images of cave art we are all familiar with, no Palaeolithic viewer was ever likely to see the art as something completely static. It was always moving in one way or another. It's difficult to believe that our ancestors – who had, after all, the same brain as us – didn't read some profound meaning into this, even if it is lost to us now. Despite the danger and disorientation, caves of remarkable depths were explored extensively, and we now know that art was engraved, pecked, drawn, spat and painted on the walls of at least 500 caves across Europe. Most are found in France and Spain, which was clearly an artistic centre for much of the period, but other examples have been found elsewhere, including in the Czech Republic, Germany, Italy, the UK and Russia, suggesting that at times, like portable art, it was far more widespread.

Cave art and its open-air equivalent, such as we've seen in Portugal's Côa Valley, weren't simply graffiti. Artists – and we don't know how many of them there were or whether they were male or female – often went to considerable effort to take artistic materials underground that had been sourced some distance from the caves. While some of the art could have been created quickly – perhaps the act of creating it was more important than the finished product – artists often created time-consuming works that required great technical skill, even in places that were uncomfortable or difficult to work in, when far more convenient blank surfaces were available close by. Something we can no longer sense was guiding what was being created and where it was placed, and if that meant a difficult job then it was still done, whatever the cost. Neither was the art simply doodling or decoration; while the rock art created on the back walls of rockshelters perhaps had a decorative element, why decorate a difficult-to-access wall of a cave when you're not hanging around to enjoy it?

In order to get closer to an understanding of these remote and alien creations, we need to break away from how we see art in the present, which often has connotations of leisure, aesthetics and entertainment. This is not to say that cave art didn't incorporate these elements, but if the non-industrial societies of the last few centuries are anything to go by, we can assume that art was a dynamic thing offering important benefits to its producers. We shouldn't think of

This remarkably well-preserved lamp, carved from red sandstone from sources in the Charente at least 70 km (45 miles) distant, was found in Lascaux's 'Shaft'. Several dozen simpler lamps with bowls pecked out of stone cobbles have been found beneath the cave's art panels. Some 21,000 years ago the soft Charentaise sandstones were clearly desired for the making of such lamps.

cave art as static pictures, either. It was more of an active dialogue between the explorer-artist and the cave itself. We've little idea what other elements of this dialogue were. Sometimes we sense that this was a private thing, at other times a group ritual probably involving music and dance. All we have to go on is the art that has remarkably survived on cave walls. Whether artists were in any way special – and given the skills exhibited by a number of them I suspect they were – they were often an integral part of the art they created. If it's fair to use a modern concept, then cave art was more like installation art, where the position, view and movement of the explorer-artist was as important as the topography, shadows and surfaces of the cave and the images they created. This was not something to create and then step back to admire. It was something meaningful that required participation. In some cases it seems that these little creative theatres were small and intimate; isolated images are sometimes hidden away, as if they were highly personal and meant to be seen only at the time they were being created. In other cases, such as the large chambers in Lascaux, Chauvet, Altamira and Niaux, there is a sense that the art was intended for an audience – that perhaps there was a shared celebration of creation that occurred alongside other rituals in the dark.

The red phase: the body meets the cave

Humans evolved as visual beings. As up to 90 per cent of the brain's information about our surroundings derives from our eyes, it is perhaps no surprise that visual culture became so central to our very way of being. But it evolved slowly, and art 'as we know it' was a relative latecomer. Before 31,000 years ago, I see no convincing evidence of figurative art on cave walls. There are contenders, for sure, but there is always some controversy related to them. If we take a critical eye to this, figurative art doesn't appear – in caves or anywhere else – until 37,000 years ago, or not much beforehand. But the depths of caves were visited, and on occasion these visits were marked with art. Prior to 40,000 years ago cave art was rare, and where it existed seems to have been restricted to making marks with the body in red pigment. Our dating of examples of this red non-figurative art in three Spanish caves – which I opened the book with – has revealed that Neanderthals were the first to create it, long before *Homo sapiens* arrived on the cave art scene. But we do have examples dated to after 43,000 years ago, by which time Neanderthals had been replaced in Western Europe. We don't know yet if this is coincidence, two phases of similar art separated by thousands of years, or a continual tradition that was shared between these two biological groups. The fact that comparable art with a minimum age of 40,000 years has been discovered in Indonesia, the other side of Eurasia, suggests that this was perhaps a phenomenon widespread among humans before this time. We have much dating to do, however.

While a wet ochre paint was used in this 'red phase', as we might name it, we shouldn't call it painting or drawing. Fingertips were covered with paint and pressed to the rock, often in sequence to create meandering lines. It was often spat at the cave wall direct from the mouth or perhaps through the intermediary of a hollow bone tube, again either in isolation or repeated in a sequence. The most intriguing elements of the red phase are hand stencils (see PL. XIII). Any parent will be familiar with positive handprints – made by covering the hand with pigment and pressing it against a surface – but these are very rare in cave art and most examples are negative stencils. These are created, counter-intuitively, by placing a hand against the cave wall and spitting a cloud of pigment at it. Perhaps accidental impressions left by hands and feet in soft muds gave their creators the idea, but it's still an odd thing to do, particularly as a task that should have been easy was often made difficult by their creation in parts of caves that were difficult to access, or at least uncomfortable to hold a position in. A lot of attention has been given to the fact that in a few caves the hands so preserved in outline forever appear to be missing one or more fingers, and much has been made of this; were they missing because of frostbite or through ritual mutilation, for example? Such speculation makes good stories, but sadly that is all they are. These types of prints are relatively few in number, accounted for perhaps by a handful (forgive the pun) of people, who could just as easily have been bending their perfectly intact fingers back for deliberate effect. We will never know.

Swan necks and duck bills, wounded men and bison-women

Time passes. First, the humans were keen to take themselves into the caves, leaving marks of their own bodies behind in the dark, and perhaps the traditions of the red phase persisted here and there still, but by 31,000 years ago something new had spread across much of France, and probably into the north of Spain. Now, they took not just the marks of their own bodies underground with them but also their observations and stories of the steppes, bringing their animal prey down into these places, and celebrating them. Caves slowly awoke from their primeval darkness, first receiving humans from the world above, and later the populations of animals on which these people were dependent for survival. Life was breathed into the caves, and swirled around their walls. As we've seen, figurative art had appeared several thousand years earlier in the form of simple engraved animals in the rockshelters of the Dordogne and the mammoth ivory carvings of southwestern Germany, but it doesn't seem to have been more widespread. Now it was; 'venus figurines' were created from France to Siberia, and the earliest recognizable tradition of figurative cave art appeared in the French Gravettian.

My colleagues Jacques Jaubert of Bordeaux University and Valérie Feruglio of Toulouse University have surveyed the art of the period, which occurs in several regional groups from the Ardèche in the southeast to the Pyrenees in the southwest, and as far north as the Paris region. It's fairly well dated. In some cases the charcoal used to draw the animals or the archaeology left in the caves by the artists has been dated by radiocarbon. In others thematic and stylistic similarities can link art to the same period. These have been great tools for what archaeologists call relative dating; where direct (absolute) dating is impossible, changes in theme, style and method over deep time reveal the broad ages of the art relative to other phases. This is no different from biostratigraphy, where palaeontologists infer ages of fossils based on their morphological characteristics. Two 20th-century giants, Henri Breuil and André Leroi-Gourhan, developed overarching relative schemes for Palaeolithic art which have stood up remarkably to the test of time. Working in the early and middle parts of the century respectively, they had different views on the grand scheme of things, but their systems reflected a broad evolution from relatively simple to increasingly sophisticated art, gradually acquiring more naturalism, perspective, composition, polychromy and depiction of movement.[1] It seems to me that there was simply more effort expended in its creation over time, too.

Jacques and Valérie collated the available chronology for Gravettian art in France, and suggested that an early phase was dominated by hand stencils and representations of mammoths. This was followed by a main, middle phase in which the typical Gravettian themes and styles dominated, and a later phase that merged into the succeeding Solutrean and in which stylistic elements one can recognize at Lascaux emerged. In my reading, taking dating imprecision into account, we can date these phases to 30,000–28,000, 27,000–26,000, and 24,000–22,000 years ago, respectively. It may be that we're missing some data, but I think it likely that there were long periods in which humans just stopped doing cave art. That might explain its rarity elsewhere; perhaps it was never that common, and at times the idea caught on and spread, and at other times it was simply lost. Perhaps new visitors saw the art that had been left on cave walls long beforehand, gave their own meaning to the magical images, and created their own. Like the other aspects of these people's material culture, things changed, appeared and disappeared.

Jacques and Valérie also noted a number of shared characteristics which link all the cave art of the period. Animals were just as often engraved onto hard cave walls or in soft cave muds as they were painted in simple monochrome. They were drawn with skill, although restricted to an outline of their profiles, a trait which persisted right to the end of cave art. They offered more accurate depictions than the earlier rockshelter art of the Dordogne, although with a tendency towards unnaturally small heads, distorted backs and bloated bellies. This wasn't artistic incompetence; the creatures' lines flow, and they seem to leap about on the walls. So it seems people were more interested in strictly adhering to artistic convention rather than to naturalism, rather like the 16th-century Mannerists. Horses' manes were drawn as a single line, like a cartoon crest; they were given unnaturally curved swan-like necks, duck-like billed mouths and drooping muzzles. Quite often a pair of legs was missing, or the legs were left without hoofs. In the modern world we have a preoccupation with completeness, but much cave art was left incomplete, as if it were sufficient to convey a general impression of the animal depicted and to emphasize a selected few traits around the head.

Recall that the 'venus' figurines belong to the earliest phase of Gravettian art, as does the art on the walls of Cussac Cave in the Dordogne and Chauvet and Cosquer Caves in the Ardèche and Provence. Although the subject matter differs, it may be significant that venuses also share this diminution of heads and unfinished feet with their wall-bound animal counterparts. If the representations in cave art were portraits in some way, we might think that steppe grasses obscured the lower legs, but we can't understand the head distortion in any prosaic way. Was it because artists couldn't 'see' their own heads unless they were reflected in water? We simply don't know, but it's one of a number of characteristics of humanity's earliest art that distinguish it from the modern world.

Two notable themes emerge in the middle phase, which is particularly well represented among a cluster of caves in the Quercy region, and in the Mayenne-Sciences Cave in the north of France. These may well stem not from observations of animal life on the steppes, but from the imaginary world. Both are representations of humans (or human-like beings), and perhaps indicate the emergence of a mythical element to the use of caves. 'Wounded men', such as the striking examples of Cougnac Cave, have a vague anthropoid shape but have numerous lines sticking out of them like porcupine quills, as if they have been wounded with javelins. Or perhaps destroyed as images. 'Bison-women' are remarkably similar to the carved venuses and may be a later persistence of them in drawn form, but they also bear some similarities in shape and stooping, animal-like posture to bison. Perhaps the theme of transformation from human to animal or vice versa was emerging?

One of the gems of cave art belongs to the earlier Gravettian, which is the panel of spotted horses in Pech Merle (Quercy). It's a beautiful natural cave, and although its art is not abundant it is an exemplar of the styles, themes and skills of the period. As Palaeolithic art specialist Michel Lorblanchet says, it's an art of the hand and mouth; black- and red-spat and finger-drawn art clusters in little groups, probably illuminated as isolated scenes that the viewer encountered as they ventured deeper into the darkness. Bison-women are found amid patterns of spat red dots, and the paired horses command a large gallery, where they are visible from a distance. Like nearby Cougnac Cave, it's difficult to escape the conclusion that these were deliberately planned ritual arenas, in which the journey of the participant through the cave and their encounters with images of real and imaginary things formed part of a wider set of ritual behaviours. But now we must let Pech Merle return to the darkness, and travel some 50 km (30 miles) north and 6,000 years forward in time to visit a great calendar of creation.

Lascaux

Like Carter and Carnarvon's first glimpse into the tomb of Tutankhamun, the story of how Robot the dog discovered Lascaux's spectacular art in 1940 is well known in archaeology. Out for a walk in the beautiful Dordogne landscape with his owner and several friends, the little rascal disappeared down a fissure. Marcel Ravidat crawled down it to rescue Robot, and found himself staring at a 'cavalcade of animals' that swirled around his head on the cave's walls and ceiling (see PL. XX). What remains to this day one of archaeology's greatest treasures had come to light once more, and although news of the discovery was slow to spread – the world had other priorities at the time – Henri Breuil was called, and so began a study that continues even now. Recently, Bordeaux-based colleagues Sylvain Ducasse and Mathieu Langlais have completely overhauled our understanding of Lascaux's art and archaeology.

As the art on its walls was produced with mineral pigments that contain no collagen, it is not possible to date it directly using the radiocarbon method. Instead, Sylvain and Mathieu used the technique to date butchered reindeer remains found scattered throughout the cave's many chambers. Prior to this, the dating of the cave's art was based on fairly flimsy evidence. Ironically, Lascaux was one of the first archaeological sites to be dated by the physicist Willard Libby, using his newly invented radiocarbon approach in the early 1950s. Until Sylvain and Mathieu's admirable revision, however, we'd relied on a handful of dates measured when results were far less reliable than they are today. To use the specific terminology, the results were both *inaccurate* and *imprecise*. Imagine if you asked me how old the English Domesday Book was. It was commissioned by William the Conqueror in 1086, hence it is about 935 years old. If my reply is 'about 935 years old', I'm being very accurate; if it's 'about 500 years old', I'm inaccurate. Laboratory dating techniques cannot arrive at one-year age estimations, however. Because of the errors and assumptions built into them they come as estimates of age ranges. So, if I replied to your question that the Domesday Book was 'somewhere between 500 and 1,000 years old', I'd technically be correct (accurate) but only because my age range estimate was big enough to encompass the real age (imprecise). The existing Lascaux dates were both inaccurate (wrong) and imprecise (wide ranging), and had become enmeshed in competing hypotheses about the site's age and cultural attribution that were impossible to resolve. The situation was, quite frankly, a mess.

Enter Sylvain Ducasse and Mathieu Langlais, both experts on the archaeology of the period. Capitalizing on major developments in radiocarbon dating, they had a number of samples analysed at the Oxford Radiocarbon Accelerator Unit, my old lab. All of them dated to the same statistical period, between 21,000 and 21,500 years ago, a pretty precise result given the antiquity of the samples. This confirmed Mathieu's and Sylvain's views of the likely age of Lascaux's activity based on the types of stone, bone and antler tools discarded in the cave. It seemed to them that the activity occurred over a very short period of time, rather than repeated visits spanning several centuries or more. Intriguingly, the evidence points right to a period in which culturally Badegoulian groups who'd been in the region for two millennia or more were replaced by new groups with a Magdalenian culture. Was the art of Lascaux the last gasp of the Badegoulians, the stamp of the new Magdalenians, or a complicated mixture of the two?

Whatever the reason for its production, Lascaux remains one of the most spectacular decorated caves. Over 2,000 paintings and engravings have been identified in the relatively small cave, clustering in its seven galleries. Some of these are large and seemingly communal, such as the 130 animals painted in the Hall of the Bulls and the Lateral Passage; others require crawling through narrow spaces. As we'll see below in the case of Niaux, the noisy scenes with stampeding groups of animals occur in those large chambers which act as natural amplifiers, whereas the crawlspaces which deaden noise have lions, the silent

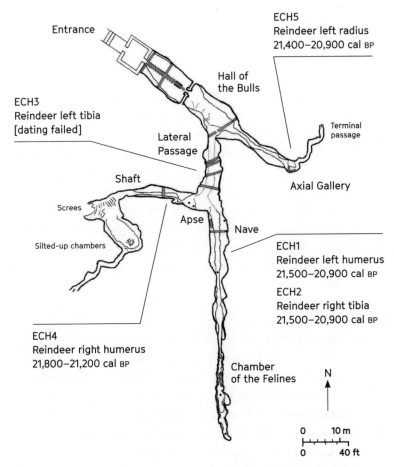

The dating of the art and activity in Lascaux Cave. Fragments of butchered reindeer remains left by Palaeolithic artists were dated by the AMS radiocarbon technique, revealing that the activity in the cave occurred over a relatively short period between 21,000 and 21,500 years ago (before present, or BP). One of these (ECH4) was found in the 'shaft' right next to the beautifully carved sandstone lamp illustrated on p. 192, others underneath the artistic panels.

predators, engraved on their walls in ways difficult to see. In a way, it's a case of art mirrors life. Over 1,000 lifelike engravings, particularly of horses and stags, cluster in the cave's central Apse. In terms of the effort it took to create them it could have been the most important part of the cave, but its fine engravings are difficult to see. Perhaps they were meant to be. Perhaps they were secret to all but the initiated, or perhaps it was the act of creating them that was important, rather than the leaving of an image to exist in perpetuity.

Lascaux's rich, detailed bichrome and polychrome paintings organized into grand, dynamic scenes catch the eye much more easily as they swirl above one's head. Visually, the painted scenes are often dominated by huge aurochs bulls and cows, but representations of horses are more numerous. Deer make up the 'trinity' of the most depicted animals in Lascaux and in Palaeolithic art. There is a great dynamism to the deer scenes, which depict social interaction and aggression typical of the rutting period. The late Norbert Aujoulat spent years studying Lascaux's art, and revealed that the three most important animals are depicted in their fine rutting coats: stocky aurochs bulls with thick head hair and gracile females in red coats; bulky horses with red and brown coats and hairy tails that reach to the ground; and red deer stags with huge antlers. Using modern analogy, their rutting periods would fall in late winter/spring (horse), summer (aurochs) and autumn (deer). As Aujoulat perceptively noted, the cave's major panels comprise a calendar of rutting. It's interesting that winter seems absent, but that's not surprising given that herbivores don't rut in winter.[2]

The food waste excavated from the cave mouth is dominated by reindeer and indicates that it was occupied in winter. This perhaps explains why there was apparently no need to depict reindeer (or humans) on Lascaux's walls; they were there in the flesh. Perhaps one way of coping with the winter was to perform the rituals to celebrate the seasons of new life to come, and as with many other caves, creation seems part of the theme; a horse falls backwards out of a crack in the Axial Gallery in the same way that some 6,000 years later bison were depicted 'dripping' out of the ceiling in Altamira. This was a great celebration of creation; perhaps some of these caves were seen as mysterious places where the animal spirits come into this world and where it is right to celebrate them.

Magdalenian cave art: Altamira to Niaux

In many technical, thematic and stylistic ways, Lascaux heralds the great *floruit* of Palaeolithic art, which spans the Late Upper Palaeolithic between around 22,000 and 13,000 years ago (see PL. XXIV). Many of the icons of cave and portable art belong to this time, particularly to the Middle Magdalenian (around 15,500 to 14,000 years ago), in which the genre reaches its highest expression, from Asturias in northwest Spain through Cantabria, the Basque Country and the Pyrenees into Ariège, Quercy, the Dordogne and beyond. This is the period to which Altamira, one of the most impressive examples, belongs. As a dedicated atheist I can honestly say that working in Altamira was the closest thing to a religious experience I've had. Occupying a high view (*alta mira*) over the coastal plain of Cantabria, it was clearly an important cave for the Solutreans and Magdalenians who camped in its daylight zone and created the art on its walls. Over 140 animals were either engraved or painted in red, yellow, violet and black, and in its famous Polychrome Chamber bison and red deer were rendered in several colours with a remarkable naturalism. The cave's Magdalenian occupants ate mainly red deer, supplemented by bison, aurochs from the plains, ibex and chamois from the mountains, and a variety of small animals available in this rich ecosystem where mountains meet the coastal plain, including birds, fish, seals and limpets. The sockets of red deer scapulae – which form a natural bowl – were used to mix pigments, and their flat surfaces, which resemble deer heads in shape, were often decorated with highly detailed images of them that are stylistically identical to deer heads engraved on the cave walls.

If we take all of Altamira's animal images into account, the Solutreans and Magdalenians of Altamira preferentially drew and ate red deer. Perhaps they saw themselves as deer people. In addition to the animals, numerous non-figurative 'signs' are dotted throughout. Many of the images are still fresh and bright. In fact, when it was discovered in 1879, the art's remarkable preservation was one reason why many critics thought it to be fake. It wasn't until the early 20th century, when more examples of cave art covered in thick (and thus very old) stalactites were recorded elsewhere, that Altamira was finally given credit for the artistic treasure it is. Other, more faded images occur on its walls and ceiling too, and our uranium-thorium dating of minute growths of stalactites overlying these has revealed that among them, an outline of a horse painted in red is at least 22,000 years old, and an odd-looking sign is at least 35,000 years old, some 20,000 years older than the famous bison and deer of the Polychrome Chamber. As we date more art from the caves of Europe it is becoming clear that many of them were visited and embellished with images on a number of occasions separated by thousands of years.

Cave art in Altamira and elsewhere often displays considerable attention to where the art was placed (it was not random); its

Panel 4 of Niaux's Salon Noir is one of the cave's most complex sets of images. Over nineteen animals cluster over a space of 4 m (13 ft) in this one alcove, including eight bison, six horses and four ibex. Note the 'S' and 'C' twists of the horns of the left bison, a classic Magdalenian technique of twisted perspective. The right-hand bison has been given two heads, one facing the front and the other turning to the rear, a typical way that brief movement was depicted.

interaction with light and shadow (adding volume and movement); preparation of the surface by scraping (probably to provide a bright, shiny surface); planning of compositions; incorporation of lumps and bumps to help convey a sense of volume; the depiction of details of the head, hoofs and fur; and clever use of conventions to convey a sense of perspective and movement. In well-studied systems, such as the Volp Caves in Ariège (Trois Frères, Enlène and Le Tuc d'Audoubert), the art clearly formed part of wider use of the caves in which the creation of space and deposition of portable art were also important. Various types of non-figurative 'signs' appeared in the Early Magdalenian: they can occur in isolation or in apparent association with figurative art, in which case they may be communicating information about the depicted animal. Human-like images are rare, and where we do have them – such as in Trois Frères and Gabillou – they almost always have a part-animal characteristic, such as the bent and antlered 'sorcerers'. There is a great degree of graphic mutability between depictions of animals, humans and signs in cave art, and over time, as Michel Lorblanchet has observed, there is a tendency for all of these to become more abstracted. We'll return to this mutability between humans and animals in Chapter 15.

I began this chapter by recounting a visit I made to Niaux with a research assistant, and my sense of its famous Salon Noir (see PL. XXII). My account was fanciful for sure, but the sense of timelessness, its vastness and remarkable acoustics are very real. It's a long cave system with art scattered around it, including various clusters of finger-drawn dots and lines which were perhaps communicating navigational information to explorers. The 15,000- to 16,000-year-old images in its vast Salon Noir are very much dominated by bison and horse, similar to the broadly contemporary images in Altamira's Polychrome Chamber and in style to the horses of Ekain (also in northern Spain) (PL. XXI). Panels of mixed horse and bison herds and individual ibex were painted within natural niches around the sides of the chamber, which could be illuminated in such a way as to ensure they stood out, animated in the flickering light, in a sea of blackness.

I can't help thinking that the animals that cavort around the walls of the Magdalenian caves were those that were dominant in the region. Some regions were horse country, others bison or ibex. Perhaps the caves were in some way totemic, locations linked to the spirits of these animals and therefore places in which it was right to celebrate their creation and perhaps to atone for hunting them in their traditional grounds. We don't know if access to the caves was restricted or open to all, or how frequently the average Magdalenian was able to create or view their marvels. But there was also much art that they would see routinely – art that, like them, was migratory; little landscapes carried around the steppes and perhaps which came and went like the animals themselves as decorated objects were gifted to others. Small, light, and often functional, the works of portable art to which we now turn depict the world of Palaeolithic *Homo sapiens* in exquisite detail.

Portable Landscapes

The shallow, gravelly river teems with life. A light snow has begun to fall and the cold is coming. Since first light the reindeer have been fording the shallow waters below the rockshelter. As the kindling in the hearth catches and spreads warmth in the dawn light, you observe the animals. The males are huge, sporting fine sets of antlers that are sharp and hard now that the velvet has fallen off them. Their nasal calls reach you through the thin air. The animals won't travel far – a day or two along the valley perhaps – but places like this are where they are most vulnerable, where you can intercept them. They are distracted, too; their antlers are heavy and cumbersome. They will make useful objects. There is much aggression in the air, as the males compete for mates. They tussle and lock antlers; some are injured already, easy picking with a well-aimed javelin. Or so you imagine as you turn the heavy object in your hands. *That time will come again.* You stand, returning the elaborately decorated spearthrower to your backpack, boots sinking into fresh snow as you climb up the plateau towards the white sky.

Art and imagination

In the paragraph above, I have tried to convey a sense of how engaging with a portable piece of art would have allowed its viewer to imagine a familiar scene at a distant time of year. In non-industrial societies (as well as in industrialized societies, of course), art is not simply for pleasure, but usually encodes meaning and information about social groups and the world that people inhabit. Images and scenes can be used to explore the world in the mind, triggering the memory, and in combination with songs and stories – the stock-in-trade of oral cultures – help to weave the cultural world and preserve critical knowledge needed for survival. As in the modern day, art was created at all scales, from impressive rock art down to decorated objects that could be carried and exchanged, as well as minute objects that adorned clothing

A 16,000-year-old river-fording scene engraved onto a cylindrical length of reindeer antler from Lortet Cave in the French Pyrenees. This image flattens out a scene that curves around the circumference of the antler: despite its great level of detail and naturalism, the object would need to be slowly turned around in order to view the whole scene.

and the body. The visual world formed a continuum from the fixed and large to the minute and portable.

We saw in Chapter 11 how the art in Portugal's Côa Valley linked the cliff faces to the portable stone plaquettes found amid the waste left at campsites beneath them. The themes and styles of the rock and portable art of the Côa and elsewhere are remarkably similar. It's as if the animals fell out of the rock face into the objects that could travel across the landscape like the animals themselves. But some objects were too large to carry, and are best seen as campsite furniture. Several Gravettian venuses were carved onto large rocks in the shelter of Laussel in the Dordogne, today displayed in Bordeaux's wonderful Musée d'Aquitaine. The site was excavated over a century ago and records are poor, but we know that two of these large and unwieldy blocks were decorated as they lay, some 2 m (6 ft) apart and close to the shelter's back wall, with a venus facing the wall on each. This

This Magdalenian high-relief carving of reindeer on antler from Montastruc (Dordogne, France) is often described as representing 'swimming reindeer', but probably renders a theme that was commonly depicted in art of the period where a male reindeer sniffs the rear of a female in mating behaviour. Note how the postures of the reindeer follow the natural outline of the antler; Magdalenian art often incorporated natural contours into its design.

A row of detailed horse heads was engraved onto this bone from the Mas d'Azil Cave in the French Pyrenees. The horse's beards were represented using a number of delicately incised parallel lines, as was the mane of the right-hand horse. The eyes have been engraved in an angular, lozenge-like shape, a very Magdalenian characteristic. Note how the mouths are depicted with drooping lips, as well as the line that demarcates the fur of the mouth and nostrils.

was perhaps a private space, seen only by walking to the back of the shelter and facing out: a little sanctuary perhaps. The low reliefs on the Laussel blocks link the bison-women on the walls of caves such as Pech Merle to the portable venuses tucked away in caves and buried in pits. Like prey animals they, too, could stay hidden in the caves and shelters and be carried around with the group.

Portable art reached its peak between 16,000 and 13,000 years ago, when iconic art forms were widespread. As we've seen, stone plaquettes used for constructing hearths and as work surfaces were engraved and painted with highly detailed animal outlines. Circular bone and stone ring objects called rondelles bearing engraved animals were probably attached to clothing and other items of hide and fur. Impact-absorbing spear shafts called *baguettes*, bearing deeply incised curvilinear decoration, were formed by sticking two half-circular sectioned rods of reindeer antler together with mastic. In Spain, doe heads were engraved on bones and cave walls; sculpted antler spearthrower crooks provided a decorative weight to thrown weapon systems; and outlines of horse, deer, chamois and ibex heads were cut out of thin, flat bone. Other bones bore complex codes of information in the form of groupings of incised lines. In some cases it's clear to us that these objects were sewn onto clothing. Other art forms were used to decorate objects that had a physical function, such as the enigmatic perforated batons of reindeer antler, and some objects seem to have been produced as art objects in their own right (see PL. XVII). Whatever the case, they were a constant celebration of the world of the hunter's prey.

Delivering life and death

We can see how function and observation were put together and carved onto objects between 16,000 and 14,000 years ago. In the Pyrenees, reindeer antlers were carved into triangular weights that could be secured to the ends of spearthrowers. The triangular parts of the antler lent themselves to the depiction of prey animals whose legs could be brought together and whose heads may be turning back to lick their flanks or call a mate, like the Lortet reindeer illustrated on p. 205. Bison, horses and mammoths were popular themes, but nothing was as popular as the *faon à l'oiseau* (fawn and bird), of which we have a number of examples. These take the form of a female red

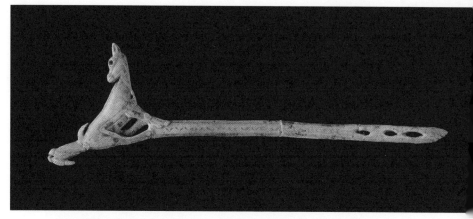

A complete *faon à l'oiseau* spearthrower carved from reindeer antler, from the Middle Magdalenian of Mas d'Azil Cave in the French Pyrenees. The open holes towards the base could hold straps of hide to secure the object to the wrist. The bases of the javelin would be secured in the crook created by the tail of the little bird perched on whatever is emerging from the doe's rear.

deer with its head turned to watch a large object emerging from its rear, on which perches a bird. Sometimes these have been (incorrectly) seen as a 'bird and turd' theme and marketed as the earliest preserved rude joke. In this interpretation the bird perches on the turd. But unless these deer were very ill indeed, their turds would be small pellets, so this cannot be the case. Instead, these seem to depict a scene that can still be witnessed today. When deer give birth, their newborn are usually still within their cauls (or amniotic sacs), and corvids will descend to feed on the cauls as they are discarded (or in some cases on the newborn too). It seems far more likely that the *faon à l'oiseau* motif reflects a common observation in Palaeolithic art, the creation of new life. The doe turns to watch the newborn emerge, just as the crow lands; will it eat the caul or the helpless calf?

The *faon à l'oiseau* theme presumably reflects an enduring story among the Magdalenians, perhaps associated with the vagaries of life and death. No wonder that so much time and skill was put into creating these spearthrowers. A small piece of amber still adheres to the eye socket of an example from Bédeilhac Cave in the French Pyrenees. Amber was an exceptionally rare material in the Palaeolithic, but it may be significant that its use also appeared around this time far to the east, in the Mezinian, as we've seen. Imagine how impressive a spearthrower of bright white, freshly carved antler would look, the doe's fur detailed in bright red ochre and her eye sparkling amber.

Chapter 14

I don't think it is a coincidence that the *faon à l'oiseau* combination only appears on spearthrowers. They are part of weapon systems designed to kill. If recent hunter-gatherers are good analogies, the Magdalenians would have sought ways to mitigate their destructive actions by ensuring that the animals they removed from the landscape – borrowed from it perhaps – were replaced by acts of creation. Here, we have creation and destruction together, in portable form.

Back to the body

I want to save discussion of a highly stylized way that Magdalenians depicted human women until we try to open up the Palaeolithic mind in Chapter 15. But we can focus down even further to the body itself. Depictions of humans are remarkably rare in Palaeolithic art. Perhaps there was a taboo against the creation of human imagery, or perhaps it was simply deemed unnecessary to depict humans as they were already participating in these landscapes, whether writ large in caves or in miniature on objects. Most examples we have are odd, as we shall see later. Let's pay two visits as we head back in time, first to a couple of Magdalenians, then to a Gravettian lady. They'll fix our attention back on people again, on our *Homo sapiens* ancestors.

Barely 3.6 cm (1.4 in.) in height, the 'Dame de Brassempouy' is one of a small number of human (or humanoid) sculptures of mammoth ivory recovered in 27,000- to 28,000-year-old levels of the Grotte du Pape at Brassempouy in Landes, France. The deep incisions of the head and rear neck could represent curled or braided hair, or a hood or other headpiece. She is broken at the neck, so we don't know whether she was part of a complete 'venus' or connected to a functional object. She is one of the few depictions of a human face we have from the Palaeolithic, and perhaps was even a portrait, if it's not anachronistic to use that term here. Are we staring at the face of a Gravettian?

Another human depiction is the so-called 'amorous pursuit', which is one of a rich set of engravings on bone from a 15,000- to 16,000-year-old occupation level in Isturitz Cave in the French Pyrenees. The cave where it was found was clearly important and repeatedly visited. Painted, engraved and sculpted art adorns its walls, and a number of portable art objects had been left behind when its

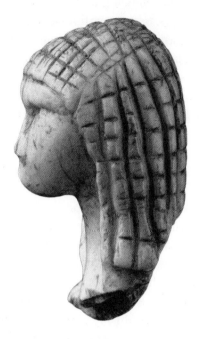

The exquisite 'Dame de Brassempouy' was carved out of ivory 27,000–28,000 years ago. She is one of the few depictions of a human face we have from the Palaeolithic, and perhaps was even a portrait. Are we face-to-face with a real person here?

The 15,000- to 16,000-year-old 'amorous pursuit' engraving from Isturitz Cave in the French Pyrenees. Note the depiction of what we assume to be necklaces, armlets and anklets, and the fletched-projectile-like 'non-figurative sign' on the thigh of the right individual. Note also the pairs of parallel lines engraved on the edge of the bone between the two individuals; these presumably recorded information now lost to us.

occupants moved on. The amorous pursuit clearly depicts humans, but it follows a typical theme of the animal depictions of the period, in which one animal follows a second. In the case of animals, such as Montastruc's reindeer, this reflects mating activity, hence the name of this piece. It's not only in their apparent behaviour that the two humans are animal-like; the outline of the left human's head and the *pointillé* dots used to depict body hair on the thighs, belly and back of the right human are created in the same way as on engravings of lions on other bones from the cave. Some characteristics are more human: the *pointillé* lines of hair hang down the head like those engraved in deep lines on the head of the Dame de Brassempouy – again, presumably long hair or a headdress of some form. But the two humans also display the unmistakable signs of society in the form of necklaces, armlets and anklets. One has a fletched-projectile-like 'non-figurative sign' on his thigh (I assume the figure is male). Similar motifs are found inside the profiles of animals in cave art, where they are usually interpreted as javelins 'killing' the animals. Could the same be said here, or is it a painted, scarred or tattooed design? Either way, perhaps the killing weapon that our *Homo sapiens* ancestors were critically dependent on for subsistence and survival was one of the most powerful cultural symbols of the time.

Return to the animal world

Most of us have seashells in our homes, however far from the sea we live. They may be strung into necklaces, displayed in jars, or holding soap in the bathroom, and they probably invoke memories of rainy holidays in Cornwall or hot ones in Corfu. When we're walking on the beach, it's difficult not to pick the beautiful little things up. We know they are the remains of houses once borne by shellfish, but that doesn't put us off of our somewhat morbid collecting habits. When we pick up shells as souvenirs we are, in fact, participating in one of the oldest documented uses of natural materials for their aesthetic properties we have evidence for. Early humans living near coasts have long appreciated the nutritional benefits of shellfish, which can often be easily gathered. As far back as half a million years ago *Homo erectus* was eating shellfish at Trinil on Java, where someone scratched irregular zigzags on one shell, one of the first examples of deliberate marking we have. Fast-forward 400,000 years and early *Homo sapiens* groups were being very selective in the shells they chose to colour, pierce and string as jewelry. The earliest widespread evidence spans the continent of Africa and Western Asia, and it was shell jewelry that spread with pioneering groups as they dispersed into Asia and Europe after 50,000 years ago.

We have a rich ethnography of shell jewelry, which shows how, across the world, carefully crafted necklaces, armlets, anklets and patterned adornments on clothing were prized and exchanged. In the 1920s the father of modern anthropology, Bronisław Malinowski, documented a complex exchange system of shell jewelry among the Trobriand Islands of Papua New Guinea. In this Kula Ring, as it was called, participants would canoe hundreds of miles, exchanging red shell jewelry in one direction and white shell jewelry in another. These *Argonauts of the Western Pacific*, as Malinowski entitled his 1922 magnum opus on them, linked together thousands of individuals through a complex exchange network, in which power could be established and maintained and obligations could be created and satisfied. We can see how attractive shells formed one of the earliest ways in which *Homo sapiens* could cement together a far-flung and mobile society.

Jewelry could express power too, particularly in the form of carnivore canines. Across the whole of the European Upper Palaeolithic, out of all of the available animal teeth that could have been worked, worn and exchanged, only a very few types were repeatedly selected. Canines of the wily fox, red or arctic, were carefully pierced for stringing in large numbers onto hats, clothes and necklaces; bear and lion canines in fewer number reminded the wearer of the largest and most dangerous predators; and while deer teeth were commonly used, it was not their chewing teeth but their relict canines that were preferred. This was a jewelry of strength and power, worn close to the body.

Personal ornaments were commonplace across Europe and the Near East back in the Aurignacian, whether shell or tooth. Through a meticulous study of the ornaments of tooth and shell available across Europe, my colleagues Francesco d'Errico and Marian Vanhaeren, two leading experts on Palaeolithic jewelry and art, were able to show how distinct regions of Aurignacian Europe had preferred shell and teeth types; they were essentially regional variations on similar – but not identical – themes. Francesco and Marian suggest, very plausibly, that these styles relate to the early emergence of what they

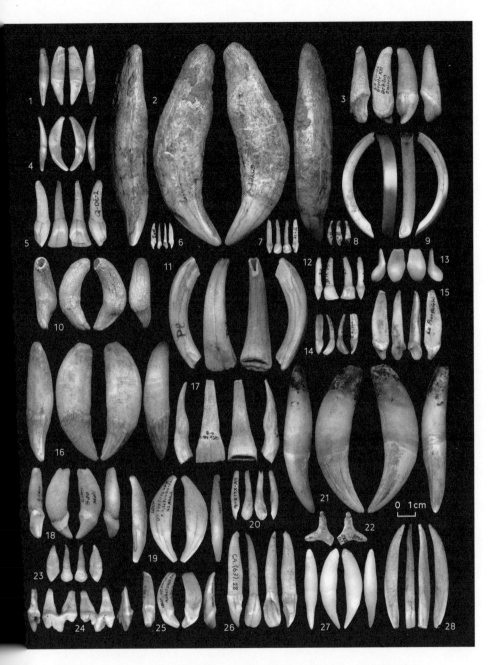

Bits of bodies worn on the body: Aurignacian teeth ornaments (which are usually carnivore canines). 1) badger canine; 2) bear canine; 3) bear incisor; 4) fox canine; 5) bovid incisor; 6) fox incisor; 7) reindeer incisor; 8) reindeer canine; 9) beaver incisor; 10) horse canine; 11) horse incisor; 12) fallow deer incisor; 13) red deer canine; 14) red deer incisor; 15) hyena incisor; 16) hyena canine; 17) horse decidual incisor; 18) lion incisor; 19) wolf canine; 20) ibex incisor; 21) lion canine; 22) shark tooth; 23) human tooth; 24) wolf molar; 25) wolf incisor; 26) moose incisor; 27) lynx canine; 28) wild boar incisor.

call 'ethnolinguistic' variation in Europe. They point out that there is often a strong correlation between what languages groups speak and the types of clothing they wear. Think of it as national language and dress in the same way that the British can be caricatured as bowler-hat wearers and the French as beret-clad. Whether or not this suggests that Aurignacians were already speaking different languages across Europe, it does show that, by 37,000 years ago or earlier, *Homo sapiens* groups were able to think of themselves both as broadly similar yet socially distinct from neighbouring groups. Social identity was emerging, and visual culture was being used as a useful expression of that identity.

When we think of the art that fortuitously survives in the protective microclimates of deep caves, and carved and pecked into hard rocks away from the destructive climates of the north, it's impossible to escape the conclusion that, as with the modern world, Upper Palaeolithic *Homo sapiens* lived in an elaborately visual world rich in symbolism and information. Life was becoming increasingly focused on society, and on the biographies of people and of the objects they exchanged between themselves. The references might always have been to the wilderness, specifically to the prey on which humans were dependent for survival, but they acted as repositories of information and as prompts for memory and storytelling; they provided opportunities for gift-giving and alliance; and they offered repeated reassurances that things were as they should be. But now we must put our spearthrowers down, close our eyes, and try to get inside the most elusive part of our *Homo sapiens* ancestors' bodies: their minds.

Chapter 15

The Mind

The Chipewyan hunter-gatherers of Canada believed that all animals and humans had their origins in the sexual union of a woman and a dog. The woman was alone on Earth, and having tired of eating only berries went out searching for other food, but found the animal. She took him back to her cave and the two grew ever closer. The animal was able to transform itself into the shape of a handsome young man, which it frequently did at night (that time of anxiety and transformations), always returning to its animal form before light, so the woman felt that the night's events were dreams. But they weren't, and soon the mother of the world was pregnant. At this point a man so tall his head reached the clouds was creating the rivers and lakes of the land, and took the dog, tore it to pieces, and threw its parts into the lands and waters, commanding each to turn into fish, birds and land animals. He gave the woman the power to kill and eat these animals in abundance. He then disappeared back to the place he came from, never to return.

We are a remarkably imaginative species, and if you think the Chipewyan are inventive just think about the notion that a bearded old war god created the entire cosmos. Barely 200 years ago most people believed in demons, witchcraft, original sin, hell, and a host of other intangible phenomena that they believed had a direct effect on their lives. Even today, sophisticated urbanites believe in ghosts, gods, bad luck, karma, reincarnation and aliens. Ah, the wonders of the imagination! If these beliefs are all difficult enough to understand, how can we possibly hope to get into the minds of Ice Age hunter-gatherers?

The answer depends on the types of questions archaeologists ask of the data. If they are too specific (did they believe in an afterlife?) we'll never know the answers, but if we keep them more general we can arrive at some understanding of how our Pleistocene ancestors' thought processes may have worked and why they engaged in some apparently odd behaviours, such as defleshing their dead or creating artworks on the walls of deep caves. My purpose in this chapter is to convey a sense of how very different the minds of early *Homo sapiens* were from our own in the way they perceived the world and tried to understand the things they observed in it. We need to consider why we all pay such a huge metabolic cost for our brains; why animals are so central to our cultural lives; how we perceive ourselves and other people; and why we like to engage in repeated rituals time and again. In these behaviours – by no means an exclusive list – lies the heart of what it is to be human.

Why such large brains?

We saw in Chapter 1 how metabolically expensive the brains of *Homo sapiens* are, and it is in the wiring and connectivity of our neurons that the secret to what distinguishes us from our nearest primate cousins will be found. Over the course of the evolution of the genus *Homo*, some of this related to improved working memory and ability to reason, and coordination, dexterity and tool manipulation. But it doesn't stop there. What really seems to have driven the evolution of Neanderthal and *Homo sapiens* brains, far in excess of what one would predict based on their body size, was the need to think in increasingly complex social ways. The larger the brain, the bigger the social group. The more capable the brain is of running through hypothetical scenarios based on increased knowledge about the world and particularly *other people*, the more complex society can be. The cognitive evolution of *Homo sapiens* probably involved the development of a mental dialogue along these lines, essentially an internal theatre in which we can play out the potential ramifications of our actions before we commit to them. We've evolved a pretty sophisticated theory of mind, in which we draw on memory based on experience and communication to *imagine* the motives, opinions, emotional states and most importantly manipulability of our kin.

At some point a symbolic system arose in which we could communicate ever more sophisticated information about the world. With language – speech structured with grammar and tense so we can refer to the past and make inferences about the future – even expert knowledge can be shared and passed down the generations. Innovations could spread more quickly, decisions essential for survival could be made with less risk, and learning that would otherwise require time and observation could be done with chat and song around the campfire as tools and clothing were repaired. Our dextrous hands, in combination with a powerful imagination, created objects that themselves carried meaning and information, providing a means external to the brain in which to preserve and communicate culture.

The two examiners of my doctoral thesis, Clive Gamble and John Gowlett of Southampton and Liverpool Universities respectively, teamed up with the evolutionary psychologist Robin Dunbar to synthesize what we know about how the uniquely social brain of *Homo sapiens* evolved. To them, the foundations laid by archaic members of the genus *Homo*, who developed technology, fire-use, cooking and the harnessing of the emotions through music and dance, were amplified considerably by our large-brained ancestors. The behaviours we've seen – the long-distance exchange, art and ornamentation, burials and, as we'll observe, rituals – were integral elements of moving towards living in societies far larger than one would predict from our primate heritage, and far more complex than our archaic ancestors had achieved. Social cognition is metabolically expensive, and as social networks grew in scale over the course of the last 100,000 years, the amount of 'strain on the brain', as Clive, John and Robin put it, increased as we became uniquely human. Larger brains went hand in hand with increasing social complexity. But that doesn't mean we left our animal past behind. Far from it.

The animal inside us all

We are still prisoners of our Pleistocene evolution as hunter-gatherers. Animals are central to our cultural worlds. Our imaginative creations, entertainments and aesthetics are dominated by animals and human-like animals. In fact, talking, human-like animals, such as breakfast cereal-loving tigers, sell things to humans far better than humans can themselves, however persuasive we think we are.[1] Just as the configuration of our bodies derives from the demands of our evolutionary past, the wiring of our brains reflects the fact that most of our existence was spent as hunter-gatherers dependent for survival largely on the procurement of animal prey.

Our very psychology has been shaped by the wild animals that we ate, with which we competed for resources critical to survival as our brains evolved, and which occasionally ate us. Our Pleistocene ancestors would have been aware that they were dependent on nature's bounty: the annual replenishment of the herds, and their predictable location in the landscape. Prey animals are good to think with; the horses, bison and other animals we've seen cavorting about the walls of caves and giving birth on spearthrowers allowed Pleistocene *Homo sapiens* to keep up a constant discussion about the world and how they fitted into it, reassuring them that they would be born into the world repeatedly in the natural order of things (see PL. XXIII).

Beyond monitoring and killing prey we don't yet know how close interaction with some herbivores was. Were reindeer or horses herded by Magdalenians? Towards the end of the Pleistocene, increasingly sedentary hunter-gatherers began to evolve close relationships with wild animals (and plants) that soon resulted in various degrees of their (and our) domestication. We will return to this in the final chapter. Wherever our evolutionary course has taken us, we've never escaped our animal origins (and that's without even beginning to discuss our love for cats and dogs). It's no surprise that from its beginnings, human art was dominated by wild animals. As we've seen, depictions of humans are remarkably rare. It may have been that there was no need to depict them amid animal scenes because, as in modern installation art, the live humans were already there, participating in the little animated shows. But it is noticeable that the relatively few examples of humans (or human-like beings; we tend to assume but don't know that human-like figures were really meant to depict real people) in Palaeolithic art are odd and animal-like. Far from emphasizing the human, cultural world, they seem to remind the viewer that there is no fixed boundary between what is human and what is animal. We enter a world of shape-shifters, sorcerers and wounded people, blurring the distinction between us and our prey.

In the modern world, we have somewhat contradictory views about animals, and I think these derive from the fact that we still haven't managed to distinguish ourselves from them completely. It certainly suits us to maintain an imaginary relationship with them. In my garden I wage a continual war with a clever, respectable enemy; to me, the squirrels who forage too aggressively at the bird feeder have personalities, strategies and emotions. Squirrels can be cute characters in children's stories, the sources of tail decorations for parkas, they can be food, or simply vermin. Think about the cute little lambs we enjoy watching frolicking in the fields, then go home to eat. The fish we keep for pleasure and the fish we eat.

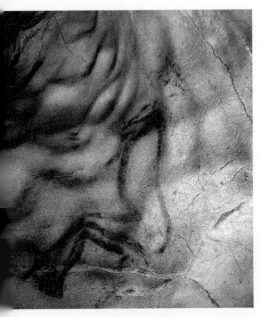
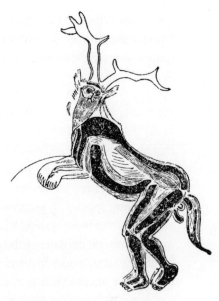

A 15,000-year-old part-human, part-animal image drawn on the wall of Trois Frères Cave in the French Pyrenees. Its limbs are distinctly human and its face shown frontally, which is otherwise exceptionally rare in Palaeolithic art. Its posture is bent, arms held out almost in imitation of an animal brandishing its claws.

Our relationships with animals are in fact some of the most complex we have evolved, tied up in our cultural worlds in ever more convoluted ways. Many of us believe – omnivores among us at least – that it is acceptable to kill herbivores to eat, but wrong to mistreat them unnecessarily; or that 'organic' meat is more acceptable because the animal has led as much of a natural, suffering-free life as possible before being (prematurely) killed.

This view closely mirrors the mindset of hunter-gatherers worldwide. Hunter-gatherers don't believe in any hard and fast distinction between humans and animals. They are all part of the natural world, and are all connected in spirit. Hunter-gatherers talk not of killing animals but of 'borrowing' them from the spirits; and in the spirit of gift exchange, they assume an obligation to pay nature back for the animal that the world has provided for them. The artistic celebrations of their prey could well have been produced as part of the ritual acts that repaid the debts incurred in the places where rebirth could be helped along. This relationship between animals and humans, who act both as executioners and spiritual midwives, can lead to totemism, which at its broadest can be regarded as a near-universal ritual expression of the interdependence of human societies and nature. It is a fundamental way of being in the world.

The visual world

Humans are visual animals. Over half of our cerebral cortex is dedicated to seeing the world, and 90 per cent of information about our surroundings derives from our eyes. We can safely assume that, as the same species, at least the more fundamental, low-level aspects of the brain's visual system, those used to detect particular stimuli, to discriminate between different types of subjects, and to establish viewing patterns and directions and the like, were the same in our Pleistocene ancestors as they are today. This means that we can use modern psychological methods to investigate the psychology of Palaeolithic visual culture. We experience the world as an abundance of colour (in reality wavelengths of light reflected or emitted by objects), which was important over the course of our evolution as diurnal animals who needed to distinguish ripe from unripe fruit, edible leaves from dead ones, and prey animals from their background landscape.

Psychologists have demonstrated a number of ways in which the way we see the world derives from the way our brains have evolved. The brain has developed a kind of computational shorthand – rules of thumb – to arrive at an estimate of what the world is at any given moment. A typical scene (say looking out of my study window as I'm doing now) requires the computation of vast amounts of information. Even in greyscale the amount of information processed by the visual system from two eyes would be enough to fill a 120-gigabyte hard drive in fifteen seconds. So the brain has evolved shortcuts, in which it forms a representative sample of reality rather than a precise and detailed reproduction. As this is very much an interpretative and evaluative process, evolution has made a strong contribution to what exactly the visual system decides is important in the model it presents to us about the world. A Palaeolithic hunter must be able to *detect* prey at some distance in the landscape, and to *discriminate* between different species. Our brains have evolved as Pleistocene hunter-gatherers, and they are obviously good at what they do – if they weren't we wouldn't be here – but they're not infallible. In some circumstances the assumptions our brains make are wrong, particularly when they make rapid, 'hair-trigger' assessments of things that turn out to be incorrect. It's easy to see why snap decisions would have been evolutionarily useful: if your eyes see something that could be a rock or a hungry bear, a stick or a poisonous snake, it's best to act quickly, erring on the side of caution, and have the visual system shout 'danger!', rather than calmly reporting 'it's probably just a rock or twig'. The visual brain can therefore be tricked; we are particularly susceptible to pareidolia, where we ascribe meaning to otherwise natural shapes. Think of those pet dogs you've seen in the clouds, or the face of the Virgin Mary in a sliced tomato. The brain's shorthand also makes us good at synecdoche, where we can easily recognize a subject even if it is incomplete, as the brain is adept at filling in the gaps, just like those incomplete drawings of animals we've seen on cave walls.

A few years back, I teamed up with Durham University's Professor of Visual Psychology, Bob Kentridge, to develop ways to research the visual psychology that underpinned the origins of art in *Homo sapiens*. It was just the sort of social and cultural connection that the human brain has evolved to support. We have a thriving research group, some of whom I've mentioned already, and we use virtual reality, eye- and body-tracking to investigate exactly why Palaeolithic

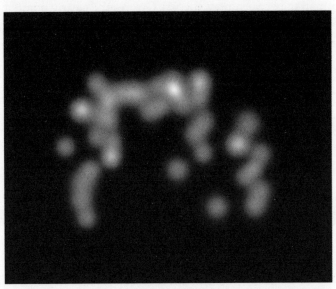

A classification image for participants' discrimination of horses using the *Bubbles* visual psychology experimental programme. Our photo of a Przewalski's horse faces to the right, its head to the floor grazing. The experiment is designed to ascertain what parts of an animal are most important to its identification.

images took the form they did and how the natural world was shaping them through the filter of the brain. We can measure what parts of an image or object attracts the eyes first, and what parts they dwell on longest, and we have many examples where this selective attention was exaggerated in art. Think of the Gravettian venuses and animal depictions with heads too small for their bodies, for example. We were most interested in whether the way that animals were depicted reflected the minimal amounts of information that the brain required in order to identify the real thing in the landscape.

To do this, we headed to the Scottish Highlands with Lisa-Elen Meyering to take profile (side-on) photographs of bison and Przewalski's horse. We then imported them into a visual psychology programme called *Bubbles*, which presents little bits of the animals' outlines to participants in random order. These 'bubbles' (actually called Gaussian windows) sample random sections of the animal images, which can be flipped so they face left and right, and can be modified throughout the experiment depending on participants' performance. With each little window they are asked whether they identify the contents as part of a horse or a bison. Resulting heat maps reveal which body parts scored the greatest number of correct identifications, and thus which were the most useful parts for discriminating between prey species. Our results clearly pointed to the overwhelming importance of the head, neck and chest, exactly those parts of the animal that are always (sometimes only) depicted,

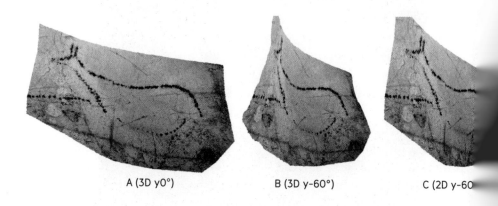

A (3D y0°)   B (3D y-60°)   C (2D y-60

Red deer drawn around 21,000 years ago in red pigment in Covalanas Cave (Cantabria, Spain). The three images show its appearance to a viewer directly in front (left) and at sixty degrees to the left (centre) and right (right). Although various flat surfaces were available in the cave, the image was deliberately placed in a concave depression in order to convey a sense of movement.

In our visual palaeopsychology research group at Durham, doctoral researcher Izzy Wisher imported three-dimensional images of art from Spain's El Castillo Cave into a virtual cave, in order to conduct visual psychological experiments. By giving the participants a virtual torch, we can ask them to move around the cave, tracking where their eyes fall as they do.

which receive the greatest attention to detail, and which, as we've seen, can even be represented at a scale apparently different from the bodies they are joined to. Perhaps it was inevitable that when figurative art appeared it was dominated by animals, which were usually incomplete aside from heads and chests.

We can also tell how the natural shapes of things – the lumps and bumps of cave walls for example – not only stimulated art but also were actively incorporated into it. Images were often fitted onto and around parts of cave walls, such as the bison that drip down from the ceiling bosses of Altamira. My colleague Derek Hodgson has developed a number of highly plausible scenarios for how our pareidolia and related mental processes can account for much of our species' earliest art, and we wanted to put these to the scientific test. A doctoral student, Takashi Sakamoto, manipulated three-dimensional photogrammetric maps he had created of Spanish cave art to simulate how the viewpoint and lighting affected the animal depicted. In a number of cases he was able to show how moving backwards and forwards in front of images caused them to change shape in the same way as animals' bodies change as they are moving. In exaggerated form this occurs with anamorphosis, where foreshortened images that are unrecognizable in frontal view resolve when they are viewed from the side, a technique used in Renaissance art.[2]

Another inventive doctoral student, Izzy Wisher, took our experiments even further, importing three-dimensional images she took of cave art in Spain's El Castillo Cave into a virtual environment. She was able to simulate the lighting that would have been used in the Palaeolithic, and used a clever series of techniques designed to test whether it was inevitable that certain animals were created in certain places, an example of the cave effectively dictating what was made and where. Putting it all together, it seems inevitable that in its origins, human art focused on prey animals, and on specific parts of them, dictated by the natural shapes of the world that the brain read in terms of predators and prey. Art was perhaps not so much the work of innovative creative types expressing themselves, but an inevitable and highly constrained dialogue between humans and the natural world.

Human symbol

In the modern world we set clear limits between what is 'real' and what is imaginary, and although opinions vary on matters such as ghosts (surely a product of pareidolia), we are normally adept at categorizing things as natural and unnatural. But as we've seen, these categories can blur. Pets take on remarkably human-like personalities, shadows solidify into dead relatives, and horror tropes focus on liminal areas such as human-animal transformation (werewolves and aliens), the dead walking (vampires, zombies) and the fallacies of trying to create artificial life (Dr Frankenstein). Our everyday lives may be dictated by the natural, but our imaginative lives embrace the unnatural. Ask an aboriginal Australian about a human-like image on a rockshelter wall and they won't tell you it's an image of a human, they will tell you it is a human, who happened to leap up into the rock, there to reside.

Ambiguity is a useful way to get a message across without distracting the brain with superfluous information. Stylization – where the natural features of a subject are reduced to a recognizable minimum – was common in early works. For example, among the mammoths, horses and other animals engraved onto the stone plaquettes at the 16,000-year-old Gönnersdorf campsite are highly stylized forms of human females that were widely spread across the Magdalenian world, painted and engraved on cave walls (in France and Spain – and, as I've argued, in Britain's only example of Palaeolithic cave art at Creswell Crags), carved out of ivory, bone, jet and amber (Germany, Russia) and even knapped in flint (Poland). The Gönnersdorf-type female images adhere to a tight design: they lack heads and feet; usually lack arms (or if present just have stubs), often lack breasts, and instead focus on large buttocks in a profile that curves boomerang-like from the torso to the thighs. Most are singular, but some were paired, and the one group of four females that exists (with breasts) appears to show clothing as well as an infant in a carrying frame. Overall, as their excavator Gerhard Bosinski observed, they depict women with arms held high (hence not depicted), buttocks thrust out behind them, and bent knees; perhaps they are dancing.

My friends Sabine Gaudzinski-Windheuser and Olaf Jöris have noted how the three-dimensional carved Gravettian venus figurines

Two typical female images engraved on a Gönnersdorf stone plaquette, either representing two individuals (dancing perhaps?) or one individual turning around, again perhaps in a dance. Note that the lines depicting the back and chest simply come to a halt, as do those of the part of the leg shown below the knee. The omission of heads and feet was intentional.

The Mind

Over 400 images were engraved onto the schist plaquettes at Gönnersdorf. Although they are widespread across Europe, the site has yielded the most numerous examples of the highly stylized Gönnersdorf-type females. Here, four human (or human-like) females face right, one apparently carrying an infant in a carrying frame.

emphasize individuality (they are all different) even if they lack faces, whereas the two-dimensional Gönnersdorf females (which are all similar) deny it, emphasizing instead a highly stylized image of the female. If Olaf is correct in his plausible view that Gönnersdorf was a place where far-flung groups came together at specific times of the year – which we saw in Chapter 12 – then this is exactly the sort of image that would be a recognizable badge and reminder that everyone belonged to the same culture, irrespective of what faces and feet they had. It was all in the dance.

Ritual, magic and belief

Around 15,000 years ago, Magdalenians created art on the walls deep in the cave of La Garma in Cantabria, Spain. They also assembled small blocks of stone and lumps of stalactite into little circles. Some of these had carved bones within them, as if they were little shrines. In one, a bear's foot bone bore a beautifully lifelike carving of an aurochs. Under a low roof, perhaps with torchlight flickering off the sparkling stalactite circles in an otherwise impenetrably dark place, a lion pelt was laid in another little enclosure. The excavators, Pablo Arias and Roberto Ontañón, were able to infer the existence of the pelt through the examination of nine cutmarked lion phalanges that were found close together in the enclosure. The position of the cuts reveals that they resulted from the careful skinning of the animal, in such a way as to leave its claws on the pelt (in no different a manner from that still practised today). Perhaps the focus of the enclosure was the lion skin itself, or perhaps it provided an impressive lining for a deposit that has long since disappeared. It might possibly have been a particularly strange place to curl up and sleep (it's just about big enough), but why this deep in a cave?

We've already seen examples of behaviour that could not have related to prosaic matters, such as the mammoth-bone enclosures and pits of eastern Europe, the burial of a pair of hands and feet at Pavlov, and the selective burial of dead males and female figurines, not to mention the creation of art underground. At Chauvet Cave in the Ardèche, in addition to the remarkable art, cave bear bones were moved around and stacked upright and a cave bear skull was placed on a rock 'table' with a fire set next to it. In Duruthy in the French Pyrenees, a small carving of a kneeling horse leant against two horse skulls, each of which defined a little enclosure in which pendants of wolf teeth were placed. In a number of other caves, such as Isturitz and Enlène in the French Pyrenees, stalactites and stalagmites were deliberately broken, either to use their parts to make little structures or to ensure a certain dull ringing sounded when they were struck; and elsewhere, such as at Niaux, artists drew their images in chambers where sound was amplified and echoed. Clayey and calcite-rich cave muds were traced with fingers, kneaded and sculpted into images. Animal bones were carefully inserted into cracks in cave walls, probably as part of the activities that also included the creation of the art. And what do we make of a raven's head buried in a little pit at Gönnersdorf?

Pablo Arias has researched the evidence for Magdalenian rituals in caves, which are surprisingly common in the circum-Pyrenean region. In one, El Juyo, stone blocks were used to create a triangular area on the cave floor, within which a small pit was dug and filled with alternating layers of sand, coloured pigments, limpets, periwinkles and mussels, and the jaws and leg bones of red and roe deer, the latter still articulated, showing that they still had meat on them. Once the pit was full a low mound was built over it by continuing the heaping of sand and archaeological objects, and by ordering small cylinders of green, red and yellow sediment into a flower-like pattern. The whole structure was then sealed with clay and marked with a circle of small standing stones, and finally several intact sagaies were left there, probably as complete javelins. This was not unique; a second structure was created nearby. In other caves, similar objects were collected together, with focal points such as deer antlers, engraved stone plaquettes and horse teeth. In these dark and frightening places there was clearly a desire to create little spaces and populate them. It's a familiar ritual, a way to bring important things together and to exercise control over them. Pablo noted that they were often created right above archaeologically sterile sediments, which shows that they were part of the first use of the caves; he has suggested that they represent foundation rituals, ways to imbue a new place with cultural identity and to begin turning it into a familiar and protective place.

Ritual areas are usually kept relatively dark, in order to heighten the emotions, focus attention, and reinforce the feeling of liminality. A participant is in a place that is partly here, yet also partly of another realm (as Pablo notes, modern churches and temples are usually poorly lit). There is a joke that archaeologists describe as 'ritual' anything that they can't understand in a more prosaic way. This used to be the case, but we know enough about rituals to make sense of how the imaginary worlds of *Homo sapiens* influenced their activities. Behavioural psychologists in particular understand the importance of how the repetition of things in suggestive places – ritualized behaviours – can reassure, calm and reinforce social bonds between participants and remind them that all is well with the world: just think of all those rows of horses in Lascaux. We need to distinguish between behavioural rituals, which are prosaic in nature and often routine and familiar, and those that turn into the expression of supernatural belief, which we might call religious rituals. We all engage in them, and those that are particularly emotive may be taken up and shared among several individuals, and turned into something cultural. Whatever your views on religion, it's difficult to escape the fact that our rituals began with people's repeated habits and grew from there. When and where this transformation began in *Homo sapiens* is unclear, but we

An aurochs (wild cattle) engraved in low relief on the phalange (paw bone) of a bear found in a small circle of stones in the 15,000-year-old La Garma Cave (Cantabria, Spain). The image is complete, even though the viewer must turn the item to see all of it. Note how the curve of the horn has been fitted perfectly to the curve of the bone's articular surface at the top, an example of how natural shapes were linked to the shape of particular images.

0   2 cm

0   1 in.

Birds provided a useful source of food, bones and feathers at Gönnersdorf (top). The wing and claw bones of ravens have been recovered from the site, revealing the careful removal of wing feathers – to which they would still be attached – for decorative use. A single raven's head (bottom) was placed in the centre of one pit, alongside a perforated slate disk. As this doesn't seem to reflect the disposal of butchery waste it seems that its burial was deliberate, in this case the creation of a little space underground for the hiding away of these objects.

might assume it was in place as soon as repeated activities such as the Blombos Cave engraved ochres in southern Africa or the use of specific shells and teeth for jewelry had appeared.

At some point, habits combined with beliefs, and certainly by 31,000 years ago I think the behaviour of the Gravettians in life and death convincingly shows that some kind of belief was central to existence. As the psychologist Pascal Boyer has observed, we are all of us bound to believe. There is a price to pay for our over-imaginative minds that appeared over the course of the evolution of *Homo sapiens*, and it doesn't take much to turn those twig-snakes and rock-bears into spirits and sky gods. When self-aggrandizers realize that people can be manipulated by making reference to the supernatural, and that they can control secret knowledge or surplus food, then the scene is set for the emergence of the weird and wonderful civilizations we create and inhabit. But it's not just the living; among *Homo sapiens* groups the dead have their social lives too, as we will now see.

Chapter 16

The World of the Dead

I'd come to Vienna for one reason, and now that I was here all I could feel was sadness. I stood above them, the laboratory's lighting falling on the red-stained bones before me. They were curled up together, these two, as if they'd just fallen asleep. Their time on Earth was so brief, some 30,000 years ago. They were ten months old when death came to them, twins perhaps. Maybe the cold got them; maybe disease or malnutrition. A flat-bottomed pit was dug to lay them in, side-by-side, wrapped in shrouds coloured with red ochre. A string of mammoth ivory beads was placed with them, before a mammoth scapula was placed on top like a lid. There they lay, undisturbed, until archaeologists brought them to light in 2006, during the excavation of a Gravettian campsite at Krems-Wachtberg. So important were they that the graves were lifted intact. And here I was, paying my respects with their discoverers Christine Neugebauer-Maresch and Maria Teschler-Nicola in their final resting place, the Austrian Natural History Museum. Brief lives, living so long ago in a very different world. I'd never had a stronger reminder of the precariousness of our time on Earth than this.

Dust to dust

There are two extreme ways of dealing with the remains of the dead. They can be dismantled, their soft bits removed and hard bits kept around; or they can be collected together and hidden, perhaps in a recognizable place to which the living can return. We do this across the world today, whether in the form of cremation and ash scattering or burial in cemeteries and tombs. The way we interact with the dead says much about our attitudes to life, how best to die, and particularly what happens to us when we're dead. Archaeologically, it's burials that tell us most about these questions, as graves protect skeletons from destruction while the manner in which people have been laid to rest and the objects associated with them can tell us about how their deaths were viewed. We have not much more than a few hundred burials for the 300,000 years of the Pleistocene over which we evolved and dispersed across the world. Most of those come from early cemeteries that appeared around the Mediterranean as hunter-gatherers in North Africa, the Near East and perhaps in southern Europe were becoming more sedentary. Prior to 15,000 years ago, we have around 100. For such a long period this is a negligible amount; most of our *Homo sapiens* ancestors are dust. We have no idea how much or how little activity their deaths provoked or how people said goodbye to them. We have to wait for the Bronze Age before any thoughts on death were put into writing, so we must instead make inferences from the scant evidence that survives.

The examples that we have often reveal odd and even complicated funerary practice, but as the numbers are so low we can probably conclude that burial was practised only in exceptional circumstances. Another universal is that some deaths are 'good' and others 'bad'. This might sound strange, as all deaths are unpleasant, but consider how you would contrast the death of a ninety-five-year-old who passed away in their sleep with the death of a child after a painful battle with cancer or the senseless murder of a random person. Deaths that are unexpected, violent, early and inexplicable cause far more distress than those that, although saddening, come gradually and naturally. I think that this dichotomy explains many of the earliest burials we have, as we'll discover.

In the modern world our contact with the dead is usually clinical and limited. Deaths most often occur in hospitals and are controlled by medication, the body is cleaned and prepared by professionals rather than kin, and funerary practice is discreet. But these practices don't characterize what most non-industrial societies have done with their dead over the course of our evolution. As with the small-scale societies that Europeans encountered as they explored the world from the 15th century onwards, our *Homo sapiens* ancestors would have had a far more proximate and visceral experience of death than most of us experience, and we can expect that human cognitive evolution was universally associated with the experience of death.

It all begins with chemistry. Insects, fish and rodents avoid, cover or remove corpses of their own when the pheromones released in life cease to limit the production of necromones, the chemical signals of decay. The funerary behaviours that minimize our contact with these potential sources of illness and infection clearly have deep evolutionary roots, concerned with simple homeostasis, the maintenance of healthy living systems. With birds, cetaceans, proboscideans and primates, chemicals are complemented by visual, auditory and tactile clues that death has occurred, which probably explains why these and other vertebrates such as giraffes, otters and sea lions gather around, manipulate and even carry dead infants. The more socially complex a species is, the more variable its responses to death, and we can probably assume that the evolutionary development of funerary behaviour – when it became 'stronger and longer' – began among early vertebrates. Emotional responses such as confusion, anger and sadness provoke particular displays, calls and interactions with the body, as the living try to understand what has happened and try to renegotiate their social lives in the sudden absence of one of the group. The emotion we recognize as 'grief' probably originated through the investigation of corpses by animals whose brains told them that the dead should be animated but whose senses revealed otherwise; a cognitive contradiction that requires explaining. Monkeys and apes revisit the scenes of death of their conspecifics out of this quest to comprehend what has occurred, and from this would eventually come memory and commemoration. Death came to be associated with danger and uncertainty. To our ancestors, while it was an inevitable part of the cycle of creation and destruction, it could at least be mitigated with the correct practice. There were ways to deal with the spirits of the dead, just as much as the spirits of the animals, at least when the natural course of things was thrown out of order.

Caching and cannibalism

Around 160,000 years ago, at a lakeside at Herto in Ethiopia, our African ancestors knapped stone tools and used them to butcher hippopotami. When they moved on, they left the cranial remains of three humans scattered among the refuse: two adults and a juvenile. We don't know if they were from kin or enemies, but the presence of stone-tool cut- and scrape-marks on them reveals that they had been completely defleshed, and their smooth and polished state suggests that they had been carried around for some time prior to arrival at Herto. They are one of a number of defleshed human remains dotting the entirety of the evolutionary skeletal record that show the practice of dismantling and even consuming parts of the dead.

For mobile hunter-gatherers this might make sense; if a person can be reduced to a few light pieces – like relics – they can be kept with the group as it moves around the landscape. Or they can be consumed and assimilated into the bodies of the living. If you think this odd, consider that Christians remember Christ by consuming his body and blood, even if only symbolically.

Alongside practices of fragmentation we see glimpses of the use of the nooks and crannies of the world to tuck the dead away in; a process I call funerary caching. Neanderthals practised it on occasion, as probably earlier humans did too. Caves, shafts and fissures provided convenient opportunities to discreetly remove corpses from around the living, which could be remembered and revisited should it be felt necessary. By 100,000 years ago, if natural crevices weren't available, *Homo sapiens* and Neanderthals began to create their own funerary caches, by excavating shallow pits to place the dead in. While it was still exceptional, burial in graves probably arose out of the need for a hole in the ground, combined with the routine practice of digging shallow pits for other purposes, like setting hearths or obtaining stone

Around 40,000 years ago at Nazlet Khater in Egypt, two adults were laid in small pits that had been dug to obtain chert for knapping. One of these had a foetus/neonate placed near to its pelvis, suggesting a death during or after childbirth: a 'bad' death. The single burial of Nazlet Khater 2 (pictured) in a chert-extraction pit could have given rise to the idea of creating graves.

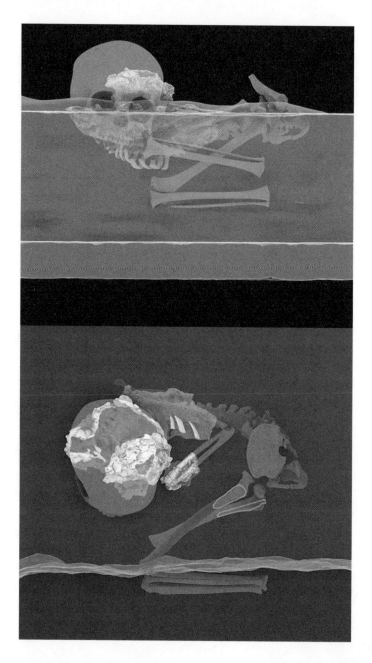

Nicknamed Mtoto (Swahili for 'child'), a two- to three-year-old was carefully laid to rest in a small pit in the cave of Panga ya Saidi in Kenya between 70,000 and 84,000 years ago. The flexed (contracted) position of the bones and close fit of the skeleton to the pit shows that it was deliberately excavated for the burial rather than repurposed. Infant bones are very fragile and the acids in soils can destroy some of them: the shaded diagram shows those that survived. The illustration opposite shows a virtual reconstruction of the burial after excavation and recording. It is, as yet, Africa's oldest human burial.

Chapter 16

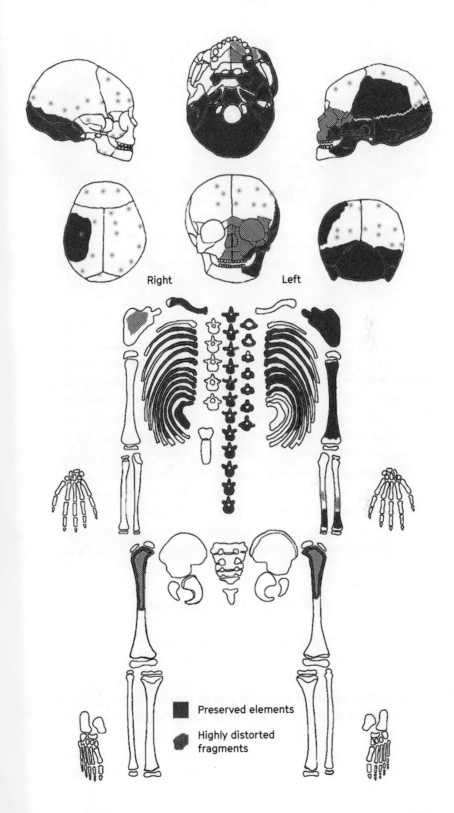

Right   Left

Preserved elements

Highly distorted
fragments

At least ten adults and infants were buried between 90,000 and 120,000 years ago in Qafzeh Cave near Nazareth, Israel. These included this adult (Burial 9), laid in a flexed position on its left side with hands in its lap, next to a six-year-old child (Burial 10), visible at the adult's feet.

for knapping. Between 100,000 and 50,000 years ago in Africa and the Near East, we have a couple of dozen examples.

At least ten adults and infants were buried in Qafzeh Cave in Israel between 90,000 and 120,000 years ago. One of the infants was lacking its feet, buried with an adult female, presumably its mother. The remains had been carefully laid in the grave, but the feet must have been deliberately removed from the rest of the corpse, for a reason we will never know.[1] Some of the burials had been placed in natural fissures as funerary caches, but others were laid in artificially excavated graves, some of which were marked by above-ground rocks. It's tempting to think that we have here evidence of one of the characteristic behaviours of *Homo sapiens* – burial – emerging out of its caching predecessor, as well as the need to memorize where the dead lie.

Bad deaths and ritual burials

I introduced the 'Red Lady of Paviland' in Chapter 9, and the mistaken notion that he was actually a she. This young adult male was the first Palaeolithic burial to be discovered (in 1823) and remains arguably the earliest of a number of simple burials we have in the Gravettian. We don't know how he died, but given his age we can assume it was accidental, and therefore a 'bad' death. He was buried in a shallow grave in a natural alcove to the side of the little cave. A complete mammoth cranium still bearing its tusks was found right by the

Chapter 16

burial: it couldn't have got up into the cave without being carried there; perhaps it served as the Ice Age equivalent of a gravestone. Thankfully for archaeology, the Red Lady was one of a rare number of individuals who were buried at the time, giving us a glimpse not only of burial practices but also of what the dead were wearing, at least when they were laid to rest. Staining on the Red Lady's bones – light ochre on the legs, darker on the torso and arms – suggests that he was wearing a two-piece combination of parka and leggings, both of which were brightly coloured, and these were probably ornamented with periwinkle shell jewelry. Several short rods carved from mammoth ivory had been broken and scattered above his chest, perhaps a ritual attempt to contain or disarm the disturbing power around the grave.

The Red Lady heralds 20,000 years of the European Upper Palaeolithic, for which we have around eighty burials. How most of the dead were treated is still unknown, but some patterns emerge from these occasional inhumations. They are usually single burials, but examples of double and in two cases triple burials are known (see PL. XXV). My colleague Enzo Formicola of Pisa University has studied their skeletons, showing how a large proportion of them had developmental or traumatic pathologies, which would have resulted in odd posture and locomotion and even pain, or else represented deaths during childbirth or through violence. He has perceptively shown how the number of incidences of major abnormalities and disabilities is far higher than one would expect in living groups, showing how those individuals who were buried were in some way unusual.

Enzo's work provides a key to understanding why burial arose in the European Upper Palaeolithic, perhaps even before (and he also makes great pasta). Thanks to his research I think we can make a convincing case for marking 'bad' deaths with burials from this time. We shouldn't think of these burials in the same way we think of burials in the modern world, where loved ones are tucked away to rest, but perhaps more as ritual containments that were practised to mitigate for sudden, untimely, violent or otherwise traumatic deaths. I've already noted how the treatment of Gravettian dead males parallels the treatment of female figurines, and if I'm right the evidence further suggests that by now, funerary practice was embedded in wider belief systems in which, perhaps, the spirits of the dead continued to exist after the body had been contained.

Further evidence of the wider belief systems that underpinned society at the time comes from Cussac Cave in the Dordogne, which snakes its way deep into the rock. The walls teem with engravings of horses, mammoths, bison and humanoids in typical Gravettian style, part of the introduction of life into dark caves some 28,000–30,000 years ago. But here, the dead were introduced too. It's one of a number of French caves in which the dead were placed around this time. The human remains are often scrappy and bear stone-tool cutmarks; clearly the dead were on occasion being defleshed deliberately or left to decay naturally before they were introduced into caves and rockshelters.

We've seen how Palaeolithic art was often concerned with creation, and this makes me wonder whether the deposition of the dead reflects an interest in rejuvenation or transitions to another world. Speculation of course, but the context of the human remains in Cussac suggests something complex like this. The cave also contained wallows – shallow pits dug by bears to hibernate in – and it's likely there was a deliberate association of the human dead with hibernating bears. The human remains were generally disarticulated, and in variable condition, although in places the preservation was excellent. Infrared spectrographic analysis of a white material found in the depressions

Around 29,000 years ago the corpse of an adult was laid face down in a bear hibernation hollow in Locus 2 of Cussac Cave (Dordogne, France). Of six adolescents and adults to be laid to rest in the cave, this is the only one which seems to have been deposited intact. The others appear to have been left to skeletonize elsewhere before being deposited in the hollows.

Chapter 16

showed that it was highly degraded human bone. Meticulous investigation of the scene (in no way dissimilar to that of a forensic crime scene) revealed that one depression was used to deposit the bones of the skull and teeth, whereas other parts of the body were placed in another depression, jumbled up and disconnected. In another, three adults and one adolescent were mixed together, including the bones of a hand still in anatomical connection, all lying beneath an impressive stalactite column on which two mammoths were engraved. Traces of red pigment around the outer edges of the hollow suggest that it was lined with coloured hides or that the remains had been carried there in a hide bag. But why the association with bears?

Anyone who has cats will know how they maintain their claws, by reaching up to a surface and letting their weight drag the claws down it. Cave bears were no different, and like the damaged furniture all cat lovers accept as inevitable, bears have left innumerable traces of their claw sharpening on cave walls. In Cussac, and a number of other French caves, humans obviously thought this significant, as they created their own finger traces on the walls right next to or on top of the claw marks. This cannot have been accidental. Clearly, their belief systems were connecting bears with both the living and the dead. Bear bones stained with ochre and canines worn as pendants are found on Gravettian sites across Europe.

Brown bears and cave bears shared the same environments and ate the same foods as humans. They can stand on their rear legs and use their hands as humans do, and their skeletons look human-like. Many non-industrial societies in circumpolar North America and Siberia see them as either humans in disguise or very closely related to humans, part of that blurring between the human and animal world that we looked at in the last chapter. Among the Siberian Khanty, bears are treated as intermediaries between humans and the spirit world. Were the dead placed in bear hollows in Cussac in order that they could journey to the spirit world like the bears? Or perhaps be reborn, just like bears coming out of winter hibernation?

Two triple burials

The red cliffs below the town of Grimaldi in Italy, close to the French border, formed the backdrop to Gravettian campsites and were on a number of occasions used to bury the dead. When I excavated there with Enzo Formicola and physical anthropologist Steve Churchill of Duke University, we would drop trowels in the late afternoon and walk the few metres to the sea, there to ease the day's muscle strains – in Steve's case by floating on the gentle waves with mirror shades and a huge cigar. Prior to our work, the burials of six adults had been excavated in Barma Grande Cave: five males and a female. Two males and a female had been buried separately, but three males were laid side-by-side in a collective grave. The first of the triple burial, an adolescent with a number of serious developmental pathologies, was laid on his left side in the centre of the grave cutting, with his head lying on an ochred bison femur. An adult male was then interred to the left, behind him, also on his left side and looking towards the adolescent. Finally, a third adolescent was buried to the right, laid on his back but looking away from the other two. The heads and torsos of all three were ochre-stained, and their remains suggest that they had been buried in coloured headgear and parkas ornamented with perforated seashells, fish vertebrae and deer canines. We don't know how they died, although the presence of adolescents and young adults who died close enough in time to be buried together suggests that it must have been a set of 'bad' deaths. Perhaps their very association in death reveals that their deaths were in some way connected.

Three males were laid together in a remarkably similar fashion at Dolní Věstonice in the Czech Republic. A congenitally deformed twenty-year-old male was laid in the centre on his back, facing to the right. His deformities had badly affected the proportion and symmetry of his limbs and his dental and pelvic morphology. He would have looked different and walked oddly. His pathologies are such that it was impossible to establish his sex on the basis of the usual skeletal traits osteoarchaeologists use, such as the shape of the pelvis. It is the derivation of his DNA from the XY (male) rather than XX (female) chromosome that established that he was the third male of the group. A seventeen- to nineteen-year-old male was laid at the grave's left, facing the central individual and stretching his hand over the latter's genital area. The third individual, a sixteen-year-old male, was placed to the right, face down and looking away from the others. The heads and torsos of the dead were ochre-stained, in the case of the head of the left-most adult so thickly that he must have been wearing a red headdress or mask. All three were ornamented with jewelry of arctic fox and wolf teeth, shells and carved mammoth ivory beads. The remains of carbonized branches suggest that the

Three males were buried together at Dolní Věstonice (Czech Republic)
around 29,000 years ago. From left to right, DV13 (seventeen to nineteen
years old at death), DV15 (twenty at death and highly pathological) and
DV14 (sixteen at death). DV13 looks towards the others, with his hand on
the pubic area of DV15; DV14 lies on his front, looking away from the others.

whole grave was covered by some kind of structure, which may have
been set alight.

The dental growth patterns of the 'Dolní Věstonice three' suggest
that they were fairly closely related, and the sequencing of their
mitochondrial and Y-chromosomal DNA showed that the pathological
central individual and the sixteen-year-old to which he turns had a
close maternal relationship, which is possibly reflected in the way
they lie close together and almost intertwined in death. The third
individual, who the other two are disengaged from, is more distantly
related to them. It's difficult to say whether the closest two were
brothers; in small-scale societies like theirs, levels of inbreeding are
usually relatively high, and with the low populations and restricted
movement of this harsh period we might expect individuals belonging
to the same group to be interbred to a degree.

The similarities between the Dolní Věstonice and Barma Grande
triple burials cannot be accidental. In each case a shallow grave large

enough to contain three burials was dug. It was obviously intended to bury three people of broadly similar age and relatively close relations together. In such small mobile groups it is unlikely that three young people should die of natural causes around the same time. Each grave is focused on a central individual, who happens to have had serious deformities probably from birth yet who had survived until adolescence and adulthood. In each case a second individual was placed closely to the central one, looking away from it, and a third to the other side, which – although looking and stretching towards the central individual – is nevertheless ignored by the other two. Does the position of the dead reveal something about their relationship in life? As we look at them, the left-hand male engages with the central figure, almost as if *wanting* to be part of the group. But it's the pair of the central and right-hand individuals who lie closer together and have a closer relationship, even though the right-hand figure looks away as if to disengage from the others. We will never know the back stories of these young people, but the triple burials at least reveal that belief systems as to how certain deaths should be treated with specific funerary practice were widespread and complex.

Fragments and collections

In the last few thousand years of the Pleistocene, things were changing. Particularly around the Mediterranean, hunter-gatherers became more sedentary, lived in larger numbers, and began to diversify the wild resources they hunted and gathered and put more effort into tending them. A more recognizably agricultural way of thinking was emerging, and the dead were part of this. Places were set aside specifically for disposing of the dead and, however small, cemeteries became commonplace.

But ancient practices continued. Around 21,000–22,000 years ago the occupants of Le Placard Cave in Charente, France, defleshed the remains of at least nine adults and nine children and adolescents. The bones of all parts of the body are present but the skulls of the adults and mandibles of the subadults are most common. This mortality curve is not what we would expect for natural deaths in non-industrial societies, where mortality among infants is high and in adolescence and adulthood it is low, only rising with old age.

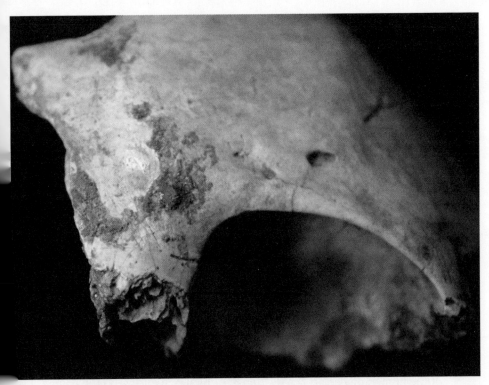

Around 14,500 years ago in Gough's Cave (UK), stone-tool cut- and smash-marks on the remains of at least four adults and one juvenile reveal that they were completely defleshed before their cranial vaults were removed from their facial bones and turned into skull cups. Exactly the same process was practised at Brillenhöhle (Germany) around the same time, and 6,000 years earlier at Le Placard Cave (France).

At Le Placard we have the opposite: an over-representation of adolescents and younger adults, which must surely have resulted from 'bad' deaths. The way their remains were treated suggests this could have been the result of inter-group violence; leg and arm bones were smashed open while still fresh, and the cranial bones were broken up. Over half of them bear marks left by the cutting and scraping of stone tools. Their positioning shows that heads were completely defleshed; cutmarks on the mandibular body show that jaws were carefully removed from the cranium, perhaps to wear as trophies, and other clusters of marks indicate the deliberate removal of eyes and ears. Finally, the cranial vaults were shaped into skull cups, a practice that is also attested several thousand years later in Germany and the UK. As I always remark ghoulishly to my students, if you're cannibalizing a corpse you need a container to drink the blood from.

Chapter 17

Into the Americas

While the Magdalenians were conducting their rituals in French and Spanish caves, *Homo sapiens* were well on their way in the last great dispersal of the Pleistocene. Native American societies are remarkably diverse, more so than many Eurasian traditional societies in fact, although as humans have been in the Americas for a far shorter time than in much of the rest of the world, much of that cultural evolution must have occurred after the Pleistocene. Now, after a century of controversy, genetics and archaeology are beginning to provide a consensus view of the arrival of Eurasian populations in the Americas.

The first human occupation of the Americas, similarly to that in Eurasia, is a story of repeated dispersals and subsequent diversification. In a sense we can see it as the post-Last Glacial Maximum continuation of the human dispersals across Eurasia, which as we've seen took people as far northeast as the Arctic coast of Siberia by 32,000 years ago. The tundra between Siberia and Alaska and beyond could be walked (or the coast canoed) as long as there was a route free of ice – this was during the period of much lower sea levels, when today's Bering Strait was a vast area of land known as Beringia that extended from Siberia to Alaska. Nowadays, specialists have a far more nuanced and critical view of the matter, thanks to carefully excavated Palaeoindian archaeological sites, a detailed understanding of the final deglaciation of the north, and a wealth of genetic data from living Native Americans, and from the bones of their Palaeoindian forebears.

Views of the dispersals into and around the Americas have been hampered by old notions that the continent was conquered by a blitzkrieg of hunters, first of mammoths around 13,000 years ago and later of bison, as well as attempts to break what became known as the 'Clovis Barrier', in which the earliest settlement of the continents was seen to have occurred no earlier than 13,000 years ago. The very origins of North American archaeology took the form of a progressive back-dating of the earliest known sites, first with the fluted points at Folsom (New Mexico), which were discovered in 1927 and were dated with the advent of radiocarbon to 12,500 years ago, then to Clovis

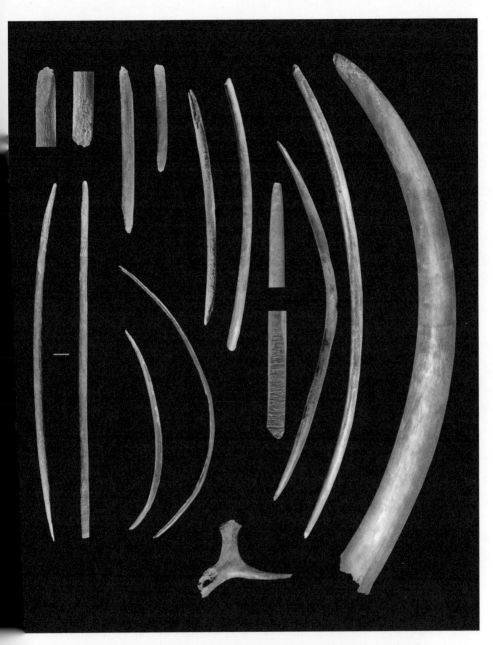

At Yana 32,000 years ago, Siberian hunter-gatherers hunted mammoth, bison, horse, reindeer and smaller animals like hare, and made artifacts such as these mammoth-ivory weapon tips. Siberian sites such as Yana were on the edge of the vast tundra of Beringia, and although the Yana River was probably the easternmost edge of human dispersal at the time, it was not long before hunters had moved further into the Beringian landbridge. A long period followed in which they were apparently restricted to Beringia, until opportunities were presented for dispersals further south into the Americas after 17,000 years ago.

Into the Americas

(also New Mexico), discovered in 1933 and dating to 13,500 years ago, and then to Monte Verde in Chile, where excavations in the 1970s and 1980s revealed a remarkable campsite that was abandoned around 14,600 years ago. These were fortuitous discoveries of course, but the sequence of their discovery added to the development of a desire to seek progressively earlier evidence of Homo sapiens dispersals.

Claims for a much older human presence than the consensus view holds are always ambiguous; well-dated collections of stones are perhaps not the deliberately knapped artifacts they are claimed to be. Nor are supposed cutmarks on animal bones convincingly the result of butchery rather than natural processes that can mimic them. We have a large, grey category of sites which *may* reveal humans in Idaho by 16,000 years ago; sites in high-altitude Mexico from around 30,000 years ago, and human footprints there 40,000 years ago; and purported evidence of mastodon butchery 130,000 years ago in California. But the arguments for these sites being genuine evidence of humans in the Americas at such early points are very unconvincing, and in time they will probably be quietly forgotten. Sensationalism aside, we do have a number of well-understood and well-dated sites that provide a reliable picture that complements the genetic evidence nicely. This is not to say that earlier sites will not appear, at least back perhaps to 17,000 years ago, but the candidates so far are to my mind far from persuasive. The situation improves after 16,000 years ago, but the story begins earlier. To pick it up we must return to Arctic Siberia, where mammoth hunters had established camps on the Yana River as early as 32,000 years ago.

What the genetics reveal

Sequencing of modern mtDNA and Y-chromosomal DNA has revealed that all indigenous people in the Americas descend from only five mitochondrial haplogroups and two paternal ones, all of which had originally derived from Asia but which had become isolated from it. This isolation probably occurred when some populations remained in eastern Beringia as others shrank back to the south when cold conditions brought a halt to their northern expansion. These people originated from the mammoth-hunting groups of Siberia, and although there is no direct link with the DNA sequenced from a Homo sapiens tooth from that region and time, this was certainly the region from which a small number of people began a major dispersal that created the human population of the entire Americas.

The lack of any Denisovan DNA in all Native Americans reinforces the conclusion that the human dispersal into the Americas occurred from the north, as the Denisovans did their interbreeding in the south of Asia, as we've seen. This also rules out the suggestion that French Solutreans dispersed around the Atlantic coast into the Americas, a brave and well-argued hypothesis based on similarities between Clovis tools dating to 13,000 years ago in North America and Solutrean tools

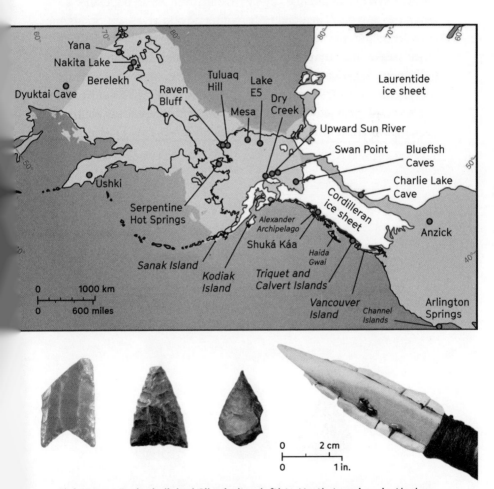

Pleistocene Beringia linked Siberia (top left) to North America via Alaska and Yukon. It was a vast tundra in its own right, harbouring human populations of varying sizes from around 32,000 years ago, as genetics reveal. The map shows important archaeological and geological sites of the Late Pleistocene. Bottom left and centre: Nenana Complex points. Bottom right: Dyuktai bone point with embedded stone microliths (reconstruction).

predating them by 8,000 years or so in France. Even without the DNA evidence, the theory has failed to convince archaeologists on either side of the pond; what its proponents need are well-dated archaeological sites of the right period containing these similar weapon tips, and in locations between the continents, which have so far failed to materialize.

To continue the genetic story: following the first dispersal of these lineages into the Americas, populations underwent a bottleneck, during which one group with very limited genetic variability gave rise to all modern populations. Genomic sequencing reveals that the ancestral group became largely isolated from Asian populations around 36,000 years ago, and fully so after 20,000 years ago. Sometime between 17,500 and 14,600 years ago – remember this is a genetic 'clock' based on assumptions about mutation rates – this earliest indigenous American population split into two groups. The Northern Native Americans (NNA) remained in the northern regions of North America and included the ancestors of modern Athabaskans, such as the Chipewyan, Cree and Ojibwa. The Southern Native Americans

In Alaska, Chindadn Points of the Nenana Complex (top) were replaced by the microblade cores of the succeeding Denali Complex (bottom) around 12,700 years ago.

Early human dispersals into the Americas. From a source population in Beringia, a dispersal southwards along the ecologically rich 'kelp highway' of the west coast or through a growing corridor between the melting Cordilleran and Laurentide ice sheets, which allowed passage after 16,000 years ago, led to human presence south of the ice by 15,500 years ago. By 14,000 years ago, groups had dispersed as far south as Argentina.

(SNA) dispersed further south and diversified, and were ancestral to the Amerindians of southern North America, Central and South America.

For archaeologists the genetic 'dating' couldn't be more important, as it provides a maximum age for the first arrival of people south of the North American ice sheets. If any of those claims for much earlier human activity in North America are to be believed, they would need to derive from a very different source population that has not yet been sampled genetically, and represent a dispersal that was ultimately unsuccessful and donated no genes to subsequent Palaeoindians.

The picture is complemented by the genetics of the first American dogs – to which we will return in the next chapter – who split from their Siberian ancestors sometime between 17,000 and 13,600 years ago. As they were domesticated by humans and dispersed with them, this forms important collaborative evidence. Genetic variation among indigenous South Americans reveals that once the northern part of this continent was reached, the dispersal split into two branches, one down the Pacific coast and one down the Atlantic.

So in the consensus view the 'when' is fairly unequivocal – nothing significantly older than 17,000 years ago – but the 'where' is still unclear. There are several potential routes that the earliest Palaeoindians could have taken. They might have moved down the Pacific coast, or through the interior, moving southwards in linear fashion or in something more akin to a multidirectional star shape. One possible route is along the extensive forests of kelp which today stretch along the north Pacific from Japan through the Aleutian

Palaeoindian specialist Mike Waters of Texas A&M University (right) and Morgan Smith examining a pre-Clovis stone knife fragment around 14,550 years old from Page-Ladson in Florida. This bifacially worked point is one of the oldest securely dated human artifacts in the Americas.

Chapter 17

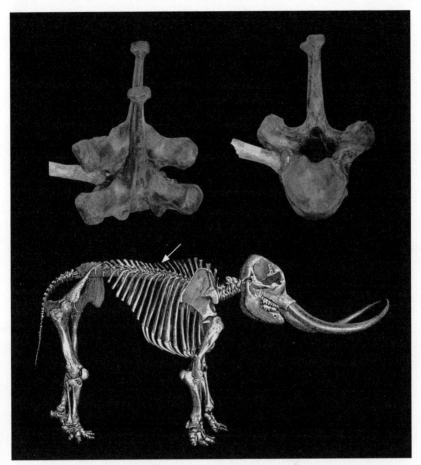

At Manis (Washington State, USA), a mastodon (*Mammut americanum*) came to rest in the bottom of a small lake 13,800 years ago. Some of its bones had marks left by butchery with stone tools, and the pictured vertebra has a fragment of a weapon tip carved from bone embedded in it. Manis is one of a small number of sites showing that Palaeoindians exploited megafauna before a supposed 'Clovis blitzkrieg' 800 years later.

Islands of Alaska and down to Baja California. This is essentially a 10,000-km- (6,250-mile-) long ecosystem, rich in fish, shellfish, marine mammals and birds, and edible seaweeds, all near to coastal inland environments.

As with the earliest dispersal of *Homo sapiens* in Europe, a pattern is visible, but debatable weight given to single-dated sites can skew the picture considerably – such dates can be very misleading if they are accepted too uncritically. The situation was clearly complex; genomics also indicates that some Native American groups shared a faint genetic connection with the populations of Sahul (the greater Australian continent during the period of much lower sea levels) and the Andaman Islands in the Bay of Bengal, even if this should not be taken to indicate direct migration into the Americas from those areas, but rather input from a common ancestral population.

Beringia

In the Pleistocene, the ancestral Americans could walk from Yana to Alaska and beyond across Beringia, formed between Eurasia and Alaska by the lowered sea levels of the Ice Age. Prior to the arrival of Europeans, the coasts around the Bering Strait were the homeland of the Yup'ik, salmon and seal hunters related to their North American neighbours the Inuit and Iñupiat. However, their homeland bears only a slight resemblance to Beringia, which was a rich tundra with no modern analogue, teeming with mammoths, mastodons, caribou and a variety of smaller animals that could be hunted and trapped. American mastodons originated in Eurasia in coniferous forests, and when these were replaced by tundra in Beringia during a cold snap around 70,000 years ago, they dispersed southwards into the mid-latitude Americas, where they remained until they became extinct at the end of the Pleistocene. Humans weren't the only mammal to discover the Americas.

After 25,000 years ago, the proliferation of at least sixteen distinct maternal DNA lineages suggests that the human population of Beringia was relatively large. As conditions improved sometime after 16,000 years ago and the Laurentide and Cordilleran ice sheets that covered large parts of North America had melted back enough to allow passage further east and south, a big population expansion into the Americas followed, with dispersals across an expanding Beringian tundra.

Around 14,000 years ago, a number of archaeological sites in Beringia – today located in northwestern Alaska – reveal the presence of groups who used weapons of bone tipped with stone microliths, a design that originated in Central Siberia a few thousand years before. These seem to have been replaced across Beringia around 13,800 years ago by groups using teardrop-shaped points, which in Alaska are referred to as the Nenana Complex, lasting until around 12,700 years ago.

Native American DNA reveals a large population expansion radiating through the Americas between 16,000 and 12,000 years ago. This happens to be the period in which the earliest unproblematic archaeological sites are found. The archaeology reveals a major population expansion at this time, with teardrop-shaped and stemmed weapon tips found across Beringia between 13,800 and 14,900 years ago that also disperse as far south as Southern California and the southern tip of South America by 13,000 years ago.

South of the Ice

The earliest unequivocal archaeological evidence for *Homo sapiens* in the Americas south of the ice dates to between 15,500 and 13,300 years ago (see PL. XXVI). There are few sites known from this period as yet, but they reveal that humans were widespread, from the Paisley Caves in Oregon and the Meadowcroft Rockshelter in Pennsylvania to Monte Verde in Chile. Some of these locations have good associations of stone tools with mammoth, mastodon, horse and camel remains. At Page-Ladson in Florida, Palaeoindians knapped fine points in mastodon country around 14,550 years ago (PL. XXVIII), and as far south as Argentina, horses and sloths were being butchered on repeated occasions between 14,000 and 13,000 years ago. Remains of a single mastodon were excavated from the sediments that had accumulated in a 'kettle hole' at Manis in Washington State, a small lake that formed in the Late Pleistocene when a great block of glacial ice melted in place. Some of this mastodon's bones bear spiral fractures, in exactly the way that fresh long bones break when you hit them, and others have cutmarks. A tip of a bone javelin point was also embedded in one of the mastodon's vertebrae. Radiocarbon dates from one of its ribs and a tusk show that the animal died around 13,800 years ago, and as there was no evidence of bone growth where the point had damaged bone, the mastodon almost certainly died shortly after it was hit.

Several other sites attest mammoth butchery around the same time, although they lack stone weapon tips, perhaps because tips of bone such as that from Manis were the main weapons, as at Yana. Other sites reveal the importance of plants, a reminder of the diversity of environments that human foragers had successfully adapted to in their eastwards dispersals through Asia.

Clovis and diversity

Clovis is a word used a lot through the early history of archaeology in the Americas. The characteristic Clovis stone tools are long, leaf-shaped and fluted points and blades, made from high-quality stone (see PL. XXIX). These, along with antler, bone and ivory points and needles, quickly spread across a wide swathe of North America to the south of the ice sheets from around 13,100 years ago, perhaps a few centuries before. Spanning the regions east of the Rockies and west of the Mississippi, Clovis tools and sites extended into northern Mexico and possibly Panama towards the end of the Clovis period, around 11,000 years ago. The available radiocarbon dates for a number of well-excavated Clovis sites suggest that the culture may have originated in the south of its distribution, probably out of the bifacial point-producing groups who left sites similar to Manis, dispersing north and east from there – although Clovis sites are most abundant in the Mississippi region, which may suggest a core population there.

The high-quality cherts and obsidians that Clovis knappers used were routinely transported far from their geological sources, and these valuable raw materials were cached in pits for future use. It's not clear what facilitated such a long-distance dispersal so quickly. We've seen how mammoths may have created landscapes that were relatively easy for hunter-gatherers to disperse through in Europe, and Gary Haynes suggests that the relatively rapid spread of Clovis peoples was made easier by locating mammoth and mastodon groups and using their tracks to explore new landscapes quickly while not getting lost.

Although Clovis is closely associated with the old ideas of a big-game hunting blitzkrieg that led to the numerous Late Pleistocene mammalian extinctions in North America, examples of Clovis megafaunal kills are remarkably rare; those species that we do have evidence for the hunting of, such as bison, did not become extinct, and the well-excavated sites we have at our disposal today show that small animals such as fish, birds, turtles, hares and even rodents were just as important resources, as well as plants. As with the Pleistocene extinctions in Sahul and Eurasia, it seems that a combination of climatic instability and environmental change was the main cause of megafaunal collapse in North America, combined here with perhaps a modest contribution from human exploitation.

Around the same time, a distinct group appeared north of Clovis in the areas between the mountains of Oregon, Idaho and Nevada.

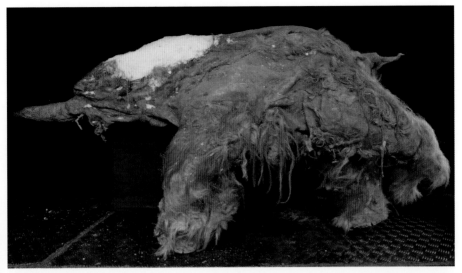

xv Yuka, a 39,000-year-old juvenile mammoth preserved in the Siberian permafrost.

xvi A mammoth engraved onto a fragment of mammoth tusk, from La Madeleine, France.

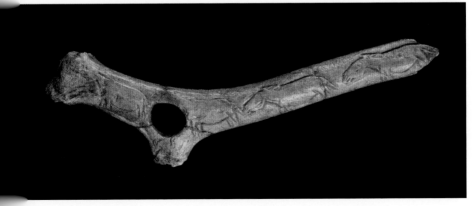

ıı A pierced baton (*bâton percée*) of reindeer antler with low relief horses, ɔm La Madeleine, France.

xviii A scene on the banks of the Vézère 15,000 years ago, engraved onto a 7-cm (2.75-in.) length of reindeer bone from La Madeleine, France. Such attention to perspective and detail is characteristic of Magdalenian art.

xix The Magdalenian sculpted frieze of the Cap Blanc rockshelter, France, depicts almost life-size horses, bison and deer. Here, shadows add volume to these lifelike carvings, which were also coloured with two shades of ochre. Similar sculptures are known from other rockshelters in France.

xx A 21,000-year-old stampede of wild cattle (aurochs) swirls around the viewer's head in Lascaux's Hall of the Bulls. This cave's numerous images of prey animals are a calendar of rutting and a celebration of life.

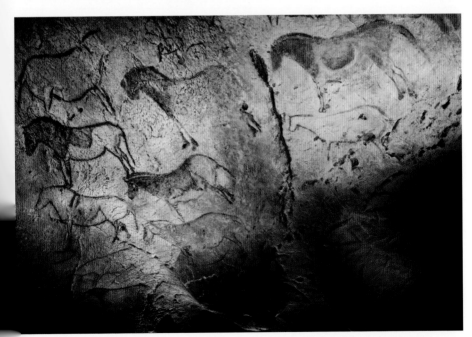

xi Around 14,500 years ago, at least thirty-four horses were painted in red and black in :kain Cave, in the Spanish Basque Country. Note the variation in completeness and the olour of their pelage. A common prey in Palaeolithic Europe, horses were the most epicted animal in Upper Palaeolithic art.

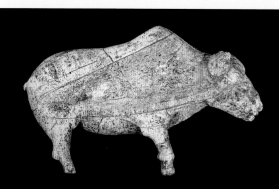

XXII (above) View over the Vicdessos Valley towards th Pyrenees from the mouth c Niaux Cave, France.

XXIII (left) 20,000-year-old carving of a bison cow from Zaraysk, Russia.

XXIV (below) Charcoal drawings in Chauvet Cave, France. Bison, rhinos, mammoths and horses graze, unaware of the stalking lions to the right.

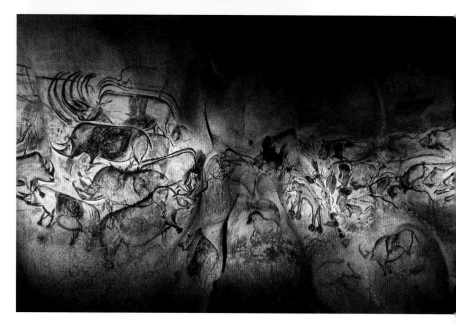

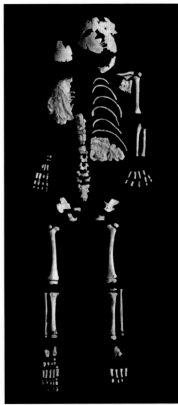

xxv (above) Around 26,500 years ago a child was buried in the Lagar Velho rockshelter in Portugal's Lapedo Valley. Ochre staining his shroud is visible.

xxvi (below) Left in wet ground 13,000 years ago, one of a number of human footprints from Calvert Island in British Columbia – early evidence of humans in the New World.

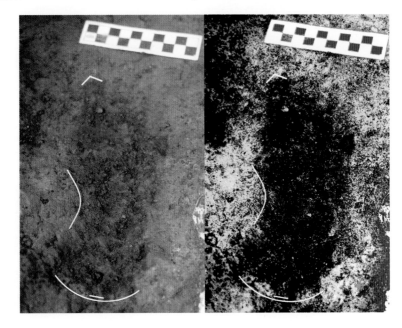

xxvii In Pleistocene North America, hunters approach a known mammoth gathering place, passing an older carcass. The dogs are fast, and can find prey and pin it down; the humans are slower, but can take advantage of a distracted target to get close enough to throw their lethal javelins. One of the dogs, made slow by injury, carries supplies. If the hunt is successful there will be plenty for all, although strict rules are followed when it comes to sharing out.

xxviii (above) In a landscape rich in mastodons, hunter-gatherers at Page-Ladson in Florida knapped fine bifacial points and repaired bone points around 14,550 years ago.

xxix (right) A variety of North American Clovis points showing fine shaping and distinctive flutes at their base to assist hafting. Note the variety in length and width: these would have tipped a variety of (thrusted) spears and (thrown) javelins, but they also could have functioned as general purpose knives.

This western Stemmed Point Tradition seems to have been completely distinct from Clovis and perhaps originated a little earlier. Whatever the case, these two groups can claim to be the earliest purely North American cultural groups, and presumably reflect populations that were already diverging into distinct territories. Further south, around the same time, groups were making fishtail-shaped stone points in Central and South America as far as Argentina and Chile. The DNA of one of the earliest Americans known to science, a male buried around 12,800 years ago at Anzick in Montana, contained the signature of the Southern Native American (SNA) lineage, ultimately rooted in Siberia.

Further diversity: Central and South America

In the 1990s, I was invited to Mexico to take samples for radiocarbon dating of sites that were said to provide dates for human activity that were much older than any other early American sites of the time. Genetics was only just beginning to contribute to the story, and archaeologists were still limited to a handful of locations which had

The anaerobic conditions of peat formation preserved the remains of a 14,600-year-old wishbone-shaped hut at Monte Verde (Chile). Wooden stakes hammered into the ground were covered by mastodon hides tied on with reeds. Inside, among stores of mastodon meat, medicinal plants have been found.

more of those dubious cutmarked or smashed bones on which to base their work. We took samples from mammoth accumulations and archaeological sites in the regions around Mexico City, and our results unequivocally showed that these genuine archaeological sites were no older than 13,000 years old, and those that were older had no evidence of human presence. That's not to say that humans weren't present before this, but probably not by more than 2,000 years or so.

The archaeology of South America reminds us how quickly hunter-gatherers can disperse over long distances. The site that reminds us the most is Monte Verde in Chile, which lies some 14,000 km (8,750 miles) south of Beringia and was occupied by 14,600 years ago. Considering its early date, dispersal there must have been fast. Monte Verde is near the coast, and canoeing along a rich marine ecosystem – kelp or not – can be fast; if our American pioneers targeted distant resource patches, their dispersal could have been more of a series of long hops between favourable areas rather than a gradual creep that took in everywhere en route.

The exceptional preservation conditions at Monte Verde revealed tents, a variety of plants from sources as diverse as the Andes and the coast, wooden spears, mortars and a variety of birds, shellfish and tools for grinding plants. It's a reminder of the varied habitats of South America that *Homo sapiens* diversified into probably as soon as they first arrived, from the wooded river valleys of the Amazon to the grasslands of Patagonia and the uplands of the Andes.

We can now turn to domestication, as we see *Homo sapiens* on the brink of transforming animals, plants, and even themselves into domestic beings. The world would still be wild for a very long time, but radically new ways of living would arise in the last few thousand years of the Pleistocene, heralding a rapid set of changes in the early millennia of the Holocene.

Chapter 18

Domestication

From 15,000 years ago, during the last few thousand years of the Ice Age, our hunter-gatherer ancestors were undergoing profound change across East Asia, the Near East and North Africa. At the same time as they were spreading through the Americas, population numbers in these other regions were rising, sedentary villages were emerging, and wild plants and animals were coming under greater control among several hunter-gatherer groups. Cemeteries set aside for burial of the dead – humans and dogs – were emerging as hitherto mobile peoples set down roots and began to invest in permanent places. The world of *Homo sapiens* was becoming something more familiar to us, as diversity developed into domestication.

The wolf: from hunter's weapon to man's grudging friend

Until now I have ignored one of *Homo sapiens'* closest companions, the dog. Let me see if I can change your view on 'man's best friend'. Over the course of the last ten millennia, humans have developed close, mutually beneficial relationships with a number of plant and animal species, but their relationship with dogs goes back farther, into the Pleistocene. The domestication of the wolf can be listed as one of the many achievements of Palaeolithic hunter-gatherers, quite probably European Gravettians or Magdalenians, and the close relationship that ensued spread rapidly across the world. By the end of the Pleistocene dogs were effectively everywhere that humans were. By and large we are a world of dog lovers (I don't mean to leave cats out of this, being a cat lover myself, but they were domesticated relatively recently). Darwin noted the remarkable variability of dogs in England alone, and used the popular pastime of dog breeding as a cultural analogy for his theory of evolution by means of natural selection. In some cases dogs were bred for great size and strength; in other cases for their cuteness and colour. The resulting myriad breeds, from the huge and intimidating to the minuscule and, quite frankly, silly, all derive from the same ancestor, the Pleistocene grey wolf (*Canis lupus*). Wolves were distributed across the entire northern hemisphere, and the distribution of early dog remains at various points within their range suggests the intensification of domestication in one or several places.

Where they coexisted with humans, free-ranging wolves were probably attracted to the animal carcasses and other food waste discarded at campsites, as well as to the same live prey as humans. Contact between the two was probably commonplace, particularly if the wolves found human food waste especially advantageous, and the high frequency of wolf remains on Palaeolithic sites shows that wolf pelts and ornaments of wolf canines were regular accoutrements of the well-dressed hunter. In rural Africa today, the populations of predators such as hyenas and wild dogs that live closest to human settlements are larger than their more remote relatives because of the higher food availability. This is ecological sympatry in action.

Wolves are not docile like sheep and cattle, and might not at first sight be the obvious candidates for domestication, let alone the earliest example of it. True, they are aggressive, but in many respects wolves *do* fit the behavioural requirements of potential domesticates: they are a social species that acts collaboratively, is well-adapted to living in groups, hunts in packs, has a strong hierarchy, and even shares in the responsibilities of caring for each other's young. All of these traits are shared with humans, as were their diets with our Palaeolithic ancestors, which they too obtained by the hunting and scavenging of large herbivores. All of these things make them almost potential humans. No wonder that the Chipewyan thought that we all descend from a female human and a male dog that could shape-shift into a human.

It is likely that wolves and humans were very familiar with each other over much of their coexistence, and as we've seen, wolves provided furs and were possibly celebrated in the ritual realm from the first time that *Homo sapiens* dispersed across Europe. It's easy to imagine that when the two were attracted to the same hunting opportunities, and to conspicuous accumulations of mammoth carcasses, then a degree of competition might emerge. Wolves can spot prey quickly and hold it in place by surrounding it and subduing it by intimidation. Perhaps human hunters realized this and began to monitor wolf hunting, closing in to assist in the kill while the wolves did their work. There are plenty of ethnographic examples of how

Much debate has focused on whether the morphologically distinct wolf-dog crania of the European Mid Upper Palaeolithic, such as this Pavlovian skull from Předmostí in Moravia, can be regarded as fully or incipiently domesticated. It was certainly smaller and had a distinctly shorter and wider muzzle than Pleistocene and modern wolves.

hunting with dogs in this way returns far larger quantities of meat than either species would obtain otherwise. Everyone's a winner. Opportunities for collaboration could easily emerge, to the point where it was recognized that a degree of sharing of mutually hunted animals would be more advantageous than competition for exclusive access. If wolves were distracting prey while hunters moved themselves into positions from which they could deliver their deadly javelins, both could reap the rewards.

Pat Shipman of Pennsylvania State University usefully recasts early wolf-dogs as 'living tools', and the long process of domestication might follow as the two came to spend more time in proximity to each other. Pleistocene dogs were still large, and could be used for carrying carcass parts, tent poles and other equipment. They could prove useful guarding against other predators, such as lions, hyenas, bears and non-domesticated wolves, and even against aggressive human groups. It doesn't follow that the loving relationship we enjoy with dogs came about quickly at all. A 'grudging toleration' might be a better description of the commensal relationship that emerged between the two. I've not mentioned before that the Chipewyan think of dogs – which eat their own faeces and cannibalize their dead – as liminal creatures, bringing chaos, sexual misconduct and social disorder. Dogs are widely associated with liminality in non-industrial societies, and even with the infernal realms – to the ancient Greeks Cerberus was the three-headed hound who stopped the dead from leaving Hades; Hekate's dog was thought to be a restless soul; and Diana, the goddess of the hunt, turned her admirer Actaeon into a deer to be ripped apart by her hounds. Beware of the dog!

How zooarchaeologists identify the early stages of domestication in animal remains is controversial. In principle, as the behaviour of a wild animal is brought under closer human control and domestication slowly occurs, its body size decreases, and as the snout becomes shorter and the teeth reduce in size they crowd in the jaws more, becoming more tightly packed together and rotating a little to fit more snugly together. At least that's the idea. Detailed measurement of the length of each tooth row (from the rearmost molar to the foremost incisor) may distinguish between modern wolves, Pleistocene wolves, and dogs, but the issue is complicated, and in practice there are many pitfalls. Dental crowding can occur naturally in wolves, although not to the degree seen in dogs over the last 150 years, and it cannot be used in isolation to distinguish between wolves and dogs. Only by using a suite of cranio-dental traits, such as the width of the braincase, length of the palette of the mouth and a host of other measurements, in addition to overall body size and weight, can one hope to arrive at a reliable distinction between a domesticated and a wild animal, and even then there is fierce debate. My zooarchaeologist colleague Kurt Gron warned me that he believes the very earliest domesticated dogs won't be morphologically distinguishable from wolves. There is still much to chew over. Fully domesticated dogs were probably smaller than wolves. Weight estimates based on ratios of soft tissues to marker bones like femurs suggest an average weight of 31 kg, compared to the 42 kg and 40 kg of Pleistocene and modern wolves respectively, but the wolves are so variable that weights can overlap between light wolves and heavier dogs.

Genetic comparison of living and fossil wolves and dogs has clarified the broad picture of wolf and dog evolution, but in no cases can this approach distinguish unambiguously between a wild wolf and one on the road to domestication. It's a remarkably difficult task. Geneticists have to deal with population bottlenecks and cross-breeding that have occurred over several millennia, let alone the confusing 'overprinting' of deliberate cross-breeding during the last few centuries. Initially, mtDNA suggested that the process of domestication occurred somewhere between 32,000 and 19,000 years ago, and while zooarchaeologists disagree as to whether it happened early or late in that range, it certainly occurred at least several thousand years before the advent of agriculture and the domestication of other plants and animals. Subsequent genomics research has refined the picture, revealing that the original wolf ancestors from which all dogs derive are now extinct. As sequences grow in number it is becoming more likely that the split between these wolves and all others occurred before the Last Glacial Maximum (LGM).[1] It's important not to mistake this split between populations for actual domestication itself, as Greger Larson – an expert on the subject – cautioned me. Genetics reveals that the earliest split was between Old and New World wolves, after which the lineage leading to domesticates split off from others. Estimates as to when this happened vary depending on how geneticists model mutation rates in wolves. Most converge on figures no later than 20,000 years ago, perhaps as early as 32,000 years ago, coinciding with the earliest remains that seem morphologically distinguishable from wolves.

Taking a broad view, several other factors point towards domesticated dogs prior to the Last Glacial Maximum, at least in Belgium, Germany, the Czech Republic and Russia. It's probably no coincidence that they accompany humans in places where they camped on the same spot for several months of the year and at which large quantities of food accumulated. In addition to cranio-dental traits of a number of specimens that differ from wolves at this time, stable isotope comparisons of the bones of Pavlovian wolves and dogs as early as 31,000 years ago reveal that the two had differing diets. Wolves obtained most of their dietary protein from horse and mammoth, whereas dogs focused more on reindeer or musk ox, despite the abundance of mammoth meat. Pat Shipman has suggested that the introduction of improved javelin technology at the time, combined with the use of early wolf-dogs, may have been critical factors allowing the semi-sedentary adaptations of the period, and one of the reasons why *Homo sapiens* in her view has been such a successfully invasive species.

The picture improves somewhat after the LGM, when we have skeletal evidence of undeniably domesticated wolf-dogs at Yakutia in Siberia by 17,000 years ago, in western Europe by 16,000 years ago,

and in the Near East, China and the far east of Russia by 12,000–
13,000 years ago. Dogs begin to appear in burials from this time
onwards, in the Magdalenian and Mezinian and even within a tent
structure at Ulakhan-Sular in Kamchatka, Russia. From this point
we can stop regarding them as a rarity; dogs are by now a relatively
common feature wherever hunter-gatherers and early agriculturalists
can be found. In the few thousand years prior to the advent of
agriculture in the Levant, hunter-gatherer burial grounds incorporate
dog burials. Sometime between 14,600 and 13,500 years ago, a man
and a woman were buried together with a dog at Bonn-Oberkassel in
Germany, and it's probably no coincidence that around the same time
a dog was buried in a shell midden in Yokosuka in Japan. Dogs, by now,
clearly enjoyed close social relationships with humans, enough to be
accorded similar treatment in death.

But let's get back to rethinking how relationships with dogs
evolved (see PL. XXVII). To rub along together, rules would have to
be enforced; transgressors would be punished when the evolving
wolf-dogs displayed unwanted aggression or took food from humans;
collaborators, on the other hand, could be rewarded with food. Over
time, wolf-dogs and humans would come to realize that working
together benefitted all. Moreover humans, who no doubt had already
woven wolves into their beliefs and customs, will have modified such
beliefs as the two came ever closer together. Eventually, the wolves'
behaviour changed; they became tolerant of their human collaborators,
less confrontational. Taming may have preceded domestication, but if
it did it leaves no skeletal markers; if cubs were reared by humans then,
while they would still grow up to be wolves, humans might begin to
assume the role of their leaders. Perhaps this is what had been achieved
in the Pavlovian and elsewhere. But we're still not dealing with pets.
Remember that the hard distinction we are used to between what is
human and what is animal was very blurred among our ancestors.
It may explain why wolves and dogs, like humans, are so rare in
Palaeolithic art: whatever our ancestors thought of the wolf-dogs it was
likely to have been very different from our view of them in the modern
world. Imagine how you might feel living alongside werewolves, with
whom you've developed a fragile cooperation. Those furry shapeshifters
on the periphery of the camp at night: they're good hunters and spirits
of the tundra; worthy companions, you'll give them that, but not to
be trusted. Their dim shadows are always shifting at the edge of the
firelight, always on the look-out for opportunities.

Village life

Our growing relationship with dogs is but one reminder of how we have never quite separated ourselves from the wild, at least until the last few centuries. But as climate change at the end of the Pleistocene made increasing sedentism and population growth possible, complex hunter-gatherer and early agriculturalist groups created ever-more visible places to live, surrounding themselves with the trappings of culture, and embarking on ways of living that would come to be encoded in morally based social laws. Across the world, *Homo sapiens* groups living in remarkably diverse environments, from the Arctic tundra to the South Asian rainforests, were wrapping themselves in the increasingly powerful clothing of villages, towns, monumental architecture, agricultural systems and the host of material and organizational trappings that accompany the transition from mobile foraging to village and town life.

During the Pleistocene, humans had already accomplished the many innovations that have been crucially important to our evolution: tool use, expanded brains and everything that came with them; the manipulation of tools, control of fire, pair bonding and hunting; living in larger groups; visual culture, language and the ability to use both to refer to other people, things and concepts; far-flung social networks maintained through long-distance exchange of valuable objects; sedentism, storage, plant processing and the accumulation of surplus; textiles and ceramics; a broad dietary spectrum that allowed them to disperse into some of the world's most varied environments and thrive there; and many more things. By 13,000 years ago, much of the world – with the exceptions of distant islands and the continent of Antarctica – had been filled by humans.

Many of the traits that are taken to define agricultural life were present, at least in incipient form, as early as 31,000 years ago. Archaeology always under-represents humanity's achievements. We can only work with what has been discovered and analysed, and that is always a small sample that a single discovery can revolutionize. In the last decade alone, several new human species have come to light, revealing a diverse and tangled human evolutionary tree even down to the last 40,000 years or so. We're amassing evidence that Neanderthals created art and were probably closer to us than we've previously given them credit for; and we've barely started with the Denisovans. After decades of scholarly debate it's now beyond doubt that we are all African, although the contribution of Neanderthals and Denisovans – and who knows what other 'ghosts' out there – is now becoming apparent. Nothing should surprise us, least of all domestication.

Let's rethink villages. Archaeologists tend to assume that 'village life' emerged with the origins of farming and the Neolithic way of doing things. Neolithic literally means 'new stone age' and is often seen as a watershed moment where much of life becomes village-based. It's a nice idea, but it's simply not true. We have seen that in Upper Palaeolithic Europe, hunter-gatherers were able to live in small villages for much or all of the year, and on the Russian Plain these villages, however temporary, had some kind of civic, communal layout. The organization and execution of major art projects, such as the 21,500-year-old masterpieces of Lascaux, required long-distance provision of diverse raw materials over a wild landscape, and artistic mastery which, just as with the knapping and carving that spread with *Homo sapiens*, must be the result of specialists at work. These were not simple, 'egalitarian' societies. Viewed in this light, I don't think that there is anything impressive about Neolithic villages.

For most people, for millennia yet, life continued in many ways as it had done since memory began. Certainly, temperatures increased, and animals and plants changed as forests swallowed up the grasslands. Coasts shrank as sea levels rose with the melting of the great ice sheets; rivers changed their courses and no longer flowed through gravelly steppe-tundra. In time, here and there, sedentary villages grew into towns, and elite groups grew from chiefdoms into city states, kingdoms and empires. In traditional thinking, 'civilization' arose. But I've failed if you still think that the vast cultural connections, imaginative worlds, exquisite art and ability to survive in some of the world's harshest environments does not deserve the term 'civilization'. Our Pleistocene ancestors were mobile hunter-gatherers and didn't need to build huge stone monuments or commit their transactions to writing. Neither did they live in uncomfortably large and dirty urban centres, suffer from the diseases born of living in close proximity to animals, risk their lives in an army fighting for a distant king's desires, or surrender their produce to an uncaring god. As many of us are coming to realize today, simpler lives may be much more civilized than the rat race.

The social processes begun in Africa 300,000 years ago by the earliest *Homo sapiens* groups and in Eurasia by the Neanderthals and

Chapter 18

Denisovans evolved, grew, were put to the test, and changed. Slowly, as our weary Pleistocene ancestors settled into a more sedentary way of life, the memory of long journeys over vast distances, the great herds of mammoths, the play of light from the campfires in the great wilderness, and rites of renewal celebrated in the darkest nooks and crannies of the Earth gradually faded. *Homo sapiens* turned increasingly inwards, preoccupied with a world filled with its own creations: the species that had domesticated itself.

I'm grateful to have had the opportunity to try to engage with our ancestors across the vast distance of Pleistocene time. The archaeologist's thrill of being the first to touch something previously held by a long-dead person will never leave me: an emotional thrill matched only by the intellectual challenge of working out how to investigate such long-dead people scientifically. I am particularly grateful to you, dear reader, for staying with me on our cold journey through our Pleistocene ancestors' past. It's time to leave them now. There is a long and complex story ahead, but that is for others to tell. Let's take off our parkas, mittens and boots, and warm ourselves back into the present by the side of our own hearths. The lights and distractions of modern life almost – just almost – drown out that distant sound of a wolf howling, way out there in the wild.

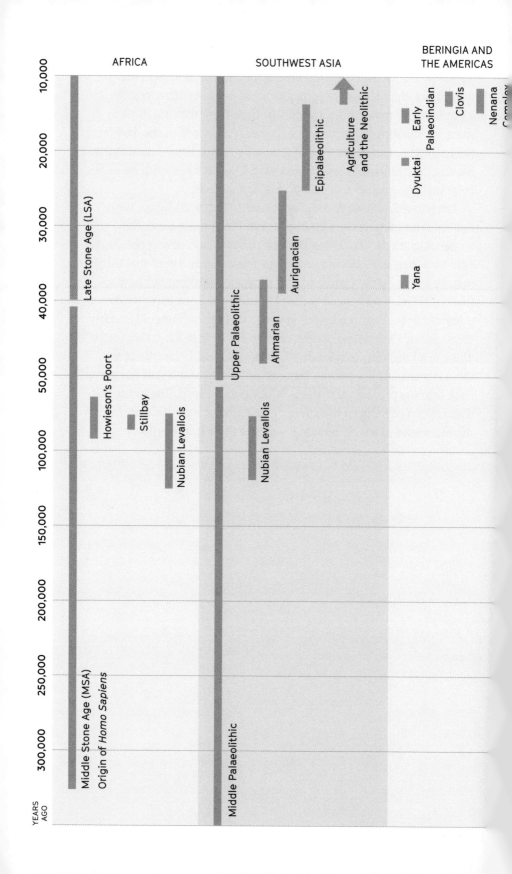

YEARS AGO

AFRICA

SOUTHWEST ASIA

BERINGIA AND THE AMERICAS

10,000
20,000
30,000
40,000
50,000
100,000
150,000
200,000
250,000
300,000

Late Stone Age (LSA)

Howieson's Poort

Stillbay

Nubian Levallois

Middle Stone Age (MSA)
Origin of *Homo Sapiens*

Upper Palaeolithic

Ahmarian

Aurignacian

Epipalaeolithic

Agriculture and the Neolithic

Nubian Levallois

Middle Palaeolithic

Early Palaeoindian

Clovis

Nenana Complex

Dyuktai

Yana

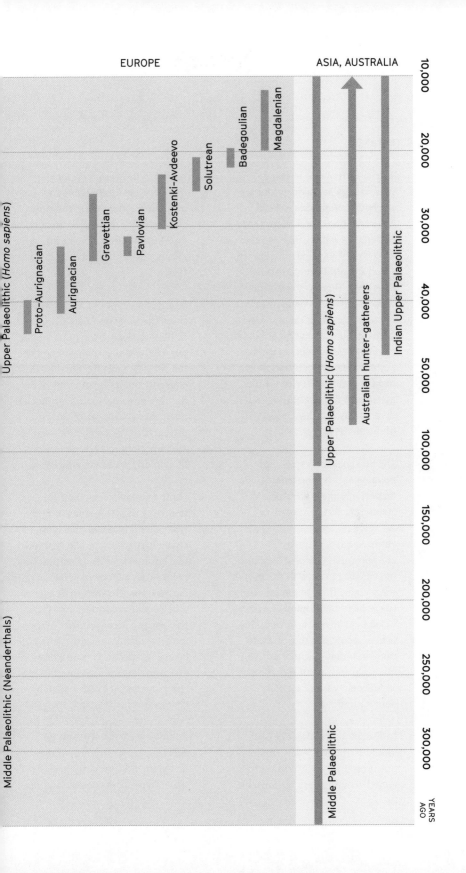

EUROPE

ASIA, AUSTRALIA

Upper Palaeolithic (*Homo sapiens*)

Middle Palaeolithic (Neanderthals)

Proto-Aurignacian

Aurignacian

Gravettian

Pavlovian

Kostenki-Avdeevo

Solutrean

Badegoulian

Magdalenian

Upper Palaeolithic (*Homo sapiens*)

Australian hunter-gatherers

Indian Upper Palaeolithic

Middle Palaeolithic

10,000

20,000

30,000

40,000

50,000

100,000

150,000

200,000

250,000

300,000

YEARS AGO

Notes

Chapter 1

1 'Racial' differences in facial morphology and skin colour are the body's responses to local environmental conditions: they can change remarkably quickly – the mark of a successful organism – and as with beauty are only skin deep. There is more genetic diversity in *one community* of chimpanzees than there is among humans *globally*, and most human genetic variation occurs *within* populations, not between them. See the excellent review of the genetics of human origins and diversity by Bradley 2008 (in further reading).

2 The biological order among mammals including lemurs, tarsiers, monkeys and apes (among the latter, humans).

3 Humans have forty-six chromosomes (spooled lengths of DNA) as opposed to the ape forty-eight. This is because two of the human chromosome pairs fused to form one long one. This was probably just one of those random mutations, that unlike many chromosomal mutations in humans was not fatal or debilitating.

4 In Europe these Miocene diets would ultimately lead to extinction of European apes. Environments were becoming very uniform in nature in northern latitudes, and the diets had limited potential for adaptation. I'm grateful to Daniel DeMiguel for sharing his insights on Miocene apes with me and for getting me to think about fall-back foods.

5 Isotopes are types of atoms which share the same number of protons in their nuclei (i.e. the same atomic number) and the same position in the periodic table (i.e. are the same element), but differ in terms of the number of neutrons in their nuclei (their mass). Isotopes of carbon, nitrogen, oxygen and strontium are important in understanding human origins, as we will see.

6 Laser ablation is a method for removing small amounts of sample from a hard material (like tooth enamel). A laser typically 0.0106th of a millimetre wide is used to heat the solid in a series of pulses. As the material absorbs the laser's energy it heats and vapourizes into CO_2 gas. The gas is *cryofocused* – trapped as condensation on a cold surface – before its specific carbon isotopes are separated and measured with a spectrometer. My colleague Simon Chenery of the British Geological Survey and I used LA-ICP MS to examine trace elements on Ice Age stone tools from the United Kingdom. By comparing these to trace elements in natural samples

of flint we were able to reconstruct how the stone tools were carried around the landscape, and therefore how mobile late Ice Age people were. We'll return to isotope analyses in Chapter 2.

7   For examples of their research, see particularly Coolidge & Wynn 2009 and Wynn & Coolidge 2016 (in further reading).

Chapter 2

1   For the history and methodological frontiers of radiocarbon (^{14}C) dating, see Bronk Ramsey 2008 (in further reading).

2   The ZooMS technique is also used in microsurgery and has been employed to characterize inks on precious manuscripts too.

3   Khoisan (alternatively, Khoe-San) is the self-designated term for the indigenous populations of southern Africa that are distinct from the sub-Saharan Bantu-speaking peoples. The Khoisan comprise the Khoekhoen nomadic pastoralists and the San hunter-gatherers. Colonial names they have also been given include Hottentots and Bushmen.

4   The genetics of African origins: for timing and diversity, see Barbieri et al. 2016 and Schlebusch et al. 2017; for metapopulations, see Scerri et al. 2019 and Klein 2019 (all in further reading).

Chapter 3

1   The term for these abrupt oscillations is Dansgaard-Oeschger (D-O) Events, after their two discoverers. The so-called 'Little Ice Age' of the 14th to 17th century AD – in which the Thames and other rivers regularly froze over – was probably the result of the most recent D-O event. Some D-O events appear to be correlated with Heinrich Events, in which massive amounts of polar ice break off (calve from) the ice sheets and float across the oceans. They take with them microscopic rock dust that has become incorporated into the ice on land (known as ice-rafted debris), which ultimately sinks and can be found (and dated) in cores drilled through the deep sea sediments. Such massive inputs of freshwater ice can profoundly influence the circulation of warm saline waters, and hence affect climate. I think of them as extreme examples of throwing three or four ice cubes into my gin and tonic.

2   American and Russian space programmes of the 1950s to 1970s serve as an excellent example of a series of increasingly expanded dispersals: the only difference is that these had a target (the Moon), whereas natural dispersals are goalless. Initially, humans adapted to low Earth orbit (Vostok 1), then to longer periods in space,

concurrent with the development of space flight (the Gemini missions). Humans then ventured beyond low orbit (the Apollo missions), and tested the ability to dock their command and lunar modules in orbit (Apollo 7). Finally, humans reached and orbited the Moon (Apollo 8), and then landed on it (Apollo 11). Having landed, the Eagle didn't hang around that long, but it still justifiably ranks as one of humanity's greatest achievements. What's more, the lessons learned in space so far will ultimately facilitate human extra-planetary dispersal. Assuming our pandemics or bombs don't destroy us first.

Chapter 4

1 These are the shells of the *swollen nassa*, which, despite the name, is not an inconvenient medical condition but a species of sea snail.

2 Iran is around 1.65 million sq. km (636,000 sq. miles) and the Arabian Peninsula 3.2 million sq. km (1.25 million sq. miles), in comparison to the United Kingdom's 242,500 sq. km (93,500 sq. miles). See Dennell 2020, 78 and 234 (in further reading).

Chapter 5

1 https://yougov.co.uk/topics/lifestyle/articles-reports/2015/09/24/you-are-not-alone-most-people-believe-aliens-exist. According to surveys, the proportion of people who believe that intelligent life exists elsewhere in the universe is 56 per cent in Germany, 54 per cent in the United States, and 52 per cent in the United Kingdom.

2 https://www.smithsonianmag.com/history/why-so-many-people-still-believe-in-bigfoot-180970045/. The various reasons why the myth remains popular are intelligently summarized in https://alumni.berkeley.edu/california-magazine/just-in/2018-10-26/so-why-do-people-believe-bigfoot-anyway. Reading the vast number of eyewitness accounts and discussions of aliens, wildmen and lost continents would be a long task... and a short route to madness. But if you think these beliefs are odd, just ask yourself this: do you believe in winged angels or bodily reincarnation?

3 Although the term 'Pygmy', referring to short stature, is often considered to be pejorative, no other handy term exists for the collective ethnic groups that comprise it, such as the Mbuti, Aka, Baka and Twa. Using one of these terms for the collective whole would be seen as pejorative too. Several genes common among pygmies and rare in Yoruba and other African and non-African populations have been identified

which are probably the cause of short stature (see Reich 2018 in further reading).

4   For the Neanderthal population estimation, see Shea 2008 (in further reading). For the concerts, see https://en.wikipedia.org/wiki/List_of_highest-attended_concerts.

5   I've obtained these dates from Trinkaus et al. 2003 (Oase) and Semal et al. 2009 (Spy); see also Higham et al. 2014 for wider discussion of the available chronology for Neanderthal extinction (all in further reading). I calibrated the two example age ranges using Oxford's OxCal online calibration programme, available at https://c14.arch.ox.ac.uk/oxcal.html.

Chapter 6

1   An unfortunate application of the name of one of Tolkien's fictitious characters which should not be confused with a real human species.

2   Which, as specialist Mike Morwood has pointed out (in Dennell & Porr 2014, in further reading),

parallels the route of the Japanese colonization of the region in 1941–2.

3   As argued by Shipman 2015, in further reading.

Chapter 7

1   This anecdote was recalled by both Leopold Martin and the artist's friend Serjeant Ralph Thomas, who purportedly took notes from the great man's reminiscences. He was indeed dapper and did wear a flower in his buttonhole, but the conversation (and the specific wording on his card) are mine. The location of *The Deluge* of 1826 is currently unknown; a famous version John Martin painted in 1834 is curated in the Yale Center for British Art. I took the story from M. L. Pendered's *John Martin Painter: His Life And Times* (London: Hurst and Blackett, 1923). I was checking up on Martin as my colleague Mark White and I had discovered in the

library of The Geological Society in London a previously uncatalogued etching of excavations in Kent's Cavern in Devon in the 1820s, which we initially (and excitedly) thought was by John Martin. Our subsequent 'research' (by which I mean a decent magnifying glass) showed, however, that it was by the Devon artist George Marten – damn those scrawly signatures! The illustration is still important to the history of excavation and the infancy of archaeology; for the story, see White & Pettitt 2009, in further reading.

2   Not to be confused with the Eifel region of Germany, also discussed

in this chapter. The names are clearly visible below the first (lowest) viewing platform.

3 Almost certainly a huge circular coracle waterproofed with bitumen, as Assyriologist Irving Finkel makes very clear in *The Ark Before Noah: Decoding the Story of the Flood* (Hodder, 2014).

4 The VEI ranks relatively small eruptions (VEI 1, at less than 100,000 cu. m or about 3.5 million cu. ft of ejecta) to the mercifully rare super eruptions (VEI 8, over 1,000 cu. km or about 240 cu. miles of ejecta, of which only eight examples are known for the last 132 million years). Eruptions at VEI 5 and greater are named in terms of their similarity to the eruption of Vesuvius in AD 79 as described by Pliny the Younger, hence the term Plinian, with eruptions above VEI 5 termed Ultra-Plinian. The Laacher See, Phlegreian Fields and Toba eruptions I discuss here are all Ultra-Plinian. The extent of the Toba ash fall, which is still coming to light, is causing an increase of the VEI scale to 9, with Toba registering at least 8.8.

Chapter 8

1 Cro-Magnon lies today in the grounds of the Hôtel Le Cro-Magnon, and you have to pay to view it. For details of the excavations, see Chapter 6 in Édouard Lartet & Henry Christy's *Reliquiae Aquitanicae: Being Contributions to the Archaeology and Palaeontology of Périgord and the Adjoining Provinces of Southern France* (Williams and Norgate, 1865–75). Digital copies of this fascinating book can be found online for free.

2 Modern population densities are estimated by dividing the available landmass (in the case of my example, minus Antarctica) by the total population.

3 World Health Organization life expectancy figures; see https://www.who.int/data/gho/data/themes/mortality-and-global-health-estimates.

Chapter 9

1 *Coast*, which aired on the BBC between 2005 and 2015. If you watch it you'll see I have a natural face for radio!

2 Radiocarbon dates for the early Upper Palaeolithic of these caves begin around 42,000 years ago. It's conceivable that these sites were occupied by *Homo sapiens* as early as this, which would put them close to the age of the Protoaurignacian and the CI-HE4 catastrophes. This is certainly the view of the Tübingen University team who excavate and study them, but as the greater majority of radiocarbon dates span the period 37,000 years ago and

younger, it is possible, I think, that the very few dates at the older age range are 'outliers', that is, materials which are older than the human occupations and have become mixed up with them. With sites excavated a long time ago, like some of these, such problems are difficult to overcome, and Bayesian modelling of the available dates (see Higham et al. 2012 in further reading) is unlikely to improve the matter as it stands. We certainly can't rule out the possibility that they are earlier, however. New discoveries of figurines and flutes derive from deposits apparently older than 37,000; it could be that these new cultural elements appeared then, and grew in importance over the next few millennia to a peak around 37,000 years ago. Whatever the case, the Swabian Jura Aurignacians were certainly some of the earliest – if not the earliest – figurative artists in Europe. Resolving this issue is important; were the very earliest *Homo sapiens* in Europe without art, or did they bring the new culture with them? I have no doubt that the Tübingen team will resolve this in the future.

3   Nick Conard and his colleagues can be seen talking about the flutes on *Sounds of Prehistory* (available on YouTube), where you can hear reproductions of the flutes played. Experimental archaeologist Wulf Hein can be heard playing 'The Star-Spangled Banner' on one too.

4   FTIR spectroscopy uses a particular technique to shine a beam of infrared light at many frequencies at a sample, measuring how much of the beam's light is absorbed by it (absorption spectroscopy). Once a complex set of absorption data has been collected, a relatively common algorithm (the Fourier Transform) is used to convert it into the required information, i.e. the amount of light absorbed at each wavelength. As the molecular structure of solids, liquids and gasses will absorb radiation differently according to their structure, the absorbance can be used to identify matter that is otherwise too small to identify visually, in this case sedimentary materials ~0.1 mg in size, on the basis of their infrared spectra.

Chapter 10

1   For the reindeer skull and pit, at Pavlov I, see Oliva 2005; for the pair of hands, also at Pavlov I, see Trinkaus et al. 2009; for the mammoth skulls, at Předmostí, and the DV3 female burial at Dolní Věstonice, see Oliva 2005 (all in further reading).

Chapter 12

1   Olaf also wonders whether the wolf was not the only animal humans were controlling, and whether wild horses were being closely herded at the time (only part tongue-in-cheek).

Chapter 13

1 If the art of Chauvet is really as old as it is said to be, it destroys both schemes completely. But I really don't think it is: references to my thoughts on the matter can be found in further reading for those of you keen to pursue the topic further or to cure your insomnia.

2 There are two bison painted on Lascaux's walls in what appears to be winter coats. Perhaps this species represented the season during which the cave was used.

Chapter 15

1 See, for example, Nancy Spears & Richard Germain, 2007. '1900–2000 in Review: the Shifting Role and Face of Animals in Print Advertisements in the Twentieth Century'. *Journal of Advertising* 36 (3), 19–33.

2 Have a look at the distorted skull at the front of Hans Holbein's *The Ambassadors*, first from the front, then from the side.

Chapter 16

1 It won't stop me speculating, however, that these were retained as relics by the living; perhaps being feet they were symbolic of travel.

Chapter 18

1 It's important not to mistake this split between genetic populations for domestication itself, as my friend, the geneticist Greger Larson, cautioned me. Sixteen basal wolf-dog breeds have now been identified genetically, the earliest split among which was between Old and New World wolves. Specific estimates as to when the lineage that lead to domesticates split off from others vary depending on how geneticists model mutation rates in wolves. Most converge on figures no later than 20,000 years ago, perhaps as early as 32,000 years ago. This estimate does coincide with the earliest remains of wolf-dogs that some zooarchaeologists suggest are morphologically distinguishable from wolves on the basis of body size and cranio-dental morphology. By the end of the Pleistocene at least five genetic lineages can be recognized, which may reflect the fact that different types of dog had emerged by this time, possibly relating to distinct contributions to their human collaborators, although the specific implication of the genetics is as yet unclear.

Further Reading

General Reading

Bahn, P. 2016. *Journey Through the Ice Age.* Oxford: Oxford University Press. An excellent introduction to Palaeolithic cave art.

Gamble, C., Gowlett, J. & Dunbar, R. 2018. *Thinking Big. How the Evolution of Social Life Shaped the Human Mind.* London & New York: Thames & Hudson. Excellent survey of the cognitive, social and behavioural changes that characterize human evolution, with much original material.

Papagianni, D. & Morse, M. 2022. *The Neanderthals Rediscovered. How Modern Science is Rewriting Their Story (3rd edition).* London & New York: Thames & Hudson.

Pettitt, P. B. 2018. The rise of modern humans. In Scarre, C. (ed.) *The Human Past (4th edition).* London & New York: Thames & Hudson. Covers the evolution and behaviour of the Neanderthals, Denisovans and *Homo sapiens* in a standard textbook that spans the entirety of prehistory.

Reich, D. 2018. *Who We Are and How We Got Here. Ancient DNA and the New Science of the Human Past.* Oxford: Oxford University Press. Highly readable introduction to the genetics of human evolution.

Stringer, C. 2013. *Lone Survivors. How We Came to be the Only Humans on Earth.* New York: St. Martin's Griffin. Published in the UK in 2012 as *The Origin of Our Species.* London: Penguin. Excellent account of the biological side of the evolution of *Homo sapiens,* written by one of the foremost experts.

Wood, B. 2019. *Human Evolution: A Very Short Introduction* (2nd edition). Oxford: Oxford University Press.

Chapter 1
Skin and Bones (pp. 12–26)

Bauernfeind, A. M. & Babbitt, C. C. 2020. Metabolic changes in human brain evolution. *Evolutionary Anthropology* 29(4), 201–11.

Böhme, M. et al. 2019. A new Miocene ape and locomotion in the ancestor of great apes and humans. *Nature* 575, 489–95.

Brace, S. et al. 2019. Ancient genomes indicate population replacement in Early Neolithic Britain. *Nature Ecology & Evolution* 3(5), 765–71 (discusses Cheddar Man's DNA).

Bradley, B. J. 2008. Reconstructing phylogenies and phenotypes: a molecular view of human evolution. *Journal of Anatomy* 212, 337–53.

Coolidge, F. & Wynn, T. 2009. *The Rise of* Homo sapiens: *The Evolution of Modern Thinking.* Chichester: Wiley-Blackwell.

DeMiguel, D., Alba, D. M. & Moyà-Solà, S. 2014. Dietary specialization during the evolution of western Eurasian hominoids and the extinction of European great apes. *PLoS ONE* 9(5). DOI: 10.1371/journal.pone.0097442.

Dunsworth, H. M. 2019. Expanding the evolutionary explanations for sex differences in the human skeleton. *Evolutionary Anthropology* 29, 108–16.

Ferraro, J. V. et al. 2013. Earliest archaeological evidence of persistent hominin carnivory. *PLoS ONE* 8(4). DOI: 10.1371/journal.pone.0062174.

Harmand, S. et al. 2015. 3.3-million-year-old stone tools from Lomekwi 3, West Turkana, Kenya. *Nature* 521, 310–16.

Hecht, E. E. et al. 2015. Acquisition of Paleolithic toolmaking abilities involves structural remodeling to inferior frontoparietal regions. *Brain Structure and Function* 220, 2315–31.

Isler, K. & Van Schaik, C. 2014. How humans evolved large brains: comparative evidence. *Evolutionary Anthropology* 23, 65–75.

Kehrer-Sawatski, H. & Cooper, D. M. 2007. Understanding the recent evolution of the human genome: insights from human-chimpanzee genome comparisons. *Human Mutation* 28(2), 99–130.

Kramer, K. & Hill, A. 2015. Was monogamy a key step on the hominin road? Reevaluating the monogamy hypothesis in the evolution of cooperative breeding. *Evolutionary Anthropology* 24, 73–83.

McHenry, H. 2004. Origin of human bipedality. *Evolutionary Anthropology* 13, 116–19.

McNabb, J. 2019. Further thoughts on the genetic argument for handaxes. *Evolutionary Anthropology* 29, 220–36.

Olalde, I. et al. 2018. The Beaker phenomenon and the genomic transformation of northwest Europe. *Nature* 555, 190–96 (discusses the DNA of Cheddar Man).

Prado-Martinez, J. et al. 2013. Great ape genetic diversity and population history. *Nature* 499, 471–5.

Pobiner, B. L. 2020. The zooarchaeology and paleoecology of early hominin scavenging. *Evolutionary Anthropology* 29, 68–82.

Reno, P. L. 2014. Genetic and developmental basis for parallel evolution and its significance for hominoid evolution. *Evolutionary Anthropology* 23, 188–200.

Sponheimer, M., et al. 2006. Isotopic evidence for dietary variability in the early hominin *Paranthropus robustus*. *Science* 314, 980–2.

Stout, D. & Chaminade, T. 2012. Stone tools, language and the brain in human evolution. *Philosophical Transactions of the Royal Society of London* Series B *Biological Sciences* 367, 75–87.

Stout, D., et al. 2015. Cognitive demands of Lower Palaeolithic toolmaking. *PLoS ONE* 10(4). DOI: 10.137/journal.pone.0128256.

Sousa, A. A. M. et al. 2017. Evolution of the human nervous system, function, structure and development. *Cell* 170, 226–47.

Tardieu, C. 2010. Development of the human hind limb and its importance for the evolution of bipedalism. *Evolutionary Anthropology* 19, 174–86.

Ungar, P. S. & Sponheimer, M. 2012. The diets of early hominins. *Science* 334, 190–3.

Wood, B. & Lonergan, N. 2008. The hominin fossil record: taxa, grades and clades. *Journal of Anatomy* 212, 354–76.

Wrangham, R. 2009. *Catching Fire: How Cooking Made Us Human.* London: Profile Books.

Wrangham, R. & Carmody, R. 2010. Human adaptation to the control of fire. *Evolutionary Anthropology* 19, 187–99.

Wynn, T. & Coolidge, F. 2016. Archaeological insights into hominin cognitive evolution. *Evolutionary Anthropology* 25, 200–13.

Chapter 2
The Molecular Frontier
(pp. 27–42)

Bronk Ramsey, C. 2008. Radiocarbon dating: revolutions in understanding. *Archaeometry* 50, 249–75.

Chan, E. et al. 2019. Human origins in a southern African palaeo-wetland and first migrations. *Nature* 575, 185–9.

Fuentes, O. et al. 2019. Interpreting and communicating genetic variation in 2019: a conversation on race. *Evolutionary Anthropology* 28, 109–11.

Green, R. E. et al. 2008. A complete Neandertal mitochondrial genome sequence determined by high-throughput sequencing. *Cell* 134(3), 416–26.

Gregory et al. 2006. The DNA sequence and biological annotation of Chromosome 1. *Nature* 441, 315–21.

Henn, B. et al. 2011. Hunter-gatherer genomic diversity suggests a southern African origin for modern humans. *Proceedings of the National Academy of Sciences (USA)* 108, 5154–62.

Klein, R. 2019. Population structure and the evolution of *Homo sapiens* in Africa. *Evolutionary Anthropology* 28, 179–88.

Llamas, B., Willerslev, E. and Orlando, L. 2017. Human evolution: a tale from ancient genomes. *Philosophical Transactions of the Royal Society of London* Series B *Biological Sciences* 372. DOI: 10.1098/rstb.2015.0484.

Marx, V. 2017. Genetics: new tales from ancient DNA. *Nature Methods* 14(8), 771–4.

Noonan, J. P. et al. 2006. Sequencing and analysis of Neanderthal genomic DNA. *Science* 314, 1113–18.

Pettitt, P. B. 2004. Ideas in relative and absolute dating. In Renfrew, C. and Bahn, P. (eds) *Archaeology: The Key Concepts.* London: Routledge, 58–64.

Richards, M. et al. 2001. Stable isotope evidence for increasing dietary breadth in the European Mid Upper Palaeolithic. *Proceedings of the National Academy of Sciences (USA)* 98, 6528–32.

Richter, D. et al. 2017. The age of the hominin fossils from Jebel Irhoud, Morocco, and the origins of the Middle Stone Age. *Nature* 546, 293–9.

Rizzi, E. et al. 2012. Ancient DNA studies: new perspectives on old samples. *Genetics Selection Evolution* 44(21).

Scerri, E. et al. 2019. Beyond multiregional and simple out-of-Africa models of human evolution. *Nature Ecology and Evolution* 3, 1370–2.

Schlebusch, C. et al. 2017. Southern African ancient genomes estimate

modern human divergence 350,000 to 260,000 years ago. *Science* 358, 652–5.

Schuster, S. et al. 2010. Complete Khoisan and Bantu genomes from southern Africa. *Nature* 463, 943–7.

Sirak, K. & Sedig, J. 2019. Balancing analytical goals and anthropological stewardship in the midst of the paleogenomics revolution. *World Archaeology* 51, 560–73.

Veeramah, K. & Hammer, M. 2014. The impact of whole-genome sequencing on the reconstruction of human population history. *Nature reviews: Genetics* 15, 149–62.

Welker, F. 2018. Palaeoproteomics for human evolutionary studies. *Quaternary Science Reviews* 190, 137–47.

Chapter 3
Climate Change and Environment   (pp. 43–53)

Basell, L. 2008. Middle Stone Age (MSA) site distributions in eastern Africa and their relationship to Quaternary environmental change, refugia and the evolution of *Homo sapiens*. *Quaternary Science Reviews* 27, 2484–98.

Fortey, R. 1997. *Life: An Unauthorised Biography*. London: HarperCollins.

Harvati, K. et al. 2019. Apidima Cave fossils provide earliest evidence of *Homo sapiens* in Eurasia. *Nature* 571, 500–4.

Hershkovitz, I. et al. 2018. The earliest modern humans outside Africa. *Science* 359, 456–9.

Hublin, J.-J. et al. 2017. New fossils from Jebel Irhoud, Morocco and the pan-African origin of *Homo sapiens*. *Nature* 546, 289–92.

Richter, D. et al. 2017. The age of the hominin fossils from Jebel Irhoud, Morocco, and the origins of the Middle Stone Age. *Nature* 546, 293–6.

Chapter 4
Dispersal: from Africa to Asia (pp. 54–66)

Blinkhorn, J. et al. 2013. Middle Palaeolithic occupation in the Thar Desert during the Upper Pleistocene: the signature of a modern human exit out of Africa? *Quaternary Science Reviews* 77, 233–8.

d'Errico, F. et al. 2005. *Nassarius kraussianus* shell beads from Blombos Cave: evidence for symbolic behaviour in the Middle Stone Age. *Journal of Human Evolution* 48, 3–24.

Dennell, R. 2020. *From Arabia to the Pacific. How Our Species Colonised Asia.* Abingdon: Routledge.

Groucutt, H. et al. 2018. *Homo sapiens* in Arabia by 85,000 years ago. *Nature Ecology and Evolution* 2(5), 800–9.

Groucutt, H. et al. 2019. Skhul lithic technology and the dispersal of *Homo sapiens* into southwest Asia. *Quaternary International* 515, 30–52.

Henshilwood, C. et al. 2004. Middle Stone Age shell beads from South Africa. *Science* 304, 404.

Holt, B. et al. 2013. An update of Wallace's zoogeographic regions of the world. *Science* 339, 74–8.

Jennings, R. et al. 2015. The greening of Arabia: multiple opportunities for human occupation of the Arabian Peninsula during the Late Pleistocene inferred from an ensemble of climate model simulations. *Quaternary International* 382, 181–99.

Stewart, M. et al. 2019. Middle and Late Pleistocene mammal fossils of Arabia and surrounding regions: implications for biogeography and hominin dispersals. *Quaternary International* 515, 12–29.

Vanhaeren, M. et al. 2006. Middle Palaeolithic shell beads in Israel and Algeria. *Science* 312, 1785–8.

Chapter 5
Contact: Neanderthals and Denisovans (pp. 67–84)

Bergström, A. et al. 2020. Insights into human genetic variation and population history from 929 diverse genomes. *Science* 367. DOI: 10.1126/science.aay5012.

Chen, F. et al. 2019. A Late Middle Pleistocene Denisovan mandible from the Tibetan Plateau. *Nature* 569, 409–12.

Dennell, R. 2019. Dating of hominin discoveries at Denisova. *Nature* 565, 571–2.

Dennell, R. 2020. *From Arabia to the Pacific. How Our Species Colonised Asia.* Abingdon: Routledge.

Doucka, K. et al. 2019. Age estimates for hominin fossils and the onset of the Upper Palaeolithic at Denisova Cave. *Nature* 565, 640–4.

Fu, Q. et al. 2015. An early modern human ancestor from Romania with a recent Neanderthal ancestor. *Nature* 524, 216–19.

Fu, Q. et al. 2016. The genetic history of Ice Age Europe. *Nature* 534, 200–5.

Gamble, C. 1993. *Timewalkers. The Prehistory of Global Colonization.* London: History Press.

Green, R. et al. 2010. A draft sequence of the Neanderthal genome. *Science* 328, 710–22.

Harvati, K. et al. 2019. Apidima Cave fossils provide earliest evidence of *Homo sapiens* in Eurasia. *Nature* 571, 500–4.

Higham, T. et al. 2014. The timing and spatiotemporal patterning of Neanderthal extinction. *Nature* 512, 306–9.

Hockett, B. 2012. The consequences of Middle Palaeolithic diets on pregnant Neanderthal women. *Quaternary International* 264, 78–82.

Jacobs, Z., et al. 2019. Timing of archaic hominin occupation of Denisova Cave in southern Siberia. *Nature* 565, 594–8.

Lachance J. et al. 2012. Evolutionary history and adaptation from high-coverage whole-genome sequences of diverse African hunter-gatherers. *Cell* 150(3), 457–69.

Morley, M. et al. 2019. Hominin and animal activities in the microstratigraphic record from the Denisova Cave (Altai Mountains, Russia). *Scientific Reports* 9. DOI: 10.1038/s41598-019-49930-3.

Moser, S. 1998. *Ancestral Images. The Iconography of Human Origins.* Ithaca: Cornell University Press.

Nielsen, R. et al. 2017. Tracing the peopling of the world through genomics. *Nature* 541, 302–10.

Pakenham, T. 1991. *The Scramble for Africa.* London: Weidenfeld and Nicolson.

Papagianni, D. & Morse, M. 2022. *The Neanderthals Rediscovered: How Modern Science is Rewriting Their Story (3rd edition).* London & New York: Thames & Hudson.

Patterson, N. et al. 2012. Ancient admixture in human history. *Genetics* 192, 1065–93.

Raghavan, M. et al. 2014. Upper Palaeolithic Siberian genome reveals dual ancestry of Native Americans. *Nature* 505, 87–91. DOI: 10.1038/nature12736.

Reich, D. et al. 2010. Genetic history of an archaic hominin group from Denisova Cave in Siberia. *Nature* 468, 1053–60.

Semal, P. et al. 2009. New data on the late Neanderthals: direct dating of the Belgian Spy fossils. *American Journal of Physical Anthropology* 138, 421–8.

Shea, J. 2008. The archaeology of an illusion: the Middle-Upper Palaeolithic transition in the Levant. In Le-Tensorer, J.-M., Jagher, R. and Otte, M. (eds) *The Lower and Middle Palaeolithic in the Near East and Neighbouring Regions.* Liège: ERAUL, 169–82.

Shipman, P. 2015. *The Invaders. How Humans and Their Dogs Drove Neanderthals to Extinction.* Cambridge, MA: Belknap Harvard.

Slon, V. et al. 2017. A fourth Denisovan individual. *Science Advances* 3(7). DOI: 10.1126/sciadv.1700186.

Arenas, M. et al. 2020. The early peopling of the Philippines based on mtDNA. *Scientific Reports* 10. DOI: 10.1038/s41598-020-61793-7.

Balme, J. 2013. Of boats and string: the maritime colonisation of Australia. *Quaternary International* 285, 68–75.

Barker, G. et al. 2007. The 'human revolution' in lowland tropical Southeast Asia: the antiquity and behaviour of anatomically modern humans in Niah Cave (Sarawak, Borneo). *Journal of Human Evolution* 52, 243–61.

Bradshaw, C. et al. 2019. Minimum founding populations for the first peopling of Sahul. *Nature Ecology and Evolution* 3, 1057–63.

Clarkson, C. et al. 2017. Human occupation of northern Australia by 65,000 years ago. *Nature* 547, 306–10.

David, B. et al. 2013. How old are Australia's pictographs? A review of rock art dating. *Journal of Archaeological Science* 40, 3–10.

Davidson, I. 2013. Peopling the last new worlds: the first colonisation of Sahul and the Americas. *Quaternary International* 285, 1–29.

Dennell, R. 2020. *From Arabia to the Pacific. How Our Species Colonised Asia.* Abingdon: Routledge.

Dennell, R. and Porr, M. (eds) 2014. *Southern Asia, Australia and the Search for Human Origins.* Cambridge: Cambridge University Press.

Field, J. & Wroe, S. 2012. Aridity, faunal adaptations and Australian Late Pleistocene extinctions. *World Archaeology* 44(1), 56–74.

Kealy, S. et al. 2018. Least-cost pathway models indicate northern human dispersal route from Sunda to Sahul. *Journal of Human Evolution* 125, 59–70.

Locatelli, E. et al. 2012. Pleistocene survivors and Holocene extinctions: the giant rats from Liang Bua (Flores, Indonesia). *Quaternary International* 281, 47–57.

Pedro, N. et al. 2020. Papuan mitochondrial genomes and the settlement of Sahul. *Journal of Human Genetics* 65, 875–87.

Shipman, P. 2015. *The Invaders. How Humans and Their Dogs Drove Neanderthals to Extinction.* Cambridge, MA: Belknap Harvard.

Álvarez-Lau, D. & García, N. 2011. Geographical distribution of Pleistocene cold-adapted faunas in the Iberian Peninsula. *Quaternary International* 233, 159–70.

Bataille, G. et al. 2018. Living on the edge. A comparative approach for studying the beginning of the Aurignacian. *Quaternary International* 474, 3–29.

Buggisch, W. et al. 2010. Did intense volcanism trigger the first late Ordovician icehouse? *Geology* 38(4), 327–30.

Falcucci, A., Conard, N. & Peresani, M. 2017. Critical assessment of the Protoaurignacian lithic technology at Fumane Cave and its implications for the definition of the earliest Aurignacian. *PLoS ONE* 12(12). DOI: 10.1371/journal.pone.0189241.

Fitzsimmons, K. et al. 2013. The Campanian Ignimbrite eruption: new data on volcanic ash dispersal and its potential impact on human evolution. *PloS ONE* 8(6). DOI: 10.1371/journal.pone.0065839.

Fortey, R. 1997. *Life: An Unauthorised Biography*. London: HarperCollins.

Hervella, M. et al. 2016. The mitogenome of a 35,000-year-old *Homo sapiens* from Europe supports a Palaeolithic back migration to Africa. *Scientific Reports* 6(25501). DOI: 10.1038/srep25501.

Hublin, J.-J. 2015. The modern human colonization of western Eurasia: when and where? *Quaternary Science Reviews* 118, 194–210.

Jöris, O. & Street, M. 2008. At the end of the ^{14}C time scale – the Middle to Upper Paleolithic record of western Eurasia. *Journal of Human Evolution* 55, 782–802.

Pinhasi, R. et al. 2011. Revised age of late Neanderthal occupation and the end of the Middle Palaeolithic in the northern Caucasus. *Proceedings of the National Academy Sciences (USA)* 108, 8611–16.

Smith, E. et al. 2018. Humans thrived in South Africa through the Toba eruption about 74,000 years ago. *Nature* 555, 511–15.

Stuart, A. 2014. Late Quaternary megafaunal extinctions on the continents: a short review. *Geological Journal* 50, 338–63.

White, M. J. & Pettitt, P. B. 2009. The demonstration of human antiquity: Three rediscovered illustrations from the 1825 and 1846 excavations in Kent's Cavern (Torquay, England). *Antiquity* 83, 758–68.

Zilhão, J. 2007. The Emergence of Ornaments and Art: An Archaeological Perspective on the Origins of 'Behavioral Modernity'. *Journal of Archaeological Research* 15, 1–54.

Bird, D. W., Bliege Bird, R., Codding, B. F. & Zeanah, D. W. 2019. Variability in the organisation and size of hunter-gatherer groups: foragers do not live in small-scale societies. *Journal of Human Evolution* 131, 96–108.

Bocquet-Appel, J.-R. & Demars, P.-Y. 2005. Estimates of Upper Palaeolithic metapopulation size in Europe from archaeological data. *Journal of Archaeological Science* 32, 1656–68.

Borgel, S. et al. 2021. Early Upper Palaeolithic foot bones from Manot Cave, Israel. *Journal of Human Evolution* 160.

Guatelli-Steinberg, D., Larsen, C. S. & Hutchinson, D. L. 2004. Prevalence and the duration of linear enamel hypoplasia: a comparative study of Neanderthals and Inuit foragers. *Journal of Human Evolution* 47, 65–84.

Hillson, S. W., Franciscus, R. G., Holliday, T. W. & Trinkaus, E. 2006. The ages at death. In Trinkaus, E. and Svoboda, S. *Early Modern Human Evolution in Central Europe: the People of Dolní Věstonice and Pavlov.* Oxford: Oxford University Press, 31–45.

Holt, B. 2003. Mobility in Upper Palaeolithic and Mesolithic Europe: evidence from the lower limb. *American Journal of Physical Anthropology* 122, 200–15.

Holt, B. & Formicola, V. 2008. Hunters of the Ice Age: the biology of Upper Paleolithic people. *Yearbook of Physical Anthropology* 51, 70–99.

Macintosh, A. A., Pinhasi, R. & Stock, J. T. 2017. Prehistoric women's manual labor exceeded that of athletes through the first 5500 years of farming in central Europe. *Science Advances* 3(11). DOI: 10.1126/sciadv.aao3893.

Migliani, A. B. et al. 2020. Hunter-gatherer multilevel sociality accelerates cumulative cultural evolution. *Scientific Advances* 6(9). DOI: 10.1126/sciadv. aax591

Shaw, C. N. & Stock, J. T. 2013. Extreme mobility in the Late Pleistocene? Comparing limb biomechanics among fossil *Homo*, varsity athletes and Holocene foragers. *Journal of Human Evolution* 64, 242–9.

Sikora, M. et al. 2017. Ancient genomes show social and reproductive behaviour of Early Upper Paleolithic foragers. *Science* 358, 659–62.

Sorensen, M. V. & Leonard, W. R. 2001. Neanderthal energetic and foraging efficiency. *Journal of Human Evolution* 40, 483–95.

Trinkaus, E. 2018. An abundance of developmental anomalies and abnormalities in Pleistocene people. *Proceedings of the National Academy of Sciences (USA)* 115, 11941–6.

Trinkaus, E. 2011. Late Pleistocene adult mortality patterns and modern human establishment. *Proceedings of the National Academy of Sciences (USA)* 108(4), 1267–71.

Villotte, S., Thiebeault, A. Sparacello, V. & Trinkaus, E. 2020. Disentangling Cro-Magnon: the adult upper limb skeleton. *Journal of Archaeological Science: Reports* 33. DOI: 10.1016/j. jasrep.2020.102475.

Barbieri, A. et al. 2018. Bridging prehistoric caves with buried landscapes in the Swabian Jura (southwestern Germany). *Quaternary International* 485, 23-43.

Cavarretta, G., Gioia, P., Mussi, M. & Palombo, M. (eds) 2001. *The World of Elephants*. Rome: Consiglio Nazionale delle ricerche. Conference proceedings on Pleistocene mammoths and elephants.

Conard, N. 2009. A female figurine from the basal Aurignacian of Hohle Fels Cave in southwestern Germany. *Nature* 459, 248-52.

Conard, N. et al. 2008. Radiocarbon dating the late Middle Palaeolithic and the Aurignacian of the Swabian Jura. *Journal of Human Evolution* 55, 886-97.

Farbstein, R. 2017. Palaeolithic Central and Eastern Europe. In Insoll, T. (ed.) *The Oxford Handbook of Prehistoric Figurines*. Oxford: Oxford University Press, 681-705. DOI: 10.1093/oxfordhb/9780199675616.013.034.

Floss, H. 2015. The oldest portable art: the Aurignacian ivory figurines from the Swabian Jura (southwest Germany). In White, R. and Bourrillon, R. (eds) *Aurignacian Genius: Art, Technology and Society of the First Modern Humans in Europe*. New York: New York University and Palethnology Society, 315-29.

Floss, H. 2018. Same as it ever was? The Aurignacian of the Swabian Jura and the origins of Palaeolithic art. *Quaternary International* 491, 21-9.

Haynes, G. 2006. Mammoth landscapes: good country for hunter-gatherers. *Quaternary International* 142/143, 20-9.

Higham, T. et al. 2012. Testing models for the beginnings of the Aurignacian and the advent of figurative art and music: the radiocarbon chronology of Geißenklösterle. *Journal of Human Evolution* 62, 664-76.

Kind, C.-J., Ebinger-Rist, N., Wolf, S., Beutelspacher, T. & Wehrberger, K. 2014. The Smile of the Lion Man. Recent Excavations in Stadel Cave (Baden-Württemberg, south-western Germany) and the Restoration of the Famous Upper Palaeolithic Figurine. *Quartär* 61, 129-45.

Kirillova, I. et al. 2016. The diet and environment of mammoths in North-East Russia reconstructed from the contents of their feces. *Quaternary International* 406, 147-61.

Lister, A. & Bahn, P. 2007. *Mammoths: Giants of the Ice Age*. London: Frances Lincoln.

Münzel, S. et al. 2011. Pleistocene bears in the Swabian Jura (Germany): Genetic replacement, ecological displacement, extinctions and survival. *Quaternary International* 245, 225-37.

Pettitt, P. B. 2008. Art and the Middle to Upper Palaeolithic transition in Europe: comments on the archaeological arguments for an Early Upper Palaeolithic antiquity of the Grotte Chauvet art. *Journal of Human Evolution* 55(5), 908-17.

Pettitt, P. B. 2017. Palaeolithic Western and Northcentral Europe. In Insoll, T. (ed.) *The Oxford Handbook of Prehistoric Figurines*. Oxford: Oxford University Press, 851–76. DOI: 10.1093/oxfordhb/9780199675616.013.041.

Porr, M. 2010. Palaeolithic art as cultural memory: a case study of the Aurignacian art of Southwest Germany. *Cambridge Archaeological Journal* 20(1), 87–108.

Van Geel, B. et al. 2008. The ecological implications of a Yakutian mammoth's last meal. *Quaternary Research* 69, 361–76.

Van Geel, B. et al. 2011. Palaeo-environmental and dietary analysis of intestinal contents of a mammoth calf (Yamal Peninsula, northwest Siberia). *Quaternary Science Reviews* 30, 3935–46.

Velliky, E. et al. 2021. Early anthropogenic use of hematite on Aurignacian ivory personal ornaments from Hohle Fels and Vogelherd caves, Germany. *Journal of Human Evolution* 150. DOI: 10.1016/j.jhevol.2020.102900.

Verpoorte, A. 2001. *Places of Art, Traces of Fire. A Contextual Approach to Anthropomorphic Figurines in the Pavlovian (Central Europe, 29–24 kyr BP).* Leiden: University of Leiden.

Wolf, S. and Conard, N. 2015. Personal ornaments of the Swabian Aurignacian. In White, R. and Bourrillon, R. (eds) *Aurignacian Genius: Art, Technology and Society of the First Modern Humans in Europe.* New York: New York University and Palethnology Society, 330–4.

Chapter 10

Cold (pp. 148–65)

Bosch, M. 2012. Human–mammoth dynamics of the Mid-Upper Palaeolithic of the Middle Danube region. *Quaternary International* 276/277, 170–82.

Gavrilov, K. 2012. Double statuette from Khotylevo 2: context, iconography, composition. *Stratum Plus* 2012(1), 1–14. [In Russian].

Gavrilov, K. & Khlopachev, G. 2018. A new female figurine from Khotylovo 2 site: canonic image and archaeological context. *Camera Praehistorica* 1(1), 8–23.

Iakovleva, L. 2012. Shell adornments from the Upper Palaeolithic in Ukraine. *Ukrainian Archaeology* 2012, 28–37.

Iakovleva, L. 2015. The architecture of mammoth bone circular dwellings of the Upper Palaeolithic settlements in Central and Eastern Europe and their socio-symbolic meanings. *Quaternary International* 359/360, 324–34.

Kozłowski, J. 2015. The origin of the Gravettian. *Quaternary International* 359/360, 3–18.

Kufel-Diakowska, B. et al. 2016. Mammoth hunting – impact traces on backed implements from a mammoth bone accumulation at Kraków Spadzista (southern Poland). *Journal of Archaeological Science* 65, 122–33.

McDermott, L. 1996. Self-representation in Upper Palaeolithic female figurines. *Current Anthropology* 37(2), 227–75.

Niţu, E.-C. et al. 2019. Mobility and social identity in the Mid Upper Paleolithic: new personal ornaments from Poiana Cireşului (Piatra Neamţ, Romania). *PLoS ONE* 14(4). DOI: 10.1371/journal.pone.0214932.

Oliva, M. 2005. *Palaeolithic and Mesolithic Moravia.* Brno: Moravian Museum.

Pettitt, P. B. 2006. The living dead and the dead living: burials, figurines and social performance in the European Mid Upper Palaeolithic. In Knüsel, C. and Gowland, R. (eds) *The Social Archaeology of Funerary Remains.* Oxford: Oxbow, 292–308.

Rice, P. 1981. Prehistoric venuses: symbols of motherhood or womanhood? *Journal of Anthropological Research* 37, 402–14.

Roebroeks, W. et al. (eds) 2000. *Hunters of the Golden Age. The Mid Upper Palaeolithic of Eurasia 30,000–20,000 BP.* Leiden: University of Leiden.

Svoboda, J. et al. 2005. Mammoth bone deposits and subsistence practices during Mid-Upper Palaeolithic in Central Europe: three cases from Moravia and Poland. *Quaternary International* 126/7/8, 209–21.

Svoboda, J. et al. 2015. Pavlov I: a large Gravettian site in space and time. *Quaternary International* 406, 95–105.

Trinkaus, E. et al. 2009. Human remains from the Moravian Gravettian: morphology and taphonomy of additional element from Dolní Věstonice II and Pavlov I. *International Journal of Osteoarchaeology* 20(6), 645–69. DOI: 10.1002/oa.1088.

Wojtal, P. & Sobeczyk, K. 2005. Man and woolly mammoth at the Kraków Spadzista Street (B) – taphonomy of the site. *Journal of Archaeological Science* 32, 193–206.

Chapter 11
Refuge (pp. 166–75)

Álvarez-Lao, D. & García, N. 2011. Geographical distribution of Pleistocene cold-adapted large mammal faunas in the Iberian Peninsula. *Quaternary International* 233, 159–70.

Aubry, T. et al. 2008. Solutrean laurel leaf production at Maîtreaux: an experimental approach guided by techno-economic analysis. *World Archaeology* 40(1), 48–66.

Banks, W. et al. 2009. Investigating links between ecology and bifacial tool types in Western Europe during the Last Glacial Maximum. *Journal of Archaeological Science* 36, 2853–67.

Clark, P. et al. 2009. The Last Glacial Maximum. *Science* 325, 710–14.

Dennell, R. 2020. *From Arabia to the Pacific. How Our Species Colonised Asia.* London: Routledge.

Dennell, R. & Porr, M. (eds) 2014. *Southern Asia, Australia and the Search for Human Origins*. Cambridge: Cambridge University Press.

Djindjian, F. 2015. Territories and economies of hunter-gatherer groups during the last glacial maximum in Europe. *Quaternary International* 412, 37–43.

Renard, C. 2011. Continuity or discontinuity in the Late Glacial Maximum of south-western Europe: the formation of the Solutrean in France. *World Archaeology* 43(4), 726–43.

Roldán García, C. et al. 2016. A Unique Collection of Palaeolithic Painted Portable Art: Characterization of Red and Yellow Pigments from the Parpalló Cave (Spain). *PLoS ONE* 11(10). DOI: 10.1371/journal.pone.0163565.

Salomon, H. et al. 2015. Solutrean and Magdalenian ferruginous rocks heat-treatment: accidental and/or deliberate action? *Journal of Archaeological Science* 55, 100–12.

Shakun, J. & Carlson, A. 2010. A global perspective on Last Glacial maximum to Holocene climate change. *Quaternary Science Reviews* 29, 1801–16.

Straus, L. G. 2015. The human occupation of southwestern Europe during the Last Glacial Maximum. Solutrean cultural adaptations in France and Iberia. *Journal of Anthropological Research* 71, 465–92.

Chapter 12
Hearth and Home (pp. 176–88)

Bodu, P. et al. 2011. Where are the hunting camps? A discussion based on Lateglacial sites in the Paris Basin. In Bon, F., Costamagno, S. and Valdeyron, N. (eds) *Hunting Camps in Prehistory. Current Archaeological Approaches*. University of Toulouse II Le Mirail: Palethnology, 231–50.

Boyle, K. 1997. Late Magdalenian carcass management strategies; the Périgord data. *Anthropozoologica* 25, 287–94.

Fontana, L. 2017. The four seasons of reindeer: Non-migrating reindeer in the Dordogne region (France) between 30 and 18 k? Data from the Middle and Upper Magdalenian at La Madeleine and methods of seasonality determination. *Journal of Archaeological Science: Reports* 12, 346–62.

Jöris, O., Street, M. & Turner, E. 2011. Spatial analysis at the Magdalenian site of Gönnersdorf (Central Rhineland, Germany). An introduction. In Gaudzinski-Windheuser, S., Jöris, O., Sensburg, M., Street, M. and Turner, E. (eds) *Site-Internal Spatial Organisation of Hunter-Gatherer Societies: Case Studies from the European Palaeolithic and Mesolithic*. Mainz: Verlag der Römisch-Germanisches Zentralmuseum, 53–80.

Langley, M. C. 2014. Magdalenian antler projectile point design: determining original form for uni- and bilaterally barbed points. *Journal of Archaeological Science* 44, 104–16.

Leesch, D. et al. 2012. The Magdalenian in Switzerland: Re-colonization of a newly accessible landscape. *Quaternary International* 272/3, 191–208.

Pétillon, J.-M. et al. 2011. Hard core and cutting edge: experimental manufacture and use of Magdalenian composite projectile tips. *Journal of Archaeological Science* 38(6), 1266–83.

Połtowicz-Bobak, M. 2012. Observations on the late Magdalenian in Poland. *Quaternary International* 272/3, 297–307.

Zubrow, E., Audouze, F. & Enloe, J. (eds) 2010. *The Magdalenian Household. Unravelling Domesticity.* New York: SUNY.

Chapter 13
The Sightless World of Palaeolithic Cave Art   (pp. 189–203)

Ducasse, S. & Langlais, M. 2019. Twenty years on, a new date with Lascaux. Reassessing the chronology of the cave's Paleolithic occupations through new ^{14}C AMS dating. *Paleo* 30(1), 130–47.

Feruglio, V. et al. 2020. Cussac cave Gravettian parietal art (Dordogne, France): Updated inventories and new insights into Noaillian rock art. *Journal of Archaeological Science: Reports* 32. DOI: 10.1016/j.jasrep.2020.102427.

Jouve, G. et al. 2020. Chauvet's art remains undated. *L'Anthropologie* 124. DOI: 10.1016/j.anthro.2020.102765.

Pettitt, P. B. & Pike, A. 2007. Dating European Palaeolithic cave art: progress, prospects, problems. *Journal of Archaeological Method and Theory* 14(1), 27–47. DOI: 10.1007/s10816-007-9026-4.

Pettitt, P. B. & Bahn, P. 2015. An alternative chronology for the art of Chauvet cave. *Antiquity* 89(345), 542–53.

Pettitt, P. B., et al. 2015. Are hand stencils in Palaeolithic cave art older than we think? An evaluation of the existing data and their potential implications. In Bueno-Ramirez, P. & Bahn, P. (eds) *Prehistoric Art as Prehistoric Culture. Studies in Honour of Professor Rodrigo de Balbin-Behrmann.* Oxford: Archaeopress, 31–43.

Sakamoto, T., Pettitt, P. B. & Ontañon-Peredo, R. 2020. Upper Palaeolithic installation art: topography, distortion, animation and participation in the production and experience of Upper Cantabrian cave art. *Cambridge Archaeological Journal* 30, 665–88.

Further Reading

Chapter 14
Portable Landscapes (pp. 204–14)

Bahn, P. 2016. *Journey Through the Ice Age*. Oxford: Oxford University Press.

Cook, J. 2013. *Ice Age Art: Arrival of the Modern Mind*. London: British Museum.

Vanhaeren, M. & d'Errico, F. 2006. Aurignacian ethno-linguistic geography of Europe revealed by personal ornaments. *Journal of Archaeological Science* 33(8), 1105–11.

Chapter 15
The Mind (pp. 215–31)

Arias, P. 2009. Rites in the dark? An evaluation of the current evidence for ritual areas at Magdalenian cave sites. *World Archaeology* 41(2), 262–94. DOI: 10.1080/00438240902843964.

Bird, D. W. et al. 2019. Variability in the organisation and size of hunter-gatherer groups: foragers do not live in small-scale societies. *Journal of Human Evolution* 131, 96–108.

Bird-David, N. 1992. Beyond 'the original affluent society': a culturalist reformulation. *Current Anthropology* 33(1), 25–47.

Boyer, P. 2008. Religion: Bound to believe? *Nature* 455, 1038–9. DOI: 10.1038/4551038a.

Coolidge, F. & Wynn, T. 2009. *The Rise of Homo Sapiens. The Evolution of Modern Thinking*. Oxford: Wiley-Blackwell.

Damasio, A. 2010. *Self Comes to Mind. Constructing the Conscious Brain*. London: Vintage.

Gamble, C., Gowlett, J. & Dunbar, R. 2014. *Thinking Big: How the Evolution of Social Life Shaped the Human Brain*. London & New York: Thames & Hudson.

Hodgson, D. & Pettitt, P. B. 2018. The Origins of Iconic Depictions: A Falsifiable Model Derived from the Visual Science of Palaeolithic Cave Art and World Rock Art. *Cambridge Archaeological Journal 28(4)*, 591–612. DOI: 10.1017/S0959774318000227.

Luís, L. et al. 2015. Directing the eye. The Côa Valley Pleistocene rock art in its social context. *Arkeos* 37, 1341–7.

Meyering, L.-E., Kentridge, R. & Pettitt, P. B. 2021. The visual psychology of European Upper Palaeolithic figurative art: using *Bubbles* to understand outline depictions. *World Archaeology* 52(2), 1–18. DOI: 10.1080/00438243.2020.1891964.

Pettitt, P. B., Meyering, L.-E. & Kentridge, R. 2021. Bringing science to the study of ancient senses – archaeology and visual psychology. *World Archaeology* 52(2), 183–204. DOI: 10.1080/00438243.2020.1909932.

Pettitt, P. B. 2020. Social ecology of the Upper Palaeolithic: exploring inequality through the art of Lascaux. In Moreau, L. (ed.) *Social Inequality Before Farming? Multidisciplinary Approaches to the Study of Social Organization and Prehistoric and Enthnographic Hunter-Fisher-Gatherer Societies.* Cambridge: McDonald Institute Conversations, 201–22.

Sakamoto, T., Pettitt, P. B. & Ontañon-Peredo, R. 2020. Upper Palaeolithic installation art: topography, distortion, animation and participation in the production and experience of Cantabrian cave art. *Cambridge Archaeological Journal 30(4), 665–88.* DOI: 10.1017/S0959774320000153.

Sharp, H. 1976. Man: wolf: woman: dog. *Arctic Anthropology* 13, 25–34.

Wengrow, D. & Graeber, D. 2015. Farewell to the 'childhood of man': ritual, seasonality, and the origins of inequality. *Journal of the Royal Anthropological Institute* 21(3), 597–619.

Chapter 16
The World of the Dead   (pp. 232–45)

Aldhouse-Green, S. H. R. & Pettitt, P. B. 1998. Paviland Cave: contextualizing the Red Lady. *Antiquity* 72(278), 756–72.

Anderson, J. R., Biro, D. & Pettitt, P. B. 2018. Evolutionary thanatology. *Philosophical Transactions of the Royal Society B: Biological Sciences* 373(1754). DOI: 10.1098/rstb.2017.0262.

Bloch, M. & Parry, J. 1994. Introduction: death and the regeneration of life. In Bloch, M. and Parry, J. (eds) *Death and the Regeneration of Life.* Cambridge: Cambridge University Press, 1–44.

Davies, D. 2017. *Death, Ritual and Belief. The Rhetoric of Funerary Rites.* London: Bloomsbury.

Formicola, V., Pontrandolfi, A. & Svoboda, J. 2001. The Upper Paleolithic triple burial of Dolní Věstonice: pathology and funerary behaviour. *American Journal of Physical Anthropology* 115, 372–9.

Hämäläinen, R. & Germonpré, M. 2007. Fossil bear bones in the Belgian Upper Palaeolithic: the possibility of a proto-bear ceremonialism. *Arctic Anthropology* 44, 1–30.

Hovers, E. & Belfer-Cohen, A. 2013. Insights into early mortuary practices of *Homo.* In Tarlow, S. and Nilsson Stutz, L. (eds) *The Oxford Handbook of the Archaeology of Death and Burial.* Oxford: Oxford University Press, 631–42.

Longbottom, S. & Slaughter, V. 2018. Sources of children's knowledge about death and dying. *Philosophical Transactions of the Royal Society B: Biological Sciences* 373(1754). DOI: 10.1098/rstb.2017.0267.

Pettitt, P. B. 2011. *The Palaeolithic Origins of Human Burial.* Abingdon: Routledge.

Pettitt, P. B. 2018. Hominin evolutionary thanatology from the mortuary to funerary realm. The palaeoanthropological bridge between chemistry and culture. *Philosophical Transactions of the Royal Society B: Biological Sciences* 373(1754). DOI: 10.1098/rstb.2018.0212.

Stiner, M. 2017. Love and death in the Stone Age: what constitutes first evidence of mortuary treatment of the human body? *Biological Theory 12(4), 248–61.* DOI: 10.1007/s13752-017-0275-5.

Villotte, S. et al. 2019. Evidence for previously unknown mortuary practices in the southwest of France (Fornol, Lot) during the Gravettian. *Journal of Archaeological Science: Reports* 27. DOI: 10.1016/j.jasrep.2019.101959.

Zilhão, J. 2015. Lower and Middle Palaeolithic mortuary behaviours and the origins of ritual burial. In Renfrew, C., Boyd, M. J. and Morley, I. (eds) *Death Rituals, Social Order and the Archaeology of Immortality in the Ancient World. 'Death Shall Have No Dominion'.* Cambridge: Cambridge University Press, 27–44.

Chapter 17
Into the Americas
(pp. 246–58)

Davidson, I. 2012. Peopling the last new worlds: the first colonisation of Sahul and the Americas. *Quaternary International* 285, 1–29.

Davis, L. & Madsen, D. 2020. The coastal migration theory: formulation and testable hypotheses. *Quaternary Science Reviews* 249. DOI: 10.1016/j. quascirev.2020.106605.

Erlandson, J. et al. 2007. The Kelp Highway Hypothesis: Marine Ecology, the Coastal Migration Theory, and the Peopling of the Americas. *The Journal of Island and Coastal Archaeology* 2(2), 161–74.

Hoffecker, J. et al. 2016. Beringia and the global dispersal of modern humans. *Evolutionary Anthropology* 25, 64–78.

Meltzer, D. 2018. The origins, antiquity, and dispersal of the first Americans. In Scarre, C. (ed.) *The Human Past (4th edition).* London & New York: Thames & Hudson, 149–71.

Mulligan, C. et al. 2008. Updated three-stage model for the peopling of the Americas. *PLoS ONE* 3(9). DOI: 10.1371/journal.pone.0003199.

Rasmussen, M. et al. 2014. The genome of a Late Pleistocene human from a Clovis burial site in western Montana. *Nature* 506, 226–9.

Speth, J. et al. 2013. Early Paleoindian big-game hunting in North America: provisioning or politics? *Quaternary International* 285, 111–39.

Waters, M. 2019. Late Pleistocene exploration and settlement of the Americas by modern humans. *Science* 365(6449). DOI: 10.1126/science. aat544.

Waters, M. et al. 2011. Pre-Clovis mastodon hunting 13,800 years ago at the Manis site, Washington. *Science* 334, 351–3.

Ameen, C. et al. 2017. A landmark-based approach for assessing the reliability of mandibular tooth crowding as a marker of dog domestication. *Journal of Archaeological Science* 85, 41–50.

Bergström, A. et al. 2020. Origins and genetic legacy of prehistoric dogs. *Science* 370, 557–64.

Germonpré, M. et al. 2015. Large canids at the Gravettian Předmostí site, the Czech Republic: the mandible. *Quaternary International* 359/360, 261–79.

Germonpré, M. et al. 2015. Palaeolithic dogs and Pleistocene wolves revisited: a reply to Morey (2014). *Journal of Archaeological Science* 54, 210–16.

Larson, G. et al. 2012. Rethinking dog domestication by integrating genetics, archaeology and biogeography. *Proceedings of the National Academy of Science (USA)* 109, 8878–83.

Shipman, P. 2015. How do you kill 86 mammoths? Taphonomic investigations of mammoth megasites. *Quaternary International* 359/360, 38–46.

Shipman, P. 2015. *The Invaders. How Humans and Their Dogs Drove Neanderthals to Extinction.* Cambridge, MA: Harvard Belknap.

Acknowledgments

If it weren't for Colin Ridler this book wouldn't have been written. I owe my deepest thanks first and foremost to him, for having identified me as the person to write this book several years ago, and for his kind, persuasive and dogged persistence with the project since he first mooted it. Colin was always there with valuable and perceptive comments, all delivered with enthusiasm. Also at Thames & Hudson, Ben Hayes was the consummate commissioning editor, steering me through a complex schedule with admirable ease, and managing the process so well I didn't really realize it was happening. Isabella Luta and Anabel Navarro relieved a lot of pressure, undertaking those vital tasks in production that allowed me to focus on the writing itself, and I shudder to think how much time I saved from their help. Mark Sapwell was simply a magical editor: I can't imagine how he can spot repetitions, contradictions and opportunities for smart writing while retaining the author's personality and perspectives. It was a great pleasure reacquainting myself with Ben Plumridge, with whom I was part of a team working on archaeological finds in Sicily some twenty years ago and with whom I share memories of a very surreal hotel. Ben took the proof editing towards the finished product with friendly efficiency. Theirs is a subtle but potent art, for which I am very grateful: I've heard about authors insisting on working with particular editors, and I can now see why.

I am greatly indebted to a number of perceptive colleagues who kindly read over draft chapters (in some cases several of them) and the text is much improved as a result. My alphabetically arranged thanks go to Stan Ambrose, Robin Dennell, Gary Haynes, Olaf Jöris, Bob Kentridge, Greger Larson, Lisa-Elen Meyering, Alice Roberts, Mike Waters and Eske Willerslev. Needless to say, while I incorporated most of their suggestions, any mistakes that remain are my own. In academia the frequent exchange of ideas is critical, and during the preparation of this book I've benefited from information received from colleagues including Thierry Aubry, Konstantin Gavrilov, Kurt Gron, Erin Hecht, Jacques Jaubert, Daniel DeMiguel, Marco Peresani and Dietrich Stout, and more widely with those I consider good friends including Paul Bahn, Francesco d'Errico, Sabine Gaudzinski-Windheuser, Christopher Henshilwood, Alistair Pike, Erik Trinkaus and João Zilhão. This is by no means an exclusive list, and it should be obvious from the text who has been particularly central to my understanding and research into early *Homo sapiens*.

I can't emphasize enough the importance of the bright undergraduate and postgraduate students at Durham University, on whom I routinely experiment with various ideas and approaches to a difficult archaeological record, and from whom I receive enthusiasm back in abundance. I reserve a particular thanks for the Palaeo team, and particularly the Visual Palaeopsychology research group at Durham, who provide a highly congenial set of friendly critics. Many an enjoyable pint or two has been sunk, strictly alphabetically, with Dana Allan,

Sam Hirst, Kirsty Jones, Barbara Oosterwijck, Takashi Sakamoto, Mark White and Izzy Wisher, and among these Bob Kentridge and Lisa-Elen Meyering have been exceptional colleagues. Sarah Semple, the Head of Department of Archaeology, has been exceptionally supportive over the period of research leave I used to write this book, which also benefited from the kind offer of the Mercator Distinguished Research Fellowship at Graduiertenkolleg 1876 'Frühe Konzepte von Mensch und Natur' at the Johannes Gutenberg University, Mainz.

Finally, my warmest thanks and love to my wife Maureen, who has put up with me spending several months 'in the zone' of writing, while she has things to research, books to write, and students to teach herself. She's an inspiration on all fronts.

Illustration Credits

a = above; b = below; c = centre; l = left; r = right.

Colour plates: I Hecht et al. 2015; II Craig Foster and Christopher Henshilwood; III Shannon McPherron, MPI EVA Leipzig; IV Jean-Jacques Hublin, MPI EVA Leipzig; V Sarah Freidline, MPI EVA Leipzig; VI Craig Foster and Christopher Henshilwood; VII Liu et al., 2015; VIII The Institute of Archaeology and Ethnography RAS, Russia; IX Centro de Colecciones Patrimoniales de Gipuzkoa, Spain. Tafelmaier, Y., 2017. Photo Yvonne Tafelmaier; x Sikora, Pitulko et al. 2019. Elena Pavlova and Vladimir Pitulko; XI Thibeault, A. & Villotte, S., 2018; XII S. Entressangle/E. Daynes/Science Photo Library; XIII Teo Moreno Moreno/ Alamy Stock Photo; xiva akg-images/Erich Lessing; xivb Naturhistorisches Museum, Vienna; xivc © University of Tübingen. Photo H. Jensen; xv Valery Sharifulin/TASS/Alamy Live News; XVI Photo Don Hitchcock; XVII © MAN/ Loïc Hamon; XVIII © The Trustees of the British Museum; XIX The Neanderthal Museum, Germany; xx Hemis/Alamy Stock Photo; XXI Gonzalo Azumendi/ Getty Images; XXII Photo Paul Pettitt; XXIII The Zaraysk Kremlin State Museum-Preserve & The Institute of Archaeology RAS, Russia; XXIV Andia/Alamy Stock Photo; xxvl José Paulo Ruas, DGPC; xxvr João Zilhão, ICREA/University of Barcelona; XXVI Duncan McLaren; XXVII Dan Burr; XXVIII Greg Harlin, Wood Ronsaville Harlin, Inc.; XXIX Mike Waters.

Black and white illustrations, by page: 2 S. Entressangle/E. Daynes/Science Photo Library; 15 Paul Pettitt; 18 Prof. Matt Sponheimer; 24 © Sonia Harmand MPK/WTAP; 33 Christopher Henshilwood & Magnus Haaland; 40 Nina

Hollfelder, Gwenna Breton, Per Sjödin & Mattias Jakobsson, 2021, The deep population history in Africa, *Human Molecular Genetics* 30(R1), R2–R10; **45** Filipa Rodrigues/STEA/João Zilhão; **46** Yau et al., 2016; **49** Paul Pettitt; **52** Prof. Israel Hershkovitz; **55** Christopher Henshilwood & Francesco d'Errico; **57** Peter Bull & Drazen Tomic; **58** Paul Pettitt; **61** Moris Kushelevitch/Alamy Stock Photo; **62, 63** Jeff Rose; **64** Redrawn from Jennings, R. et al., 2015; **65** Paul Pettitt; **66** Liu et al., 2015; **79** Omry Barzilai & Natalia Gubenko, Israel Antiquities Authority; **83** Paul Pettitt; **87** Mishra et al., 2013; **91** Photo Graeme Barker; **96** Zwyns et al., 2019. Photo Nicolas Zwyns; **101** Dr. M. Baales (Olpe, Germany); **108** Erik Trinkaus; **109** Photo Marco Peresani; **111** Prof. Jamie Woodward; **113** Collection MNHN, France. Photo D. Henry-Gambier; **114** Thibeault, A. & Villotte, S., 2018; **116–17** Sikora et al., *Science*, 2017; **123** Erik Trinkaus; **124** Sparacello et al., 2018; **125** S. Villotte, A. R. Ogden & E. Trinkaus. © Lavoisier SAS 2018; **126** Erik Trinkaus; **131** Hemis/Alamy Stock Photo; **137** Sommer/ROCEEH University of Tübingen; **139** Photos H. Jensen, University of Tübingen (rows 1-3, 5), S. Wolf (rows 4, 6-8); montage: G. Häussler; **140** © University of Tübingen. Photos H. Jensen & J. Lipták; **143** © University of Tübingen. Photo Hildegard Jensen; **146** © Ulmer Museum, Ulm, Germany. Photo Oleg Kuchar; **149** Paul Pettitt; **150** Mission archéologique des grottes de Saulges. Photo Hervé Paitier; **153** Jiří Svoboda; **154** Jiří Svoboda/Institute of Archaeology, Brno, Czech Republic. Photo Rebecca Farbstein; **157l** DeAgostini/A. Dagli Orti; **157r** Heritage Images/Werner Forman Archive; **162–4** © L. Iakovleva; **169** CW Images/Alamy Stock Photo; **171–2** Photo Thierry Aubry; **174** DeAgostini/G. Dagli Orti; **184** Olaf Jöris; **187** Römisch-Germanisches Zentralmuseum, Mainz, Germany. Photo Gerhard Bosinski, MONREPOS picture archive; **192** WHPics/Alamy Stock Photo; **199** Sylvain Ducasse & Mathieu Langlais; **202** Hemis/Alamy Stock Photo; **205** The Print Collector/Alamy Stock Photo; **206a** © The Trustees of the British Museum; **206b** Photo © RMN-Grand Palais (Musée d'Archéologie nationale)/Thierry Le Mage; **208** Photo © RMN-Grand Palais/Gérard Blot; **210a** Historic Images/Alamy Stock Photo; **210b** Photo © RMN-Grand Palais (Musée d'archéologie nationale)/Loïc Hamon; **213** M. Vanhaeren & F. d'Errico, 2006; **219l** Granger Historical Picture Archive/Alamy Stock Photo; **219r** Photo 12/Alamy Stock Photo; **221** MATLAB/L.-E. Meyering; **222** Takashi Sakamoto; **223** Photo Izzy Wisher and with thanks to Gobierno de Cantabria, Spain; **225** Photo Lisa-Elen Meyering; **226** Volker Iserhardt, Römisch Germanisches Zentralmuseum, Mainz, Germany; **229** Proyecto La Garma. Photo Pedro A. Saura; **230a** © MONREPOS Bildarchiv, Germany; **230b** Römisch-Germanisches Zentralmuseum/E. Turner; **235** Belgian Middle Egypt Prehistoric project of Leuven University; **236–7** Jorge González, University of South Florida/Elena Santos, Complutense University of Madrid-CENIEH; **238** Pascal Goetgheluck/ Science Photo Library; **240** © N. Aujoulat, CNP, MCC; **243** Jiří Svoboda; **245** © The Trustees of the Natural History Museum, London; **247** After Nikolskiy & Pitulko (2013), reproduced with permission of JAS. Photo Vladimir Pitulko; **249** Waters et al., 2019. Reprinted with permission from AAAS; **250** University of Alaska Museum of the North; **251** ML Design; **252** Photo Mike Waters; **253** Waters et al., 2011. Reprinted with permission from AAAS; **257** Tom D. Dillehay; **261** © Mietje Germonpré.

Index